KB085608

GRAMMAR
BITE

이 책과 함께 미래를 디자인하는 나를 위해 응원의 한마디를 적어 보세요.

GRAMMAR BITE
Grade 1

CONCEPT
문법 개념 이해부터 내신 대비까지 완벽하게 끝내는
문법 필수 개념서

BOOK GRADE

WRITERS
미래엔콘텐츠연구회
No.1 Content를 개발하는 교육 전문 콘텐츠 연구회

PROOFREADER
Mark Holden

COPYRIGHT
인쇄일 2024년 5월 27일(2판14쇄)
발행일 2018년 9월 10일

펴낸이 신광수
펴낸곳 ㈜미래엔
등록번호 제16-67호

교육개발2실장 김용균
개발책임 이보현
개발 정규진, 한고운, 김은송, 정유진

디자인실장 손현지
디자인책임 김기욱
디자인 장병진, 윤지혜

CS본부장 강윤구
CS지원책임 강승훈

ISBN 979-11-6233-738-7

"흔들리지 않고 피는 꽃이
어디 있으랴"

활짝 핀 꽃은 사람들의 눈을 즐겁게 하고 기분을 좋게 합니다.
그런데 이 꽃은 처음부터 그렇게 환하게 우리에게 왔을까요?
그렇지 않습니다.
거친 땅을 뚫고 싹을 틔우고, 줄기를 세우고,
비바람을 견뎌 내고서야 드디어 화려한 꽃을 피웁니다.

영어 공부도 마찬가지입니다.
하루아침에 우리말처럼 영어가 술술 나오지는 않으니까요.
영어 속담에 이런 말이 있습니다.
Little drops of water make the mighty ocean.
작은 물방울이 모여 거대한 바다를 이룬다는 말이지요.
영어 공부는 반복입니다.
어제 배운 것을 잊어버리지 않게 오늘 다시 반복하고,
오늘 배운 것은 내일 또 다시 보면서 익숙하게 내 것처럼 만들어야 합니다.
이렇게 반복하다 보면 어느 순간, 화려한 꽃처럼
영어가 어렵지 않게, 술술 피어오르는 경험을 하게 될 것입니다.

영어 공부는 성실함과 꾸준함입니다.
오늘도 하루 학습 목표를 세우고, 목표한 바를 해내는 여러분이
결국 최후의 영어 승자가 될 것입니다.

GRAMMAR BITE 가 여러분을 응원합니다.

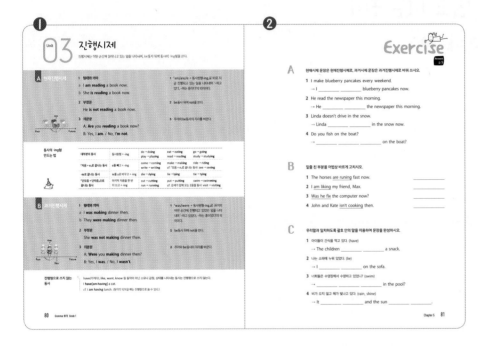

문법 개념은 꼼꼼히!

❶ 개념 익히기

Unit에서 배워야 할 핵심 문법들의 원리와 쓰임을 명확한 설명과 예문을 통해 쉽게 이해할 수 있습니다.

❷ 개념 확인하기

Unit에서 배운 문법의 기본적인 내용을 확인하면서 익힐 수 있는 문제들로 구성하였습니다.

서술형 대비는 문장쓰기로!

단어 배열하여 문장 완성하기, 문장의 빈칸에 알맞은 말 쓰고 이 문장을 바탕으로 비교 문장 쓰기 및 문장 바꿔 쓰기를 통해 문장 구성 능력의 기본기를 쌓을 수 있습니다.

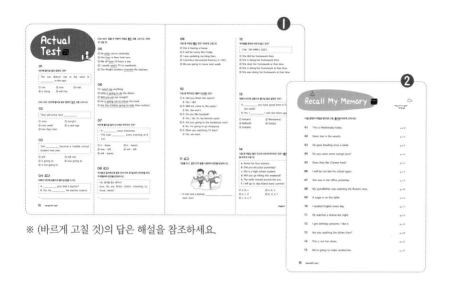

내신 대비는 확실하게!

❶ 실력 완성하기

학교 시험에 나올 만한 문제들로 구성하여 배운 내용을 종합적으로 확인하며 내신 시험까지 대비할 수 있습니다.

❷ 반복 학습하기

첫 챕터부터 해당 챕터까지의 주요 문법 내용을 반복적으로 확인함으로써 완벽하게 내 것으로 만들 수 있습니다.

※ (바르게 고칠 것)의 답은 해설을 참조하세요.

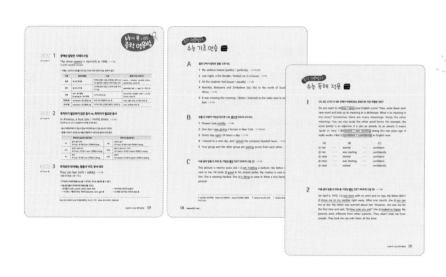

수능 빈출 어법, 지금부터!

수능 어법에 나오는 문법 대부분이 중학교 문법이므로, 중학교 때부터 수능을 차근차근 준비할 수 있도록 하였습니다. 수능에 자주 출제되는 중학 문법을 살펴보고, 연습문제와 독해로 적용해 봅니다.

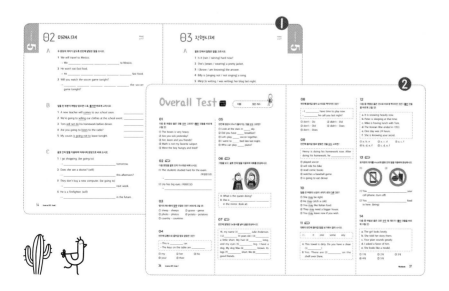

복습하고, 확인하고!

❶ Workbook으로 실력 쌓기

Unit별로 더 많은 연습문제를 풀어 봄으로써 문법을 보다 완벽하게 익힐 수 있습니다.

❷ 총괄평가로 진짜 실력 확인하기

Workbook 마지막에 총괄평가를 수록하여 전체 내용에 대한 자기 실력을 점검해 볼 수 있습니다.

GRAMMAR BITE
Contents
차례

| INTRO | 꼭 알아두어야 할 문법 POINTs | 6 |

Chapter 1 그때그때 달라, 혼자서는 안 돼, 주어의 짝꿍 **be동사**

Unit 01 be동사의 현재형과 과거형 · · · 18
Unit 02 be동사의 부정문과 의문문 · · · 20

Chapter 2 현재로 과거로 갑옷을 바꿔 입는, 주어의 행동대장, **일반동사**

Unit 01 일반동사의 현재형 · · · 30
Unit 02 일반동사의 과거형 · · · 32
Unit 03 일반동사의 부정문과 의문문 · · · 34

Chapter 3 이름을 불러 주면 나에게로 와서 하나의 의미가 되는 **명사**

Unit 01 셀 수 있는 명사 · · · 44
Unit 02 셀 수 없는 명사 · · · 46
Unit 03 관사 · · · 48

Chapter 4 명사의 대리인 **대명사**

Unit 01 인칭대명사, 재귀대명사 · · · 58
Unit 02 this, that, it · · · 60
Unit 03 one, some, any · · · 62

수능에 꼭 나오는 중학 영문법 · · · 71

Chapter 5 과거부터 미래까지 시간을 품고 있는 타임머신, **시제**

Unit 01 현재시제, 과거시제 · · · 76
Unit 02 미래시제 · · · 78
Unit 03 진행시제 · · · 80

Chapter 6 함께하면 특별한 의미가 돼, 동사의 도우미 **조동사**

Unit 01 can, may · · · 90
Unit 02 must, have to, should · · · 92

Chapter 7   의도한 바를 이렇게 전해 봐, 알아두면 유용한 **문장의 종류**

     Unit 01   who, what, which 의문문   **102**

     Unit 02   when, where, why, how 의문문   **104**

     Unit 03   명령문, Let's ~, There is/are ~   **106**

     Unit 04   감탄문, 부가의문문   **108**

Chapter 8   문장의 형태를 지배하는 **동사의 종류**

     Unit 01   감각동사   **118**

     Unit 02   수여동사   **120**

수능에 꼭 나오는 중학 영문법   **129**

Chapter 9   동사인 듯 동사 아닌 동사 같은 너, to부정사와 동명사

     Unit 01   명사처럼 쓰이는 to부정사   **134**

     Unit 02   형용사, 부사처럼 쓰이는 to부정사   **136**

     Unit 03   명사처럼 쓰이는 동명사   **138**

Chapter 10   말과 글을 살찌우는 **형용사와 부사**

     Unit 01   형용사   **148**

     Unit 02   부사   **150**

     Unit 03   원급, 비교급, 최상급   **152**

Chapter 11   나를 이끌어 줘, 명사의 가이드 **전치사**

     Unit 01   시간을 나타내는 전치사   **162**

     Unit 02   장소를 나타내는 전치사   **164**

     Unit 03   그 밖의 전치사   **166**

Chapter 12   너와 나를 이어 주는 오작교, **접속사**

     Unit 01   and, but, or, so   **176**

     Unit 02   when, while, before, after   **178**

     Unit 03   because, if, that   **180**

수능에 꼭 나오는 중학 영문법   **189**

GRAMMAR BITE
INTRO

" 영문법은 중학교에서
꽉! 잡아야 합니다 "

1 영문법에 대한 두려움을 먼저 없애자

중학교에 들어가면 영문법이 너무 어렵다고 많이들 말합니다. 막연히 어려울 것으로 생각하고 보면 정말 어려워지고, 어려우니 자꾸 공부하기 싫어질 수밖에 없습니다. 우리말 체계와 많이 다른 영어는 당연히 어려운 게 맞습니다. 그러니 조급한 마음을 버리고, 한번 보고 잘 이해가 되지 않는다고 쉽게 포기하면 안 됩니다. 여러 번 읽고, 또 읽어 이해할 수 있도록 합니다.

2 문법 용어, 외우지 말고 이해하자

to부정사, 동명사, 수여동사 .... 벌써 머리가 아픈가요? 사실 대부분의 문법 용어는 한자어로 되어 있어 언뜻 이해하기 어려울 수 있습니다. 용어에 대한 이해를 포기하고 무작정 외워 버리기도 하지요. 하지만 워낙 많은 문법 용어가 있으니 일일이 외운다는 것은 한계가 있습니다. 조금 시간이 걸리더라도 용어 자체가 어떤 의미인지를 정확하게 파악하면 문법 개념 설명을 훨씬 쉽게 이해할 수 있습니다. 예를 들어 '동명사(動名詞)'는 '동사+명사'를 합한 것입니다. 동사원형에 –ing를 붙인 것인데, 이는 동사의 의미를 가지면서 명사의 역할을 하는 것을 말합니다. 결국, 동명사는 명사이기 때문에 주어나 목적어, 보어로 쓰일 수가 있습니다.

3 우리말과 다른 영어 문장 구성을 파악하자

'나는 너를 사랑한다.'를 영어로 표현하면 I love you.입니다. 분명한 차이가 있죠? 우리말은 주어가 먼저 나오고 동사는 문장의 끝에 오는 경우가 보통입니다. 그러나 영어는 동사가 주어 바로 다음에 나옵니다. 우리는 이미 우리말 구조에 익숙합니다. 때에 따라서는 우리말과 비교하면서 영어 문장 구성의 특성을 파악하는 것도 좋은 방법입니다. 기본 문장 구성을 알고 나면 점차 영어 순서에 따라 문장을 쓰고, 또 해석하게 될 것이니까요.

4 주어, 동사, 목적어 등 문장의 구조를 분석해 보자

문장 속에서 단어들은 각자의 역할이 있습니다. 문장의 구성을 좀 더 정확하게 이해하기 위해서는 알고 있거나 학습한 문법 지식을 활용하여 주어와 동사를 먼저 나눈 다음, 이어지는 단어들이 목적어인지, 보어인지, 수식어구인지 등을 구분하는 습관을 가져 보세요. 이렇게 문장 성분별로 분석하는 훈련이 되면 점차 긴 문장도 어렵지 않게 이해하고 해석해 낼 수 있습니다.

5 Step by Step, 단계별 학습으로 한 걸음씩!

항상 너무 과한 욕심은 화를 부릅니다. 수학처럼 문법도 단계별로 차근차근 접근하는 것이 좋습니다. 중학교 학년별 교과서에 나오는 문법을 중심으로 단순한 문장부터 확실하게 개념을 이해해야 합니다. 형용사나 부사의 역할을 정확히 알지 못한 상태에서 to부정사의 형용사적 용법이나 부사적 용법을 이해하기란 쉽지 않습니다. 더디더라도 기본 핵심부터 기초를 탄탄히 다져 놓아야 한 단계 더 발전할 수 있습니다.

6 학습한 문법은 여러 번의 문장쓰기를 통해 복습하자

학습한 문법 내용을 바탕으로 문장을 해석해 내는 실력에 머무르지 않고 그 이상을 원한다면 단어들을 다양하게 바꿔 가며 여러 번 문장을 써 봄으로써 문장의 형태를 익히는 것이 중요합니다. 눈으로만 읽고 해석하는 것보다 직접 완전한 문장을 쓸 때 기억에 더 오래 남고 영어 실력 향상에도 큰 도움이 됩니다.

7 문제를 풀고 나면 왜 틀렸는지 오답 체크는 필수!

학교 시험에는 다양한 형태의 문제가 나옵니다. 문법 문제가 아니더라도 틀린 문제는 왜 틀렸는지 점검하는 과정이 꼭 필요합니다. 문법 문제는 이 과정이 더욱 중요합니다. 특히 어법상 맞는지 틀린지를 판단하는 문제는 맞으면 왜 맞는지, 틀리면 왜 틀리는지를 반드시 짚어 보고 오류를 고쳐 다시 써 보세요. 이러한 과정은 무조건 많은 문제를 풀어 내는 것보다 문법 개념을 확실히 내 것으로 만들어 어떤 유형의 문제가 나와도 실수 없이 해결해 낼 수 있는 실력을 갖게 해 줍니다.

꼭 알아두어야 할
문법 POINTs

01 | 문장을 만드는 필수 요소

동사

주어의 상태나 동작을 나타내는 말로
주어의 인칭과 수, 문장의 시제에 따라 형태가 달라져요.

I am fourteen years old.
나는 14살**이야**.

I go to Mirae Middle School.
나는 미래중학교에 **다녀**.

주어

행동의 주체로 명사, 대명사, 의문사
등이 주어로 쓰여요.

My name is Suho.
내 이름은 수호야.

목적어

동사의 대상이 되는 말로
명사나 대명사 등이 목적어로 쓰여요.

I like English very much.
나는 **영어를** 매우 좋아해.

**I will give you some help
with your grammar.**

내가 **여러분에게** 문법 공부하는 데
도움을 좀 줄게.

보어

주어나 목적어를 보충 설명해 주는 말로
명사나 형용사 등이 보어로 쓰여요.

My favorite sport is basketball.
내가 가장 좋아하는 운동은 **농구**야.

**My smile makes everyone
happy.**

내 미소는 모든 사람들을
행복하게 해 줘.

보어

목적어

02 | 인칭대명사와 be동사

수	인칭		현재형	과거형	현재형의 줄임말	현재형의 부정	과거형의 부정
단수	1인칭	I	am	was	I'm	I am not[I'm not]	I was not[I wasn't]
	2인칭	You	are	were	You're	You are not[You're not / You aren't]	You were not[You weren't]
	3인칭	She	is	was	She's	She is not[She's not / She isn't]	She was not[She wasn't]
		He			He's	He is not[He's not / He isn't]	He was not[He wasn't]
		It			It's	It is not[It's not / It isn't]	It was not[It wasn't]
복수	1인칭	We	are	were	We're	We are not[We're not / We aren't]	We were not[We weren't]
	2인칭	You			You're	You are not[You're not / You aren't]	You were not[You weren't]
	3인칭	They			They're	They are not[They're not / They aren't]	They were not[They weren't]

03 | 인칭대명사의 격

수	인칭	주격	목적격	소유격	소유대명사	재귀대명사
단수	1인칭	I	me	my	mine	myself
	2인칭	you	you	your	yours	yourself
	3인칭	she	her	her	hers	herself
		he	him	his	his	himself
		it	it	its	-	itself
복수	1인칭	we	us	our	ours	ourselves
	2인칭	you	you	your	yours	yourselves
	3인칭	they	them	their	theirs	themselves

04 | 명사의 복수형 만드는 법

구분	변화 형태	예
대부분의 경우	명사＋-s	dogs, books, phones, computers, pencils, sports
-s, -x, -ch, -sh로 끝나는 경우	명사＋-es	buses, classes, boxes, foxes, watches, dishes
「자음＋o」로 끝나는 경우	명사＋-es	potatoes, tomatoes, heroes 예외: pianos, photos *cf.* radios, studios
「자음＋y」로 끝나는 경우	y를 i로 바꾸고＋-es	baby → babies, candy → candies, city → cities, country → countries, lady → ladies, fly → flies *cf.* boy → boys, day → days
-f, -fe로 끝나는 경우	f, fe를 v로 바꾸고＋-es	knife → knives, wife → wives, leaf → leaves, thief → thieves, wolf → wolves 예외: roofs, cliffs, beliefs
단수형과 복수형이 같은 경우		deer → deer, fish → fish, sheep → sheep
불규칙하게 변하는 경우		man → men, woman → women, child → children, tooth → teeth, foot → feet, mouse → mice, goose → geese

05 | 일반동사의 3인칭 단수 현재형 만드는 법

구분	변화 형태	예
대부분의 경우	동사원형 + -s	likes, eats, buys, knows, loves, comes, sees, sleeps, plays, speaks, learns, reads
-o, -s, -ch, -sh, -x로 끝나는 경우	동사원형 + -es	does, goes, passes, misses, watches, teaches, washes, brushes, fixes, mixes
「자음 + y」로 끝나는 경우	y를 i로 바꾸고 + -es	study → studies, try → tries, cry → cries, worry → worries, carry → carries, copy → copies, fly → flies cf. enjoy → enjoys, buy → buys
불규칙하게 변하는 경우	have → has	

06 | 일반동사의 과거형 만드는 법

구분	변화 형태	예
대부분의 경우	동사원형 + -ed	played, walked, looked, talked, watched, missed, listened, rained, wanted, started
-e로 끝나는 경우	동사원형 + -d	lived, danced, liked, moved, loved, invited, smiled, changed, hated, hoped
「자음 + y」로 끝나는 경우	y를 i로 바꾸고 + -ed	cry → cried, try → tried, worry → worried, carry → carried, copy → copied, study → studied cf. enjoy → enjoyed, stay → stayed
「단모음 + 단자음」으로 끝나는 경우	마지막 자음을 한 번 더 쓰고 + -ed	plan → planned, drop → dropped, stop → stopped, chat → chatted cf. visit → visited, enter → entered

07 | 동사의 -ing형 만드는 법

구분	변화 형태	예
대부분의 경우	동사원형 + -ing	going, playing, eating, doing, watching, talking, speaking, reading, walking, learning, calling, singing, teaching
「자음 + e」로 끝나는 경우	e를 빼고 + -ing	come → coming, give → giving, ride → riding, live → living, make → making, write → writing, smile → smiling, dance → dancing cf. see → seeing
-ie로 끝나는 경우	ie를 y로 바꾸고 + -ing	die → dying, lie → lying, tie → tying
「단모음 + 단자음」으로 끝나는 경우	마지막 자음을 한 번 더 쓰고 + -ing	sit → sitting, cut → cutting, run → running, get → getting, put → putting, swim → swimming, begin → beginning cf. visit → visiting

08 | 동사의 불규칙 변화형

구분	원형	과거형	과거분사형	-ing형	3인칭 단수 현재형	뜻
A-A-A형 (원형, 과거형, 과거분사형이 같은 동사)	cost	cost	cost	costing	costs	비용이 들다
	cut	cut	cut	cutting	cuts	베다, 자르다
	hit	hit	hit	hitting	hits	치다
	hurt	hurt	hurt	hurting	hurts	다치다
	let	let	let	letting	lets	~하게 하다
	put	put	put	putting	puts	놓다
	read[ri:d]	read[red]	read[red]	reading	reads	읽다
	set	set	set	setting	sets	놓다
	shut	shut	shut	shutting	shuts	닫다
	spread	spread	spread	spreading	spreads	퍼지다
A-B-B형 (과거형과 과거분사형이 같은 동사)	bring	brought	brought	bringing	brings	가져오다
	build	built	built	building	builds	짓다
	buy	bought	bought	buying	buys	사다
	catch	caught	caught	catching	catches	잡다
	feed	fed	fed	feeding	feeds	먹이다
	feel	felt	felt	feeling	feels	느끼다
	fight	fought	fought	fighting	fights	싸우다
	find	found	found	finding	finds	발견하다
	get	got	got/gotten	getting	gets	얻다
	have	had	had	having	has	가지다; 먹다
	hear	heard	heard	hearing	hears	듣다
	hold	held	held	holding	holds	잡다; 개최하다
	keep	kept	kept	keeping	keeps	유지하다
	lay	laid	laid	laying	lays	놓다; 낳다
	leave	left	left	leaving	leaves	떠나다
	lend	lent	lent	lending	lends	빌려주다
	lose	lost	lost	losing	loses	잃어버리다
	make	made	made	making	makes	만들다
	meet	met	met	meeting	meets	만나다
	pay	paid	paid	paying	pays	지불하다
	stand	stood	stood	standing	stands	서다
	say	said	said	saying	says	말하다
	sleep	slept	slept	sleeping	sleeps	자다
	sell	sold	sold	selling	sells	팔다
	send	sent	sent	sending	sends	보내다
	sit	sat	sat	sitting	sits	앉다
	spend	spent	spent	spending	spends	소비하다
	teach	taught	taught	teaching	teaches	가르치다
	tell	told	told	telling	tells	말하다
	think	thought	thought	thinking	thinks	생각하다
	win	won	won	winning	wins	이기다

구분	원형	과거형	과거분사형	-ing형	3인칭 단수 현재형	뜻
A-B-C형 (원형, 과거형, 과거분사형이 다른 동사)	be	was/were	been	being	is	~이다; 있다
	bear	bore	born	bearing	bears	참다; 낳다
	begin	began	begun	beginning	begins	시작하다
	bite	bit	bitten	biting	bites	물다
	blow	blew	blown	blowing	blows	불다
	break	broke	broken	breaking	breaks	깨뜨리다
	choose	chose	chosen	choosing	chooses	선택하다
	do	did	done	doing	does	하다
	draw	drew	drawn	drawing	draws	그리다
	drink	drank	drunk	drinking	drinks	마시다
	drive	drove	driven	driving	drives	운전하다
	eat	ate	eaten	eating	eats	먹다
	fall	fell	fallen	falling	falls	떨어지다
	fly	flew	flown	flying	flies	날다
	forget	forgot	forgotten	forgetting	forgets	잊다
	forgive	forgave	forgiven	forgiving	forgives	용서하다
	freeze	froze	frozen	freezing	freezes	얼다
	give	gave	given	giving	gives	주다
	go	went	gone	going	goes	가다
	grow	grew	grown	growing	grows	자라다
	hide	hid	hidden	hiding	hides	숨기다
	know	knew	known	knowing	knows	알다
	lie	lay	lain	lying	lies	눕다; 놓여 있다
	ride	rode	ridden	riding	rides	타다
	ring	rang	rung	ringing	rings	울리다
	rise	rose	risen	rising	rises	오르다
	see	saw	seen	seeing	sees	보다
	sew	sewed	sewn/sewed	sewing	sews	바느질하다
	shake	shook	shaken	shaking	shakes	흔들다
	show	showed	shown	showing	shows	보여 주다
	sing	sang	sung	singing	sings	노래하다
	sow	sowed	sown/sowed	sowing	sows	(씨를) 뿌리다
	speak	spoke	spoken	speaking	speaks	말하다
	steal	stole	stolen	stealing	steals	훔치다
	swim	swam	swum	swimming	swims	수영하다
	take	took	taken	taking	takes	가지고 가다
	throw	threw	thrown	throwing	throws	던지다
	wake	woke	woken	waking	wakes	깨다
	wear	wore	worn	wearing	wears	입다
	write	wrote	written	writing	writes	쓰다
A-B-A형 (원형과 과거분사형이 같은 동사)	become	became	become	becoming	becomes	되다
	come	came	come	coming	comes	오다
	run	ran	run	running	runs	달리다

09 | to부정사 vs. 동명사를 목적어로 가지는 동사

구분	예	
to부정사만을 목적어로 가지는 동사	want, hope, wish, expect, plan, decide, promise, need, learn, refuse 등	
동명사만을 목적어로 가지는 동사	enjoy, finish, mind, stop, give up, keep, avoid, quit, delay, put off, practice, deny 등	
둘 다를 목적어로 가지는 동사	like, love, hate, begin, start, continue, intend 등	
둘 다를 목적어로 가지지만 의미가 달라지는 동사	remember + to부정사: ~할 것을 기억하다	remember + 동명사: ~했던 것을 기억하다
	forget + to부정사: ~할 것을 잊다	forget + 동명사: ~했던 것을 잊다
	try + to부정사: ~하려고 노력하다	try + 동명사: 시험 삼아 ~해 보다
	regret + to부정사: ~하게 되어 유감이다	regret + 동명사: ~했던 것을 후회하다

10 | 자주 쓰이는 동명사 표현

표현	뜻	표현	뜻
go -ing	~하러 가다	can't help -ing	~하지 않을 수 없다
spend + 시간[돈] + -ing	~하는 데 시간[돈]을 쓰다	be busy -ing	~하느라 바쁘다
It's no use -ing	~해 봐야 소용없다	have trouble[difficulty, a hard time] -ing	~하는 데 어려움을 겪다
be worth -ing	~할 가치가 있다	There is no -ing	~할 수 없다
How[What] about -ing?	~하는 게 어때?	keep[stop, prevent] + 목적어 + from -ing	…가 ~하는 것을 막다
feel like -ing	~하고 싶다	on -ing	~하자마자
look forward to -ing	~할 것을 고대하다	be used[accustomed] to -ing	~하는 데 익숙하다

11 | 자주 쓰이는 동사구

표현	뜻	표현	뜻
take care of(= look after)	~을 돌보다	cut down	~을 자르다
bring up	~을 기르다	put off	~을 미루다, 연기하다
call off	~을 취소하다	hand in	~을 제출하다
turn on[off]	~을 켜다[끄다]	turn down[up]	(소리 등을) 낮추다[높이다]
speak well[ill] of	~을 칭찬하다[욕하다]	run over	(차가) ~을 치다
look up[down] to	~을 우러러보다[경멸하다]	laugh at	~을 비웃다

12 | 형용사를 부사로 만드는 법

구분	변화 형태	예
대부분의 경우	형용사 + -ly	sadly, badly, largely, slowly, kindly, really, usually beautifully, carefully, suddenly
-y로 끝나는 경우	y를 i로 바꾸고 + -ly	happy → happily, easy → easily, lucky → luckily, heavy → heavily, noisy → noisily
형용사와 부사의 형태가 같은 경우		fast(빠른, 빨리), early(이른, 일찍), hard(열심인, 열심히), long(긴, 길게), short(짧은, 짧게), low(낮은, 낮게), high(높은, 높게), late(늦은, 늦게), near(가까운, 가까이), most(대부분의, 가장), enough(충분한, 충분히)
「부사 + -ly」가 다른 뜻의 부사가 되는 경우		hard – hardly(거의 ~ 않다), short – shortly(곧), high – highly(매우), late – lately(최근에), near – nearly(거의)
예외		good(좋은) → well(잘)

13 | 비교급과 최상급 만드는 법

구분	변화 형태	예
대부분의 경우	원급 + -er/-est	small – smaller – smallest tall – taller – tallest old – older – oldest hard – harder – hardest
-e로 끝나는 경우	원급 + -r/-st	large – larger – largest nice – nicer – nicest wise – wiser – wisest
「단모음 + 단자음」으로 끝나는 경우	마지막 자음을 한 번 더 쓰고 + -er/-est	big – bigger – biggest hot – hotter – hottest fat – fatter – fattest
「자음 + y」로 끝나는 경우	y를 i로 바꾸고 + -er/-est	easy – easier – easiest happy – happier – happiest pretty – prettier – prettiest
-ful, -ous, -ive, -able, -less, -ly, -ing, -ed 등으로 끝나는 대부분의 2음절 단어와 3음절 이상의 단어인 경우	more/most + 원급	useful – more useful – most useful famous – more famous – most famous active – more active – most active potable – more potable – most potable hopeless – more hopeless – most hopeless quickly – more quickly – most quickly shocking – more shocking – most shocking excited – more excited – most excited
불규칙하게 변하는 경우	good/well – better – best many/much – more – most	bad – worse – worst little – less – least

14 | 전치사

시간을 나타내는 전치사		
in vs. **on** vs. **at**	in: ~에	연도, 계절, 월, 오전, 오후, 저녁 앞에 쓴다. She was born **in** 2000.
	on: ~에	날짜, 요일, 특정한 날 앞에 쓴다. I will go to London **on** September 12th.
	at: ~에	시각, 순간, 나이, 밤 앞에 쓴다. The park closes **at** 6.
before vs. **after** vs. **in**	before: ~ 전에	Let's meet at the bus stop **before** dinner.
	after: ~ 후에	They play tennis **after** school.
	in: ~ 후에	뒤에 일정 기간의 시간이 와서 '지금부터 ~ 후에'라는 의미를 나타낸다. The final exams are **in** two weeks.
for vs. **during**	for: ~ 동안	뒤에 숫자와 함께 시간의 길이를 나타내는 명사(구)가 온다. Sandy was sick **for** two days.
	during: ~ 동안	뒤에 특정 기간을 나타내는 명사(구)가 온다. He swam every day **during** the summer.
until vs. **by**	until: ~까지	동작이나 상태가 한 시점까지 계속됨을 나타낸다. I sleep **until** 9 o'clock every Sunday.
	by: ~까지	동작이나 상태가 끝나는 시점을 나타낸다. Cinderella had to return home **by** midnight.

장소를 나타내는 전치사		
in vs. **at**	in: ~ (안)에	비교적 넓은 장소 앞에 쓰며, 어떤 공간 안에 있는 것을 나타낼 때도 쓴다. I live **in** Seoul. There are some fruits **in** the refrigerator.
	at: ~에	비교적 좁은 장소 앞에 쓰며, 특정한 지점을 나타낼 때도 쓴다. I was waiting for her **at** the airport. Turn right **at** the corner, and go straight up.
on vs. **over** vs. **under**	on: ~ (위)에	표면과 맞닿아 있는 것을 나타낸다. She lives **on** the second floor.
	over: ~ 위에	표면과 떨어져서 위에 있는 것을 나타낸다. Build a bridge **over** the river!
	under: ~ 아래에	표면과 떨어져서 아래에 있는 것을 나타낸다. A boat is passing **under** the bridge.
between vs. **among**	between: ~ 사이에	둘 사이에 쓴다. What is the difference **between** this and that?
	among: ~ 사이에	셋 이상의 사이에 쓴다. Jenny is **among** the top students in her class.

여운이 있는
카툰

비가 그치면

이 비가 그치면 무지개가 뜰 거야.
내가 있으니 아무 걱정하지 마.

에.. 에쳐!

하지만 감기는 피해 갈 수 없었다.

GRAMMAR
BITE

핵심 문법만 콕! 쉽게 이해하는
중등 영문법

바른답·알찬풀이

Grade
1

Mirae N 에듀

GRAMMAR BITE
바른답 · 알찬풀이

GRAMMAR
BITE

Grade 1

Answers

Unit 01　Exercise　p.19

A　**1** is　**2** are　**3** was　**4** are　**5** is

B　**1** am　**2** is　**3** are　**4** was　**5** are

C　**1** Two bananas are on the table.
　2 She is in the gym.
　3 It was very hot yesterday.
　4 They were expensive.

Unit 02　Exercise　p.21

A　**1** Yes, he is　**2** No, I wasn't, was
　3 No, they aren't, are

B　**1** aren't[are not]　**2** Is　**3** ○　**4** isn't[is not]

C　**1** Is your uncle
　2 The book wasn't
　3 Were you busy
　4 Hamburgers aren't

Writing Practice　pp.22~23

A　**01** She is tall.
　02 We are middle school students.
　03 Many people were on the street.
　04 I am not strong.
　05 Were you sick
　06 They are my little brothers.
　07 Is he smart?
　08 It was very cold
　09 Tom and I are in the same club.
　10 The movie was not funny.

B　**01** a am　b We are in the first grade.
　02 a is　b My uncle isn't[is not] a doctor.
　03 a is　b Jenny was in the music room
　04 a is　b Are you tired?
　05 a were
　　　b They are not[They aren't, They're not] short

Actual Test　pp.24~27

※ (바르게 고칠 것)의 답은 해설을 참조하세요.

01 ③　**02** ⑤　**03** ④　**04** ⑤　**05** Is[is]　**06** ④　**07** ②
08 It was very windy yesterday.　**09** ④　**10** He is in the gym　**11** ②　**12** is not　**13** ④　**14** ①　**15** Peter was 13 years old last year. He is 14 years old this year.
16 ⑤　**17** ③　**18** ③　**19** ③　**20** ②　**21** Are you a member of the soccer club?　**22** ①　**23** I amn't → I am not[I'm not], My best friend are → My best friend is　**24** ①　**25** (1) Is → Was　(2) were → was　**26** ④
27 ③　**28** ②, ④

01 주어 We, You, They의 be동사의 현재형은 are이다.

02 Clara and Emma는 복수 주어이므로 is를 are로 고쳐야 한다.

03 주어가 I이고 yesterday가 있으므로 과거형 was가 알맞다.

04 주어가 They이고 last month가 있으므로 과거형 were가 알맞다.

05 주어가 he이고, 새로운 선생님에 대해 묻고 답하므로 be동사의 현재형 Is[is]가 알맞다.

06 '연필들'은 복수이므로 pencils로 나타내며, 복수형의 be동사 현재형은 are이다.

07 be동사의 부정형은 be동사 뒤에 not을 쓴다. (no → not)

08 어제의 날씨를 나타내므로 주어는 it, be동사는 was를 사용한다.

09 3인칭 단수 주어 Ms. Kim은 be동사 is를 쓰므로, 빈칸 뒤의 are와 어울릴 수 없다.

10 「주어 + be동사 + 장소를 나타내는 말」의 순서로 쓴다.
해석 A: Jason은 지금 집에 있나요?
　B: 아니. 그는 지금 체육관에 있어.
　A: 네, 감사합니다.

11 Her name은 3인칭 단수 주어이므로 be동사 are가 아니라 is를 사용한다.
해석 A: Alice, 저 소녀가 너의 여동생이니?
　B: 응. 그녀의 이름은 Olivia야.
　A: 그녀는 참 사랑스럽구나. 그녀는 초등학생이니?
　B: 아니. 그녀는 7살이야.

12 She는 be동사 현재형 is를 사용하며, be동사의 부정형은 be동사 뒤에 not을 쓴다.

13 last night은 과거이므로 it의 be동사 과거형 was가 적절하며, No 다음에는 was의 부정형 wasn't가 와야 한다.

14 is의 과거형은 was이므로 He was sick.이 되어야 한다.

15 last year는 과거이고 Peter는 3인칭 단수 주어이므로 is의 과거형 was로 쓰며, this year는 현재를 나타내므로 is로 쓴다.

16 wasn't는 was not의 줄임말이므로 wasn't not의 not을 삭제하여 wasn't로 쓰거나 was not으로 써야 올바르다.

17 ① wasn't → weren't[were not] ② was → is ④ is → are ⑤ is → was

18 ③은 you 뒤에 장소를 나타내는 말이 와서 '~에 있다'라는 의미를 나타내고, 나머지는 직업, 이름, 특정한 날이 와서 '~이다'라는 의미를 나타낸다.

19 ③은 주어가 James로 3인칭 단수이므로 빈칸에 is가 들어가지만, 나머지는 모두 are[Are]가 들어간다.

20 '너는 친구 집에 있었니?'라는 물음에 '응, 나는 학교에 있었어.'라고 답하는 것은 어색하다.

21 be동사의 의문문은 be동사를 주어 앞으로 보내므로 Are you ~?로 시작한다.

22 Am I pretty?는 상대방에게 자신에 대해 묻는 것이므로 대답할 때는 you를 사용해서 No, you aren't. / Yes, you are.로 한다.

23 am not은 amn't로 줄여 쓰지 않으며, My best friend는 3인칭 단수 주어이므로 be동사로 is를 쓴다.

해석 안녕, 내 이름은 수호야. 나는 14살이야. 나는 대한중학교 학생이야. 나는 농구를 잘하지만 배드민턴은 잘 못해. 나의 가장 친한 친구는 Chris야. 그는 영국 출신이야. 우리는 같은 반이야. 그와 나는 아주 친해.

24 첫 번째 문장은 주어가 It이고 today가 현재를 나타내므로 is, 두 번째 문장은 주어가 I이고 now가 현재를 나타내므로 am, 세 번째 문장은 She가 주어이고 last night이 과거를 나타내므로 was, 네 번째 문장은 주어가 The girls로 복수이고 yesterday가 과거를 나타내므로 were가 알맞다.

25 여행이 좋았는지 묻고 있으므로 Is를 Was로 고쳐야 한다. The weather는 3인칭 단수 주어이고 과거의 날씨에 대해 말하고 있으므로 were를 was로 고쳐야 한다.

26 차례대로 not, Are, is, Were가 빈칸에 들어가야 한다.

27 지금 날씨는 be동사 현재형으로, 날씨가 좋음은 nice(좋은)로 나타낸다.

28 ① was → were ③ Is → Was ⑤ They's → They're[They are]

Recall My Memory
p. 28

01 are → is   **02** were → was   **03** Are → Is   **04** ○
05 ○   **06** Is → Are   **07** was → were   **08** ○   **09** Was → Were   **10** ○   **11** is → are   **12** is → are   **13** Were → Was   **14** isn't → aren't[are not]   **15** was → were

---

Chapter **2** 현재로 과거로 갑옷을 바꿔 입는, 주어의 행동대장, 일반동사

Unit 01   Exercise
p. 31

A 1 studies   2 plays   3 washes   4 has   5 sees

B 1 fixes   2 fly   3 misses   4 ○   5 go

C 1 Mike has brown eyes.
2 My mom watches TV every evening.
3 The children wake up at 7 in the morning.

Unit 02   Exercise
p. 33

A 1 lost   2 ran   3 drank   4 visited   5 made

B 1 won   2 played   3 stopped   4 mixed   5 rode

C 1 saw a movie a week ago
2 ate cereal this morning
3 went swimming last weekend
4 had a piano lesson yesterday

Unit 03   Exercise
p. 35

A 1 My mother doesn't[does not] have a car.
2 Does Mr. Smith live in Seoul?
3 They didn't[did not] get up early this morning.
4 Did she go to the beach last summer?

B 1 Did   2 doesn't[does not] have   3 exercise
4 didn't[did not] play   5 ○

C 1 Does she play   2 don't like   3 Did he cook
4 didn't study

Writing Practice
pp. 36~37

A 01 We play basketball
02 Dad made a pizza
03 I do not go jogging
04 Did he draw this picture?
05 They went camping
06 I bought white sneakers
07 He does his homework

08 Does your sister play the violin?

09 I did not watch TV

10 She has a house

B **01 a** go **b** He goes to school

02 a gets up **b** I got up early

03 a Do you eat **b** Does she eat a sandwich

04 a likes **b** She doesn't[does not] like baseball.

05 a studied **b** Did they study English

Actual Test

pp. 38~41

01 ① **02** ② **03** ② **04** ④ **05** ②, ④, ⑤ **06** ②
07 ② **08** ② **09** ⑤ **10** ⑤ **11** ⑤ **12** ④ **13** Does,
like **14** ③ **15** (1) exercise → exercises (2) don't goes
→ doesn't[does not] go (3) use → uses **16** ④ **17**
② **18** ③ **19** His friends don't[do not] play tennis on
Sundays. **20** He didn't[did not] tell the truth to me.
21 Does he take care of sick animals? **22** Did she
find the money? **23** ① **24** (1) plays (2) has (3)
watches **25** ② **26** (1) Did (2) cried (3) Did (4) didn't
(5) slept **27** (1) rode (2) made (3) read (4) didn't go
28 ⑤ **29** (1) went (2) shopped (3) ate (4) liked (5)
had **30 b** losed → lost **d** didn't broke → didn't
break **f** ate → eat **g** swimmed → swam

01 carry → carries

02 plan → planned

03 일반동사 grow가 쓰인 의문문이고, 주어가 potatoes로 복수이므로
Do가 알맞다.

04 동사가 walks이므로 3인칭 단수 주어가 들어가야 하는데, ④ The
girls(소녀들)는 복수이므로 빈칸에 들어갈 수 없다.

05 동사가 과거형 went이므로 과거를 나타내는 부사(구)가 빈칸에 알맞
다. ① 토요일마다 ③ 내일

06 주어가 1인칭일 때 일반동사 현재형의 부정문은 don't를 이용하고, 일
반동사 과거형의 부정문은 인칭이나 수와 관계없이 didn't를 이용해 만
든다.

07 첫 번째 빈칸에는 주어(Many children)가 복수이므로 동사원형 like
가 알맞다. 두 번째 빈칸에는 주어(this child)가 3인칭 단수이고 but
(하지만)으로 보아 부정문이 되어야 하므로 doesn't like가 알맞다.

08 ①, ④, ⑤에는 Do가 들어가고, ③에는 뒤에 형용사 kind가 나오므로
be동사 Is가 들어간다.

09 걸어서 학교에 갔냐는 질문에 자전거를 타고 갔다고 했으므로 빈칸에는
과거형 의문문에 대한 부정의 대답이 들어가야 한다.

10 학교 근처에 사냐는 질문에 멀리 산다는 대답이 이어지고 있으므로 빈
칸에는 부정의 응답이 알맞다. Do you ~?로 시작하는 의문문의 부정
의 응답은 No, I don't.이다.

11 A의 질문에 last weekend가 나오므로 과거의 일을 묻고 답하는 내용
이 되어야 한다.

12 ④ doesn't gets → doesn't get

13 주어가 3인칭 단수인 일반동사 현재형의 의문문: 「Does + 주어 + 동사
원형 ~?」

14 ① Are → Do ② doesn't travel → don't[do not] travel ④
doesn't has → doesn't have ⑤ don't knows → don't know

15 (1), (3) 주어가 3인칭 단수일 때 일반동사의 현재형: 「동사원형 + -(e)s」
(2) 주어가 3인칭 단수일 때 일반동사 현재형의 부정문: 「doesn't
[does not] + 동사원형」

해석 Peter는 좋은 습관들을 가지고 있다. 그는 일찍 일어난다. 그는 매
일 운동을 한다. 하지만 그는 또한 나쁜 습관들도 가지고 있다. 그는
일찍 잠자리에 들지 않는다. 그는 휴대 전화를 너무 많이 사용한다.

16 주어가 3인칭 단수일 때 일반동사 현재형의 의문문: 「Does + 주어 + 동
사원형 ~?」

17 주어가 3인칭 단수일 때 일반동사 현재형의 부정문: 「doesn't[does
not] + 동사원형」

18 일반동사 과거형의 의문문: 「Did + 주어 + 동사원형 ~?」

19 주어가 복수일 때 일반동사 현재형의 부정문: 「don't[do not] + 동사
원형」

20 일반동사 과거형의 부정문: 「didn't[did not] + 동사원형」

21 주어가 3인칭 단수일 때 일반동사 현재형의 의문문: 「Does + 주어 + 동
사원형 ~?」

22 일반동사 과거형의 의문문: 「Did + 주어 + 동사원형 ~?」

23 ①은 일반동사의 부정문에 쓰이는 do, 나머지는 모두 일반동사로 쓰이
는 do이다.

24 주어가 모두 3인칭 단수이므로 동사도 3인칭 단수 현재형으로 쓴다.

해석 진수는 보통 방과 후에 농구를 한다. 세호는 간식을 먹고, 미나는
TV를 본다.

25 b Does → Is **c** doesn't likes → doesn't like **d** play → plays
f speaks → speak

26 (1), (3) 일반동사 과거형의 의문문이므로 Did가 들어간다. (2), (5) 과거의
일이므로 동사의 과거형이 알맞다. (4) 일반동사 과거형 의문문에 대한
부정의 대답은 「No, 주어 + didn't.」이다.

해석 A: Sally는 울었나요?

B: 네, 그랬어요. 그녀는 영화 마지막에 울었어요.

A: Fred는 영화를 재미있게 보았나요?

B: 아니오, 그렇지 않았어요. 그는 영화 보는 내내 잤어요.

27 (1), (2), (3) 지난 주말에 한 일을 나타내므로 동사의 과거형을 쓴다. (4) 일반동사 과거형의 부정문은 「didn't[did not]+동사원형」으로 쓴다.

해석 지난 주말에 수지는 자전거를 탔다. 그리고 그녀는 점심 식사를 만들었다. 그녀는 책도 읽었다. 그러나 그녀는 쇼핑은 가지 않았다.

28 b waked → woke **d** sended → sent

29 어제의 일에 대한 내용이므로 동사의 과거형을 쓴다.

해석 어제는 멋진 날이었다. 나의 친구 Katie가 서울에 왔다. 우리는 인사동에 갔다. 그곳은 한국에서 매우 유명한 곳이다. 우리는 멋진 옷을 쇼핑했다. 그리고 우리는 한국의 길거리 음식을 먹었다. Katie는 그 음식을 매우 좋아했다. 우리는 재미있는 시간을 보냈다. 우리는 매우 행복했다.

30 b lose의 과거형: lost **d** 일반동사 과거형의 부정문: 「didn't[did not]+동사원형」 **f** 일반동사 과거형의 의문문: 「Did+주어+동사원형 ~?」 **g** swim의 과거형: swam

Recall My Memory   p.42

01 watchs → watches **02** ○ **03** Are → Is **04** buyed → bought **05** am → was **06** plays → play **07** ○ **08** have → has **09** were → was **10** Do → Does **11** ○ **12** wrote → write **13** wasn't → isn't[is not] **14** didn't finished → didn't finish **15** readed → read

Chapter **3** 이름을 불러 주면 나에게로 와서 하나의 의미가 되는 명사

Unit 01   Exercise   p.45

A 1 dogs **2** tomatoes **3** cities **4** Deer **5** mice

B 1 foxes **2** countries **3** leaves **4** photos **5** teeth

C 1 ladies **2** Monkeys **3** knives **4** oxen, sheep

Unit 02   Exercise   p.47

A 1 is **2** advice **3** two cups of **4** New York **5** sunglasses

B 1 a bowl of **2** three bottles of **3** two pairs of **4** four pieces of **5** two loaves of **6** a sheet of

C 1 two glasses of milk **2** salt **3** Water flows

Unit 03   Exercise   p.49

A 1 the **2** an **3** a **4** The **5** a

B 1 an **2** ✕ **3** ✕ **4** A **5** the

C 1 a uniform
2 play the guitar
3 An elephant, a long nose
4 The moon, a month

Writing Practice   pp.50~51

A 01 The man on TV is
02 An ant has six legs.
03 have a slice of bread
04 went to the museum by bus
05 visits the dentist twice a year
06 My uncle grows potatoes
07 Two women sat
08 The sun rises in the east.
09 He bought three bottles of juice
10 I brush my teeth

B **01 a** a rabbit **b** keeps four fish

02 a a glass of milk **b** drank two glasses of water

03 a a cake

  b I bought three pieces[slices] of cake.

04 a the piano **b** The children play soccer well.

05 a A bird, The bird

  b An owl is in the tree. The owl is brown.

Actual Test

01 ② **02** ② **03** ① **04** ④ **05** ⑤ **06** need five boxes **07** two glasses of milk **08** ① **09** Many children like sweet things. **10** ② **11** Two mice are **12** ③ **13** ⑤ **14** ③ **15** ④ **16** They drank three bottles of juice. **17** ⑤ **18** ② **19** ④ **20** ③ **21** cereals → cereal **22** ① **23** a party → the party, cakes → cake, shoe → shoes **24** ① **25** ⑤ **26** The students go to school by school bus. **27** ② **28** the[The] **29** ②

01 paper는 셀 수 없는 명사로 뒤에 -s를 붙일 수 없다.

02 빈칸 앞에 부정관사 an이 있으므로 첫 발음이 모음으로 시작하는 apple이 알맞다.

03 fish는 단수형과 복수형이 같다.

04 country의 복수형은 countries이다.

05 class의 복수형은 classes, leaf의 복수형은 leaves이다.

06 box의 복수형은 boxes이다.

07 milk는 셀 수 없는 명사이므로 glass와 같이 담는 그릇을 나타내는 말로 수량을 표현한다.

08 feet은 foot의 복수형으로 부정관사 a와 함께 쓸 수 없다. a big feet → big feet

09 child의 복수형은 children이며 주어가 복수형이므로 동사는 like를 사용한다.

10 salt는 셀 수 없는 명사로 뒤에 -s를 붙일 수 없다.
해석 A: 수프는 어때요?
  B: 너무 많은 소금이 들어 있어요.
  A: 마실 것 좀 드릴까요?
  B: 네, 물 한 잔 주세요.

11 mouse의 복수형은 mice이다.

12 반바지는 항상 복수형 shorts로 나타낸다.

13 group은 셀 수 있는 명사이다.

14 goose의 복수형은 geese이며, 주어가 복수이므로 동사는 live를 쓴다.

15 ① health는 셀 수 없는 명사이므로 뒤에 -s를 붙일 수 없다. ② photo의 복수형은 photos이다. ③ boy의 복수형은 boys이다. ⑤ 고유한 이름을 나타내는 명사는 셀 수 없으므로 단수로 취급한다. are → is

16 juice는 셀 수 없는 명사이므로 bottle과 같이 담는 그릇을 나타내는 말로 수량을 표현한다.

17 ① rices → rice ② sheet → piece[slice] ③ loafs → loaves ④ coffees → coffee

18 가위는 복수형 scissors로 나타내고 동사도 are로 고쳐야 한다.

19 우리말을 영어로 표현하면 I go to church every Sunday[on Sundays].이다. 장소가 본래의 목적으로 쓰일 때는 장소 앞에 정관사 the를 쓰지 않는다.

20 umbrella는 첫 발음이 모음이므로 부정관사 an을 사용한다.

21 cereal은 셀 수 없는 명사이므로 뒤에 -s를 붙일 수 없다.
해석 A: 너는 아침을 먹니?
  B: 아니. 너는 어때?
  A: 나는 매일 아침 시리얼 두 그릇을 먹어.

22 earth는 세상에 하나뿐이므로 정관사 the를 붙인다.

23 party는 앞서 언급되었으므로 다시 말할 때는 정관사 the와 함께 써야 한다. cake를 조각으로 수량을 표현할 때 복수형으로 쓸 수 없다. 신발은 항상 복수형 shoes로 나타낸다.
해석 나는 어제 Tom의 생일 파티에 갔다. 많은 사람들이 파티에 있었다. 음식은 맛있었다. 나는 케이크 세 조각과 피자 두 조각을 먹었다. Tom은 많은 선물을 받았다. 그것들 중에서 그는 신발 한 켤레를 매우 좋아했다. 모든 사람이 즐거운 시간을 보냈다.

24 보기와 ①은 '~마다', ②와 ⑤는 막연한 어떤 하나, ③과 ④는 '한 개'를 나타낸다.

25 동사가 eat이므로 이때의 deer는 복수를 나타내며, a/an은 복수 명사와 함께 쓸 수 없다.

26 장소가 본래의 목적으로 쓰일 때와 「by + 교통수단」으로 쓰일 때는 정관사 the를 쓰지 않는다.

27 (A) 하나의 고유한 섬 이름 앞에는 정관사 the를 쓰지 않는다. (2) sun은 세상에 하나뿐이므로 정관사 the와 함께 쓴다. (C) 「by + 교통수단」에는 정관사 the를 쓰지 않는다.
해석 A: 주말 잘 보냈니?
  B: 응, 나는 가족과 함께 제주도에 갔었어.
  A: 좋았겠다. 날씨는 좋았니?
  B: 응, 아주 좋았어. 하루 종일 해가 비쳤어. 우리는 자동차를 빌려서 자동차로 많은 유명한 장소들을 방문했어.

28 정관사 the는 상황상 무엇을 가리키는지 알 수 있을 때, 명사 뒤에 꾸며주는 말이 있어서 가리키는 것이 분명할 때, 앞에서 말한 명사를 다시 말할 때 사용한다.

29 ① bed → the bed ③ drums → the drums ④ is → are ⑤ an European tour → a European tour

Recall My Memory
p. 56

01 waters → water　**02** don't like → doesn't[does not] like　**03** were → was　**04** leafs → leaves　**05** ○　**06** isn't → aren't[are not]　**07** glass → glasses　**08** ate → eat　**09** a interesting film → an interesting film　**10** ○　**11** childs → children　**12** go → went　**13** the badminton → badminton　**14** Was → Were　**15** ○

Chapter **4** 명사의 대리인 대명사

Unit 01　Exercise
p. 59

A　**1** them　**2** Our　**3** his　**4** myself　**5** her

B　**1** He　**2** her　**3** itself　**4** Their　**5** yours
　6 themselves

C　**1** his movies　**2** call me　**3** is hers
　4 hurt himself

Unit 02　Exercise
p. 61

A　**1** That　**2** these　**3** It　**4** This　**5** Those

B　**1** These　**2** That　**3** It　**4** those　**5** This

C　**1** This girl　**2** These flowers
　3 Is that your grandfather
　4 It is ten thirty

Unit 03　Exercise
p. 63

A　**1** some　**2** any　**3** one　**4** any　**5** ones

B　**1** some　**2** one　**3** any　**4** it　**5** ones

C　**1** any pets　**2** new ones　**3** some butter
　4 needs one

Writing Practice
pp. 64~65

A　**01** Is that bike his?
　02 It is dark
　03 I save some pocket money
　04 Do you know yourself
　05 These are not her shoes.
　06 He did not eat any food
　07 I like yellow ones
　08 She saw herself
　09 Their grandparents love them.
　10 This T-shirt goes well with those jeans.

B　**01 a** This, your umbrella　**b** That is my umbrella.
　02 a She, It
　　b He has two rabbits. They are so cute.
　03 a some juice
　　b They didn't[did not] drink any juice.
　04 a Those gloves, mine
　　b These gloves are yours.
　05 a myself　**b** He often talks to himself.

Actual Test
pp. 66~69

01 ②　**02** ③　**03** ②　**04** ③　**05** ④　**06** ②　**07** ⑤　**08** ③, ⑤　**09** ③　**10** ③　**11** himself　**12** These are white wolves.　**13** (1) mine　(2) my　**14** ⑤　**15** ⑤ you → yourself　**16** ③　**17** ⑤　**18** ①　**19** ④　**20** ④ Her → Their　**21** ②　**22** ④　**23** ③　**24** ③　**25** (1) one　(2) some　**26** (1) them　(2) ones　**27 b** some → any　**e** me → myself　**g** one → it　**28** (1) This　(2) it　(3) that　(4) its

01 ②는 '주격 - 소유격' 관계이고, 나머지는 '주격 - 목적격' 관계이다. ④ her는 목적격과 소유격 둘 다 되지만 나머지 넷과 다른 하나를 고르는 문제이므로 여기서는 목적격으로 보는 것이 적절하다.

02 '드레스의 색'이므로 3인칭 단수 It의 소유격 Its가 알맞다.

03 빈칸에는 You and Fred를 가리키는 주격 대명사가 필요하므로 You가 알맞다.

04 a cat을 가리키는 주격 대명사가 필요하므로 It이 알맞다.

05 빈칸은 동사 call의 목적어 자리이므로 목적격 대명사가 들어가는데, our는 소유격이다.

06 빈칸 뒤에 명사가 없으므로 '~의 것'이라는 소유대명사가 들어가는데, her는 소유격 또는 목적격이므로 빈칸에 들어갈 수 없다.

07 over there로 보아 멀리 있는 복수 명사 socks를 가리키므로 those가 알맞다.

08 첫 번째 빈칸은 명사 앞에 쓰여 소유 관계를 나타내는 소유격 자리이고, 두 번째 빈칸은 「소유격＋명사」를 대신하는 소유대명사 자리이므로 소유격과 소유대명사의 형태가 같은 his와 Katie's가 알맞다.

09 Henry and I는 They가 아니라 We로 대신한다.

10 '너의 것'이라는 의미가 되어야 하므로 yours로 고쳐야 한다.

11 소년이 거울 속의 자신을 보고, 혼잣말하는 상황이므로 전치사 at과 to의 목적어로 the boy의 재귀대명사가 와야 한다.

12 This is ~의 복수형은 These are ~이다. 복수형으로 써야 하므로 하나를 나타내는 부정관사 a를 빼고 wolf의 복수형인 wolves를 쓴다.

13 (1) '나의 것'을 뜻하는 소유대명사 mine이 알맞다. (2) 명사 bike 앞에 '나의'를 뜻하는 소유격 my가 알맞다.
해석 A: Brian, 이것이 네 자전거니?
B: 아니, 그것은 내 것이 아니야.
A: 저것이 네 것이니?
B: 응, 그것이 내 자전거야.

14 they의 재귀대명사는 themselves이다.

15 목적어 you가 주어 you와 같은 대상이므로 재귀대명사 yourself로 고쳐야 한다.

16 동사가 are로 복수 동사이고 뒤에 복수 명사 pants가 나오므로 That이 아니라 Those로 써야 한다.

17 목적어 me는 주어 I와 같은 대상이므로 재귀대명사 myself로 고쳐야 한다.

18 some은 주로 긍정문에, any는 부정문과 의문문에 주로 사용된다.

19 보기와 ④는 재귀대명사가 동사의 목적어로 쓰였고, 나머지는 '직접' 했다는 것을 강조하기 위해 쓰였다.

20 두 여동생의 이름으로, 복수 명사 names 앞의 소유격이므로 Their가 와야 한다.
해석 나의 아빠는 수의사이고 나의 엄마는 선생님이다. 나는 두 명의 여동생이 있다. 그들의 이름은 Lily와 Alice이다. Lily는 키가 크고 날씬하다. Alice는 키가 작고 뚱뚱하다. 그들은 매우 귀엽다.

21 ②는 강조하기 위해 쓰인 재귀대명사이므로 생략할 수 있다.

22 ④는 소유대명사이고, 나머지는 소유격으로 쓰였다.

23 ③은 지시형용사로 쓰였고, 나머지는 지시대명사로 쓰였다.

24 ③은 인칭대명사로 쓰였고, 나머지는 비인칭 주어로 쓰였다.

25 (1) 정해지지 않은 것을 대신하는 one이 알맞다. (2) '몇몇'을 나타내며 긍정문에 쓰이는 some이 알맞다.

26 (1) 앞 문장의 these shoes를 대신하는 대명사 them이 알맞다. (2) 특정하지 않은 것을 가리키는 부정대명사가 알맞다. shoes가 복수형이므로 ones로 쓴다.

27 b 부정문에서는 주로 any가 쓰인다. e 주어와 목적어가 같은 대상일 때는 목적어를 재귀대명사로 쓴다. g 잃어버린 것은 새로 산 우산이므로, a new umbrella를 대신하는 it으로 써야 한다.

28 (1) right here로 보아 가까이 있는 것을 가리키므로 this, (2) 앞에서 언급한 my house를 대신하므로 it, (3) across the field로 보아 멀리 있는 것을 가리키므로 that, (4) 앞에서 언급한 말의 이름을 의미하므로 it의 소유격 its가 알맞다.
해석 A: 바로 여기 이것이 우리 집이야.
B: 와, 아주 근사하구나. 들판 가로질러 있는 저것이 네 말이니?
A: 응, 그것의 이름은 Jet야.

Recall My Memory
p. 70

01 that → those **02** have → had **03** That → It **04** finishs → finishes **05** by the bus → by bus **06** some → any **07** ○ **08** ourself → ourselves **09** glass → glasses **10** ○ **11** Were → Was **12** don't cook → doesn't[does not] cook **13** a hour → an hour **14** ○ **15** sheeps → sheep

수능에 꼭 나오는 중학 영문법

수능 기초 연습
p. 72

A 1 myself 2 surround 3 yourself 4 are
  5 their

B 1 were 2 it 3 ○ 4 is 5 herself

C ①

C 문장의 주어인 A guy and a big dog가 복수이므로 복수 동사 run으로 고쳐야 한다.

해석 한 남자와 큰 개가 들판으로 달린다. 그 개는 그 남자를 뒤쫓는다. 그 남자는 들판에서 욕조를 본다. 그는 욕조로 달려가 그것을 뒤집어쓴다. 그 개는 그저 짖고 또 짖는다. 결국, 그것은 가버린다. 그런 다음 그 남자는 욕조에서 나와 집으로 간다.

수능 독해 적용

pp. 73~74

I ③ **2** ② **3** ⑤

I (A) 주어 he가 자신을 숨긴 것이므로 he의 재귀대명사 himself가 알맞다. (B) 첫 문장의 a big rock을 가리키므로 it이 알맞다. (C) gold는 셀 수 없는 명사이므로 gold가 알맞다.

해석 옛날에 한 왕이 길에 큰 바위를 놓아두었다. 그러고 나서 그는 숨어서 그것을 지켜봤다. 대부분의 사람들이 바위로 다가와서는 그저 돌아서 지나갈 뿐이었다. 그들은 "길들이 깨끗하지가 않아. 왕이 일을 안 하는군."이라고 말했다. 그때 한 농부가 나타났고 그 돌을 발견했다. 그는 그 돌을 길가로 옮겨 놓았다. 왕은 매우 행복해졌고 그 농부에게 많은 금을 주었다.

2 ②는 앞의 computers를 가리키므로 it을 them으로 고쳐야 한다.

해석 나의 할머니는 70세이다. 그녀는 컴퓨터들에 관심이 있어서, 공립 도서관에서 그것들에 대해 배웠다. 수업 시간에 그녀는 훌륭한 학생이었다. 그녀는 선생님 말씀에 귀를 기울였고 많은 질문들을 했다. 그녀는 많이 배웠다. 나는 그녀가 매우 자랑스럽다.

3 (A) 주어인 men's clothes가 복수이므로 복수 동사 have가 알맞다. (B) 주어인 rich women이 자기 자신에게 옷을 입히지 않았다는 의미로, 주어와 목적어가 같은 대상이므로 재귀대명사 themselves가 알맞다. (C) 앞에 나온 the buttons를 가리키므로 them이 알맞다.

해석 오른손잡이 사람들은 오른쪽에 있는 단추를 왼쪽에 있는 구멍으로 쉽게 끼운다. 대부분의 사람들이 오른손잡이라서, 남성복은 오른쪽에 단추가 있다. 하지만 여성은 어떤가? 처음에 단추는 매우 비쌌고, 단지 부유한 사람들의 옷에만 그것들을 달았다. 옛날에 부유한 여성들은 보통 자기 자신이 옷을 입지 않았다. 하녀들이 그들에게 옷을 입혀 주었다. 그래서 양재사들은 단추를 하녀의 오른쪽에 두었고, 이것은 여성의 왼쪽에 그것들을 두게 했다.

Chapter **5** 과거부터 미래까지 시간을 품고 있는 타임머신, 시제

Unit 01 Exercise
p. 77

A **1** **a** was **b** is **2** **a** plays **b** played
3 **a** lived **b** live

B **1** walks **2** Did **3** doesn't[does not] drink **4** ○
5 rides

C **1** painted **2** sets **3** didn't go fishing
4 Does she exercise

Unit 02 Exercise
p. 79

A **1** be **2** is going to **3** stay **4** am not going to
5 to join

B **1** will clean his room
2 is going to play tennis
3 won't[will not] go
4 Is he going to go, he isn't, will travel

C **1** will write
2 won't watch
3 is going to help
4 Are you going to visit

Unit 03 Exercise
p. 81

A **1** am making **2** was reading **3** isn't driving
4 Are you fishing

B **1** are running **2** like **3** Is he fixing
4 weren't[were not] cooking

C **1** are having **2** was lying **3** Were you swimming
4 isn't raining, is shining

Writing Practice
pp. 82~83

A **01** They are taking a walk
02 She goes to bed
03 I will do my best
04 He was not wearing a hat.

05 I will not climb a mountain

06 Is she going to buy

07 The boys were dancing

08 The singer came to Korea

09 Is she sitting on the bench?

10 We are going to have his birthday party

B **01** a rode b He will ride his skateboard

02 a is lying

b She is not[She isn't, She's not] lying to the teacher.

03 a were making b I am making spaghetti

04 a are going to go

b Are they going to go to the library?

05 a isn't[is not] sunny

b It won't[will not] be sunny in London

Actual Test

pp. 84~87

01 ③ **02** ④ **03** ④ **04** Is[is] **05** ① **06** ④ **07** ⑤
08 Are you listening to music? **09** ① **10** ④ **11** are running **12** ⑤ **13** ⑤ **14** ③ **15** is not sleeping
16 ② **17** ② **18** Mike went hiking yesterday. He saw some beautiful flowers. **19** ③ **20** ① **21** ① **22** was taking **23** was putting on **24** ⑤ **25** does not like → did not like, will go → go, playing → play **26** ② **27** ⑤

01 변하지 않는 진리는 현재시제를 사용한다.

02 미래를 나타내는 will과 과거를 나타내는 a year ago는 함께 사용될 수 없다.

03 미래를 나타내는 next year와 과거를 나타내는 was going to는 함께 사용될 수 없다.

04 동사 teaches로 보아 현재의 상태에 관해 이야기하고 있으므로 Is[is]를 사용한다.

05 과거를 나타내는 yesterday가 있으므로 plays를 played로 고쳐야 한다.

06 be going to의 부정형은 not을 be동사 뒤에 쓴다. is going not to return → is not going to return

07 첫 번째 빈칸에는 tomorrow가 미래를 나타내므로 will이, 두 번째 빈칸에는 매일 반복되는 일을 나타내는 현재시제 leaves가 적절하다.

08 현재진행시제의 의문문: 「Be동사 + 주어 + 동사원형-ing ~?」

09 have가 '소유'의 개념을 가질 때는 현재진행형으로 쓸 수 없다. is having → has

10 '너는 지금 서점에 가는 중이니?'라는 물음에 '아니, 나는 쇼핑을 갈 예정이야.'라고 답하는 것은 어색하다.

11 남자와 여자가 달리기하는 중이므로 현재진행형을 사용해야 한다.

12 과거진행시제: 「was/were + 동사원형-ing」

13 last week는 과거를 나타내고 동사 have로 보아 일반동사 의문문이므로 Did[did]가 알맞다.

14 b ate → eat e moved → moves f will go → go

15 현재진행시제의 부정문: 「am/are/is not + 동사원형-ing」

16 five years ago는 과거를 나타내므로 meet을 met으로 고쳐야 한다.

17 ① is dancing → was dancing ③ am wanting → want ④ will eat → eat ⑤ was walking → is walking

18 yesterday는 과거를 나타내므로 go를 went로, see를 saw로 바꿔 쓴다.

19 진행시제의 의문문은 be동사를 주어 앞으로 보내므로 Was she watching a movie?가 되어야 한다.

20 첫 번째 빈칸에는 계획이 있는지 묻는 말이므로 Do가 들어가고, 두 번째 빈칸에는 어젯밤의 일을 나타내야 하므로 arrived가 들어가야 한다.

해석 A: 안녕, 지수야. 오늘 오후에 무슨 계획 있니?
B: 응, 나는 공원에서 개를 산책시킬 거야. 너는 어때?
A: 어젯밤에 캐나다에서 내 사촌이 도착했거든. 그래서 우리는 도시를 둘러볼 거야.

21 ①에는 Is, 나머지에는 모두 was[Was]가 들어가는 것이 적절하다.

22 7시 30분에 샤워하는 중이었으므로 과거진행형으로 쓴다.

23 7시 45분에 옷을 입는 중이었으므로 과거진행형으로 쓴다.

24 첫 번째는 now가 현재진행시제와 어울리므로 crying이, 두 번째는 tomorrow가 미래시제와 어울리므로 will이, 세 번째는 then이 과거진행시제와 어울리므로 was가, 네 번째는 three days ago가 과거시제와 어울리므로 bought가 들어간다.

25 before는 과거시제와 어울리므로 does not like를 did not like로, Every Sunday는 현재시제와 어울리므로 will go를 go로, be going to는 뒤에 동사원형이 오므로 playing을 play로 고쳐야 한다.

해석 나는 탁구와 농구를 좋아한다. 매주 토요일에 나는 Sam과 탁구를 한다. 그는 전에는 탁구를 좋아하지 않았지만, 지금 그는 그것을 즐긴다. 매주 일요일에 나는 체육관에 가서 James와 농구를 한다. 그는 농구를 정말 잘한다. 내일은 토요일이다. 그래서 Sam과 나는 함께 탁구를 할 예정이다.

26 B가 영어 말하기 대회에서 이미 일등을 한 상황이므로 과거시제를 사용해야 한다. win → won

A: 축하해! 너 영어 말하기 대회에서 일등했구나.

B: 고마워. 네 덕분에 그것을 해냈어. 네가 나를 많이 도와줬잖아.

A: 천만에. 너는 최선을 다했어.

27 첫 번째는 last week이 과거시제와 어울리므로 was가, 두 번째는 is going to가 미래의 일을 나타내므로 미래를 나타내는 부사 soon이, 세 번째는 every Monday가 현재시제와 어울리므로 have가, 네 번째는 now가 현재진행시제와 어울리므로 Are가 들어간다.

Recall My Memory
p. 88

01 This → It **02** Deers → Deer **03** ○ **04** ○ **05** Does → Do **06** will be not → will not be **07** ○ **08** was watering → is watering **09** A sugar → Sugar **10** studied → study **11** watches → watched **12** it → them **13** Are → Were **14** This is → These are **15** ○

Chapter **6** 함께하면 특별한 의미가 돼, 동사의 도우미 조동사

Unit 01 Exercise
p. 91

A **1** b **2** a **3** b **4** c **5** d

B **1** Can **2** may **3** can't **4** may not

C **1** I can't[cannot] see
2 May[Can] I try on
3 could pass
4 is able to speak

Unit 02 Exercise
p. 93

A **1** must **2** must not **3** don't have to **4** should
5 must not

B **1** has to **2** had to **3** will have to **4** ○
5 doesn't have to

C **1** must be
2 has to take care of
3 shouldn't eat
4 don't have to do

Writing Practice
pp. 94~95

A **01** Can you sing
02 We should be quiet
03 The story must be true.
04 Students have to keep the rules.
05 It may snow tonight.
06 Dogs cannot see red.
07 People should not drive fast
08 She has to come home
09 Sam is able to speak Korean
10 Amy doesn't have to go to school

B **01** **a** has to finish
b She doesn't have to finish her homework today.
02 **a** may be **b** He must be late for class.
03 **a** shouldn't[should not] throw
b We should throw trash in the trash can.
04 **a** can't[cannot] help
b She will be able to help you later.
05 **a** must get up **b** Jack had to get up early

Actual Test
pp. 96~99

01 ③ **02** ① **03** ③ **04** ④ **05** ② **06** ② **07** ⑤ **08** ⑤ **09** ③ **10** ⑤ **11** ⑤ **12** She may be sleeping. **13** must not take **14** ① **15** ④ **16** ① **17** ④ **18** ③ **19** had to **20** won't be able to have **21** ② **22** may not keep the secret **23** ③ **24** He wasn't able to read the English words. **25** **c** is → be **g** must → have to **26** ③ **27** (1) can do 20 push-ups (2) can ride a bike (3) can't[cannot] make pasta (4) can't[cannot] play the violin **28** (1) should not talk (2) should turn off (3) should return

01 너무 크게 말하고 있어서 아기를 깨울지도 모른다는 추측의 의미가 되어야 하므로 may가 알맞다.

02 must는 '~임이 틀림없다'라는 의미로 확신이 강한 추측을 나타낸다.

03 can 다음에는 동사원형이 와야 하는데, ③은 빈칸 뒤에 fixing이 있으므로 can이 들어갈 수 없다.

04 Can you ~?로 물을 때는 Yes, I can. 또는 No, I can't.로 답한다. 빈칸 뒤에 춤을 잘 못 춘다는 말이 이어지므로 빈칸에는 부정의 대답이 알맞다.

05 Can I ~?는 '내가 ~해도 될까?'라는 뜻으로 허락을 구하는 표현이다.

06 시험공부를 해야 한다는 의미가 되어야 하므로 should가 알맞다.

07 '~해야 할 것이다'라는 미래의 의무는 will have to로 나타낸다.

08 don't have to: ~할 필요가 없다

09 can(~할 수 있다) = be able to

10 must not(~해서는 안 된다) → don't have to(~할 필요가 없다)

11 부탁할 때는 can[could] 또는 will[would]을 쓴다. ⑤ should는 의무를 나타낸다.
해석 A: 나 좀 도와주겠니?
　　　B: 물론이지. 그게 뭔데?
　　　A: 우리는 가족 여행을 떠날 예정이야. 우리 개 좀 돌봐 주겠니?
　　　B: 좋아. 물론이지.

12 perhaps는 '아마도'라는 뜻으로 추측의 may로 바꿔 쓸 수 있다. may는 뒤에 동사원형이 와야 하므로 is는 be로 쓴다.

13 「must not + 동사원형」: ~하면 안 된다

14 may와 can은 둘 다 허가의 의미로 쓰인다.

15 must와 have to는 둘 다 의무의 의미로 쓰인다.

16 ①은 허가, 나머지는 능력을 나타낸다.

17 ④는 허가, 나머지는 추측을 나타낸다.

18 ③은 강한 추측, 나머지는 의무를 나타낸다.

19 had to: ~해야 했다

20 조동사는 두 개를 연달아 쓸 수 없으므로 can을 be able to로 고쳐야 한다.

21 must not(~하면 안 된다) ≠ don't have to(~할 필요가 없다)

22 「may not + 동사원형」: ~하지 않을지도 모른다
해석 A: Jenny에게 그 비밀을 말하지 마.
　　　B: 왜 안 되는데?
　　　A: 그녀는 입이 가벼워. 그녀는 그 비밀을 지키지 않을지도 몰라.
　　　B: 오, 나는 그것을 몰랐어. 알겠어, 그녀에게 그것을 말하지 않을게.

23 **a** don't have to → doesn't have to **b** have to → has to
d has to → had to

24 '~할 수 없다'는 「be not able to + 동사원형」으로 쓴다. 주어가 3인칭 단수이고 과거시제이므로 be동사는 was를 쓴다. 이때 8단어로 써야 하므로 was not을 wasn't로 줄여 쓴다.

25 **c** should 뒤에 동사원형이 와야 한다. **g** 조동사는 두 개를 연달아 쓸 수 없으므로 둘 중 하나를 조동사를 대신하는 말로 바꿔 써야 한다.

26 ① are → be ② plays → play ④ Does your mom can drive a car? → Can your mom drive a car? ⑤ cans → can

27 할 수 있는 것은 can, 할 수 없는 것은 can't[cannot]로 나타내며, 뒤에 동사원형을 쓴다.

28 「should + 동사원형」: ~해야 한다, 「should not + 동사원형」: ~하지 말아야 한다

Recall My Memory p. 100

01 has to → must **02** ○ **03** have to → has to **04** a happiness → happiness **05** ○ **06** ○ **07** washed → wash **08** wins → won **09** They were → It was **10** can't → couldn't[could not] **11** is → be **12** ○ **13** wasn't → weren't[were not] **14** is runing → is running **15** an uniform → a uniform

Chapter **7** 의도한 바를 이렇게 전해 봐, 알아두면 유용한 문장의 종류

Unit 01 Exercise p. 103

A **1** What **2** Whose **3** What **4** Who **5** Which

B **1** Who **2** What **3** Whose **4** Which

C **1** Who[Whom] did you meet **2** Which is your cup **3** What will you do **4** Whose car is he

Unit 02 Exercise p. 105

A **1** How **2** When **3** Where **4** Why **5** How long

B **1** How **2** When **3** Why **4** Where

C **1** Where are **2** When do you
3 How often do you **4** Why is she

Unit 03 Exercise p. 107

A **1** Turn **2** go **3** Don't **4** Let's not **5** Be

B **1** There is **2** There are **3** There isn't **4** Is there

C **1** Let's take **2** Don't talk
3 There were many people

A　**1** a hot day (it is)　**2** exciting the final game was
　3 tall buildings (those are)　**4** well Daniel dances

B　**1** aren't you　**2** doesn't he　**3** should we
　4 didn't she　**5** do they

C　**1** How delicious　**2** What a long bridge
　3 didn't do, did she　**4** will come, won't he

Writing Practice

A　**01** Who is your best friend?
　02 How high he jumps!
　03 When will the meeting begin?
　04 What is the woman doing?
　05 Don't worry about the exam.
　06 How long does the movie last?
　07 What a cute puppy you have!
　08 Which dish did she order
　09 There were five ducks
　10 was cold yesterday, wasn't it

B　**01 a** is a tiger
　　b There are four elephants in the zoo.
　02 a Where did the accident
　　b Why did the accident happen?
　03 a Be nice　**b** Don't be rude to your friends.
　04 a How many pencils
　　b How much paper do you need?
　05 a don't you
　　b Sam doesn't[does not] eat carrots, does he?

Actual Test

01 ①　**02** ⑤　**03** ④　**04** ③　**05** Who sits　**06** ⑤　**07** ③　**08** ④　**09** How　**10** ①　**11** ①　**12** There was a dog in the house.　**13** ③　**14** Where do you go to school　**15** ⑤　**16** ②　**17** ①　**18** ②　**19** ④　**20** ③　**21** There are many students in the playground now.　**22** ②　**23** closed → close　**24** ⑤　**25** ③　**26** You won't be late again, will you?　**27** fast she talks　**28** a beautiful day (it is)　**29** ④　**30** there is → there are, being → be, Let's be follow → Let's follow

01 영어라고 답했으므로 가장 좋아하는 과목이 무엇인지 물을 때 쓰는 What이 알맞다.

02 내 것이라고 답했으므로 누구의 것인지 물을 때 쓰는 Whose가 알맞다.

03 lots of pens는 복수이므로 There is 뒤에 올 수 없다.

04 생일이 언제인지 물을 때는 Where가 아니라 When을 쓴다.

05 '누구'는 who이고, 의문사가 문장의 주어일 때 3인칭 단수로 취급한다.

06 which 뒤에 선택을 제시할 때는 and가 아니라 or를 쓴다.

07 '누구를'은 who[whom]이고, 의문사가 문장의 목적어이므로 뒤에 「조동사 + 주어 + 동사원형」이 온다.

08 「What + a/an + 형용사 + 명사 + 주어 + 동사!」에서 명사가 복수이므로 a/an을 쓰지 않는다.

09 여행이 어땠는지, 우체국에 어떻게 가는지를 묻고 있으므로, '어떻게'라는 의미의 How를 쓴다.

10 ① '얼마나 키가 큰'은 How tall이며, 나머지 빈칸에는 이유를 물을 때 쓰는 Why가 알맞다.

11 앞 문장의 동사가 are이고 긍정이므로 부가의문은 aren't로 쓴다. 어젯밤 늦게까지 자지 않고 있었으므로 피곤하다는 긍정의 대답인 yes로 답해야 한다.

12 「There was + 단수 명사 + 장소」: ~에 …이 있었다

13 지금 어디에 가는 중인지 묻는 말에 '지금 곧.'이라는 대답은 어색하다.

14 대한중학교에 다닌다고 했으므로 어느 학교에 다니는지 묻는 말이 되도록 「Where + do동사 + 주어 + 동사원형 ~?」의 순서로 쓴다.

15 Let's의 부정형은 Let's don't가 아니라 Let's not이다.

16 다음 버스가 언제 도착하냐고 물었으므로 5분 후에 도착할 거라는 대답이 자연스럽다.

17 '너는 배드민턴을 좋아하지, 그렇지 않니?'라고 물었으므로 '응, 그것은 내가 가장 좋아하는 운동이야.'라고 답하는 것이 자연스럽다.

18 how much: 얼마(가격), how old: 몇 살의, how often: 얼마나 자주, how long: 얼마나 오래(기간)

19 왜 결석했는지를 묻는 말이 자연스러우므로 when을 why로 고쳐야 한다.
해석 A: 안녕, Daniel. 너는 오늘 Robert를 봤니?
　　B: 아니, 그는 학교에 오지 않았어.
　　A: 오, 그는 오늘 왜 결석했니?
　　B: 왜냐하면 그가 다리를 다쳤기 때문이야.

20 부가의문문의 내용이 긍정이든 부정이든 상관없이 지금 가야 한다고 긍정의 내용으로 답하고 있으므로 No를 Yes로 고쳐야 한다.
해석 A: 우리는 지금 갈 필요가 없지, 그렇지?
　　B: 아니, 우리는 지금 가야 해.
　　A: 알았어. 그러면 서두르자.

21 「There are + 셀 수 있는 명사의 복수형」: ~들이 있다

22 첫 번째 빈칸에는 부정 명령문을 만드는 Don't가, 두 번째 빈칸에는 감탄문을 만드는 What이, 세 번째 빈칸에는 뒤에 형용사 kind가 있으므로 동사 be가, 네 번째 빈칸에는 '~이 있니?'라는 의미의 Is there ~?의 there가 들어가는 것이 알맞다.

23 명령문은 동사원형으로 시작하며, 문장 앞이나 뒤에 please를 붙이면 공손한 표현이 된다.

24 How many 뒤에는 셀 수 있는 명사의 복수형이 오므로 brother를 brothers로 고쳐야 한다.

25 5분이 필요하다고 답했으므로, how much time을 이용해서 몇 분이 필요한지 묻는 말이 적절하다.

26 부정문 뒤에는 긍정의 부가의문문이 오며, 앞에 won't가 있으면 부가의문문에는 will을 쓴다.

27 「How + 형용사/부사 (+ 주어 + 동사)!」

28 「What + a/an + 형용사 + 명사 (+ 주어 + 동사)!」

29 ① Be watch → Watch ② Don't afraid → Don't be afraid ③ Let's playing → Let's play ⑤ There were → There was

30 rules는 복수 명사이므로 there are를 쓴다. 명령문은 동사원형으로 시작하므로 being을 be로 고쳐야 한다. Let's 뒤에 일반동사가 올 때는 be가 필요하지 않다.

해석 많은 학생들이 매일 도서관을 이용한다. 그래서 도서관에는 몇 가지 규칙이 있다. 첫째, 시끄럽게 하지 마라. 둘째, 다른 사람들에게 친절해라. 셋째, 도서관에서 먹거나 마시지 마라. 넷째, 각각의 책을 다시 제자리에 갖다 놓아라. 이런 규칙들을 지켜서 도서관에서 즐거운 시간을 보내자.

Recall My Memory

p.116

01 There are → There is **02** rose → rises **03** one → ones **04** ○ **05** do → be **06** ○ **07** Where → When **08** himself → themselves **09** cleaning → clean **10** knifes → knives **11** wasn't he → didn't he **12** is going → is going to **13** ○ **14** What → How **15** visitted → visited

---

Unit 01 Exercise
p. 119

A **1** salty **2** feel like **3** lovely **4** good **5** fun

B **1** smells **2** look **3** tastes **4** sounds **5** feel

C **1** smells bad
2 look like angels
3 feels comfortable
4 tastes like strawberries

Unit 02 Exercise
p. 121

A **1** for **2** to **3** ✕ **4** ✕ **5** of

B **1** me their new car[their new car to me]
2 you some snacks[some snacks for you]
3 a story to her students[her students a story]
4 a delicious meal for his parents[his parents a delicious meal] **5** ○

C **1** her a letter **2** me a favor
3 a carnation for his teacher
4 her dictionary to him

Writing Practice
pp. 122~123

A **01** I feel cold
02 ask a question of you
03 Flowers smell good.
04 show me your passport
05 Oranges taste sweet and sour.
06 looked like a tree
07 sent a present to me
08 sounds very beautiful
09 gave some chocolate to him
10 made his dog a nice house[made a nice house for his dog]

B **01** **a** smells **b** That food tastes salty.
02 **a** read us
b She wrote them a letter.[She wrote a letter to them.]
03 **a** looks like **b** He feels like a hero.

04 a bought a bag for
   b Mom made a bag for me.[Mom made me a bag.]
05 a taught magic to
   b Harry showed magic to him.[Harry showed him magic.]

Actual Test

pp. 124~127

01 ③　**02** ④　**03** ⑤　**04** ①　**05** ④　**06** ⑤　**07** ①
08 ③　**09** ⑤　**10** ②, ④, ⑤　**11** ④　**12** ④　**13** for me
14 ②, ③　**15** Grace taught children English at the community center.　**16** ③　**17** This fish smells bad.
18 It sounded like a beautiful song to my ears.　**19** ①, ②　**20** (1) two free movie tickets me → two free movie tickets to me[me two free movie tickets]　(2) greatly → great　**21** Give him some milk.　**22** ②, ③
23 ②　**24** ③　**25** ② → tells funny stories to the children[tells the children funny stories]　⑤ → get some snacks for the children[get the children some snacks]　**26** (1) lent her camera to　(2) bought Lisa
27 looks like a sheep　**28 b** powerfully → powerful　**g** to → for　**29** (1) Amy math　(2) stories to　(3) pasta for

01 감각동사 look 다음에는 형용사가 온다.

02 간접목적어(me) 앞에 전치사 to가 있으므로, 전치사 for를 쓰는 수여동사 buy는 빈칸에 들어갈 수 없다.

03 explain은 수여동사가 아니므로 간접목적어와 직접목적어를 가질 수 없다.

04 수여동사 teach와 send는 「수여동사 + 직접목적어 + to + 간접목적어」의 어순을 가진다.

05 감각동사 taste 다음에는 형용사가 오므로, 부사 sweetly는 올 수 없다.

06 감각동사 feel 다음에는 형용사가 오므로, 부사 terribly는 올 수 없다.

07 ①은 빈칸에 to가 들어가지만, 나머지는 모두 for가 들어간다.

08 수여동사 write는 전치사 to를, make는 for를 쓴다.

09 「감각동사 + 형용사」 또는 「감각동사 + like + 명사」의 형태로 써야 한다.

10 감각동사 look은 뒤에 형용사가 오므로, 부사 sadly와 greatly는 올 수 없다.

11 ④의 동사 name은 「주어 + 동사 + 목적어 + 목적격보어」의 형태를 이루지만, 나머지는 수여동사로 「주어 + 동사 + 간접목적어 + 직접목적어」의 형태를 이룬다.

12 ④의 동사 catch는 뒤에 목적어가 필요하지만, 나머지 동사들은 주격 보어가 필요하다.

13 수여동사 buy는 간접목적어가 직접목적어 뒤로 갈 때 간접목적어 앞에 전치사 for를 쓴다.

14 빈칸 뒤에 형용사 difficult가 있으므로, 감각동사 look과 sound가 알맞다. 동사 see, hear, watch는 뒤에 목적어가 필요하다.

15 수여동사 teach는 「수여동사 + 간접목적어 + 직접목적어」의 어순으로 쓴다.

16 수여동사 send는 전치사 for가 아니라 to를 쓴다.

17 감각동사 뒤에는 부사 badly가 아니라 형용사 bad가 와야 한다.

18 감각동사 뒤에 명사구 a beautiful song이 있으므로 전치사 like가 필요하다.

19 수여동사 ask는 「수여동사 + 간접목적어 + 직접목적어」 또는 「수여동사 + 직접목적어 + of + 간접목적어」의 형태를 이룬다.

20 수여동사 give는 「수여동사 + 간접목적어 + 직접목적어」 또는 「수여동사 + 직접목적어 + to + 간접목적어」의 형태를 이루며, 감각동사 sound는 뒤에 부사가 아니라 형용사가 온다.
해석 A: Fred, 너 오늘 기분 좋아 보인다.
　　B: 나 오늘 기분이 아주 좋아. 민호가 내게 두 장의 무료 영화 표를 줬거든. 오늘 밤에 영화 보러 가자.
　　A: 그거 좋아.

21 수여동사 give는 「수여동사 + 간접목적어 + 직접목적어」의 순서로 쓴다.

22 ① to me her story → me her story[her story to me]　④ for → to　⑤ he → him

23 (A) 수여동사 make는 전치사 for를 쓴다. (B) 수여동사 write는 전치사 to를 쓴다. (C) 감각동사 look 뒤에는 형용사가 온다.
해석 어제는 엄마의 생신이었다. 언니와 나는 그녀를 위해 뭔가 특별한 것을 했다. 먼저, 나는 엄마에게 생일 케이크를 만들어 드렸다. 나의 언니는 엄마에게 멋진 선물을 사 드렸다. 그녀는 또한 엄마에게 생신 카드를 써 드렸다. 엄마는 매우 행복해 보이셨다.

24 c sadly → sad　**e** looks → looks like

25 수여동사 tell과 get은 「수여동사 + 간접목적어 + 직접목적어」의 형태로 쓰며, 간접목적어와 직접목적어의 위치를 바꿀 때 tell은 간접목적어 앞에 전치사 to를, get은 for를 쓴다.
해석 Jason과 그의 친구들은 매주 토요일에 보육원을 방문한다. Jason은 아이들에게 재미있는 이야기를 들려준다. 그들은 웃는다. Brian과 Sally는 장난감을 청소한다. Jane과 Bobby는 아이들에게 간식을 가져다준다.

26 수여동사 lend는 「수여동사 + 직접목적어 + to + 간접목적어」, 수여동사 buy는 「수여동사 + 간접목적어 + 직접목적어」의 순서로 쓴다.

27 「look like + 명사」: ~처럼 보이다

28 **b** 감각동사 feel은 뒤에 형용사가 오므로, 부사 powerfully를 형용사 powerful로 고쳐야 한다. **g** 수여동사 make는 간접목적어가 직접목적어 뒤에 위치할 때 간접목적어 앞에 전치사 for를 쓴다.

29 수여동사 teach는 「수여동사 + 간접목적어 + 직접목적어」, 수여동사 read는 「수여동사 + 직접목적어 + to + 간접목적어」, 수여동사 cook은 「수여동사 + 직접목적어 + for + 간접목적어」의 형태를 이용하여 쓴다.

Recall My Memory
p. 128

01 looked → looked like **02** the butter me → the butter to me[me the butter] **03** What tall boy → What a tall boy **04** Is → Are **05** Where → Why **06** don't have to → must not **07** ○ **08** ○ **09** does he → doesn't he **10** woman → women **11** well → good **12** ○ **13** some → any **14** ○ **15** to → for

수능에 꼭 나오는 **중학 영문법**

수능 기초 연습
p. 130

A **1** perfect **2** broke **3** equal **4** lie **5** listened

B **1** pretty **2** ○ **3** ○ **4** ○ **5** sitting

C ③

C 소유, 감정, 상태 등을 나타내는 동사는 진행형으로 쓰지 않으므로 ③ is liking을 likes로 고쳐야 한다.
해석 이 사진은 20년이 되었다. 나는 풍선을 들고 있다. 나의 아버지는 내 옆에 계신다. 그는 줄무늬 재킷이 잘 어울린다. 나의 어머니가 그의 옆에 계신다. 그녀는 한복을 입고 있다. 그녀는 그것을 입기를 좋아한다. 정말 멋진 가족사진이다!

수능 독해 적용
pp. 131~132

1 ③ 2 ③ 3 ④

1 (A) rise는 목적어를 갖지 않는 동사로 '오르다'라는 뜻이고, raise는 목적어를 갖는 동사로 '올리다'라는 뜻이다. 뒤에 목적어 your English score가 있으므로 raise가 알맞다. (B) ago는 과거시제와 함께 쓰이는 부사이므로 started가 알맞다. (C) feel은 뒤에 형용사를 주격보어로 가지므로 confident가 알맞다.

해석 영어 점수를 올리고 싶은가? 그렇다면, 각각의 새로운 단어를 적고 사전에서 그것의 의미를 찾아라. 이야기 속에서 그것의 의미는 무엇인가? 때로 많은 의미들이 있다. 다른 의미들을 공부해라. 여러분은 또한 다른 단어 형태들을 공부할 수도 있다. 예를 들어, 'pretty'라는 단어는 형용사이다. 그것은 또한 부사이기도 하다. 부사로, 그것은 '꽤' 또는 '매우'를 의미한다. 나는 2년 전에 이것을 하기 시작했다. 그것은 실제로 효과가 있다. 나는 이제 영어에서 자신감을 느낀다.

2 글의 전반적인 시제가 과거이므로 조동사 can을 과거형 could로 고쳐야 한다.
해석 1976년 4월 6일에, 나는 팔과 다리가 없이 태어났다. 나의 아버지는 나를 어머니에게 곧바로 보여 주지 않았다. 한 달 후, 그녀는 마침내 나를 볼 수 있었다. 나의 아버지는 그녀를 걱정했다. 하지만 그녀는 처음으로 나를 보고서 말했다. "넌 정말 귀엽구나!" 그녀는 아주 행복해 보였다. 나의 부모님은 다른 부모님들과 달랐다. 그들은 사람들에게 나를 숨기지 않았다. 그들은 항상 그들과 함께 나를 데리고 나갔다.

3 (A) 목적어가 없는 문장이므로 목적어를 갖지 않는 동사 arise의 과거형 arose가 알맞다. arise는 '생기다, 발생하다'라는 뜻이고, raise는 목적어를 갖는 동사로 '올리다, 일으키다'라는 뜻이다. (B) '~할 수 있다'라는 의미의 「be able to + 동사원형」 구문이므로 to rebuild가 알맞다. (C) once가 과거의 한때를 나타내므로 동사의 과거형 lived가 알맞다.

해석 오래전에 한 위대한 문명이 중앙아메리카와 남부 멕시코 지역에서 발생했다. 이것이 마야 문명이었다. 마야인들은 피라미드가 있는 큰 도시들을 가지고 있었다. 마야 문명은 기원후 1300년경에 끝났다. 마야인들은 그것을 다시 세울 수가 없었다. 그들의 문명은 사라져 버렸고 거대한 피라미드들만을 남겼다. 그것들은 우리에게 "한 위대한 문명이 한때 여기에 존재했다."라고 말해 준다.

Chapter **9** 동사인 듯 동사 아닌 동사 같은 너, to부정사와 동명사

Unit 01   Exercise   p. 135

A 1 목적어 2 주어 3 보어 4 주어 5 목적어

B 1 tell → to tell 2 buying → to buy 3 to going
→ to go 4 This → It 5 to not play → not to play

C 1 hope to see 2 is to learn 3 It, to play
4 promised not to watch

Unit 02   Exercise   p. 137

A 1 b 2 c 3 e 4 a 5 d

B 1 to being → to be 2 to sit → to sit on
3 in order study → in order to study
4 help → to help 5 for get → to get

C 1 something to eat 2 glad to see
3 to play badminton 4 a house to live in

Unit 03   Exercise   p. 139

A 1 목적어 2 주어 3 목적어 4 목적어 5 보어

B 1 ○ 2 is 3 washing 4 to seeing
5 not working

C 1 practice playing 2 is teaching 3 Reading is
4 is busy studying

Writing Practice   pp. 140~141

A 01 finished washing the clothes
02 need paper to write on
03 were surprised to see a snake
04 is to spend the holidays
05 decided not to fight
06 looking forward to going camping
07 mind waiting for a minute
08 turned on the radio to listen to music
09 want some water to drink
10 It is important to exercise

B 01 **a** enjoy watching
b is watching[to watch] movies
02 **a** stopped taking
b We stopped to take a break.
03 **a** need to get up **b** I keep getting up early.
04 **a** clothes to buy **b** happy to buy clothes
05 **a** wants to become
b is becoming[to become] an astronaut

Actual Test   pp. 142~145

01 ④ 02 ④ 03 ④ 04 ③ 05 It, to study 06 ⑤
07 I am planning to visit Jeju Island. 08 ⑤ 09 ④
10 exercise to be 11 go swimming 12 ② 13 ①
14 ① 15 something to drink 16 ① 17 ② 18 ②
19 ③ 20 ① 21 finish cleaning 22 ④ 23 ① 24
⑤ 25 to bother → bothering 26 ⑤ 27 ② 28
You don't have to be afraid of playing with the dog.
29 To getting → To get, to do → doing

01 What[How] about -ing?: ~하는 게 어때?

02 to부정사의 부정형은 to 앞에 not이나 never를 쓴다.

03 avoid는 목적어로 동명사를 사용한다.

04 wish는 목적어로 to부정사를 사용한다.

05 to부정사가 주어일 때 주어 자리에 It을 쓰고 to부정사를 문장 뒤로 보낼 수 있다.

06 to부정사 주어는 3인칭 단수로 취급하므로 are를 is로 고쳐야 한다.

07 plan은 목적어로 to부정사를 사용한다.
해석 A: 안녕, 지수야. 너는 이번 주말에 무엇을 할 거니?
B: 나는 제주도를 방문하는 것을 계획 중이야.
A: 좋겠다.

08 for와 in은 전치사이므로 뒤에 동명사가 목적어로 온다.

09 sorry와 같이 감정을 나타내는 형용사 다음에 to부정사가 와서 감정의 원인을 나타내므로 for를 to로 고쳐야 한다.
해석 A: Charlie, 일어나렴! 학교에 갈 시간이야.
B: 엄마, 제발요. 5분만 더요.
A: 깨워서 미안하지만, 학교에 지각하면 안 되잖니.
B: 알겠어요, 엄마.

10 '~하기 위해서'는 to부정사로 나타낸다.

11 '~하러 가다'는 go -ing로 나타낸다.

12 to부정사의 부정형은 to 앞에 not이나 never를 쓴다.

13 보기와 ①은 목적어, ②와 ④는 보어, ③과 ⑤는 주어로 쓰였다.

14 보기와 ①은 형용사, ②는 주어로 쓰인 명사, ③은 보어로 쓰인 명사, ④는 결과를 나타내는 부사, ⑤는 감정의 원인을 나타내는 부사로 쓰였다.

15 something과 같은 대명사는 to부정사가 뒤에서 꾸며 준다.

16 목적의 의미를 나타내는 to부정사는 「in order to + 동사원형」으로 바꿔 쓸 수 있다.

17 water는 동사 drink의 직접적인 목적어이므로 전치사가 필요하지 않다. 나머지 빈칸에는 ① in, ③ with, ④ about, ⑤ with가 들어간다.

18 ②의 밑줄 친 부분은 현재진행형의 동사원형-ing이고, 나머지는 동명사로 쓰였다.

19 동명사 주어는 3인칭 단수로 취급하므로 are를 is로 고쳐야 한다.

20 to부정사는 live, grow up 등의 동사 뒤에 쓰여 '(그래서, 그 결과) ~하다'라는 결과의 의미를 나타낸다.

21 finish는 동명사를 목적어로 사용한다.

22 동사 quit는 목적어로 동명사를 사용하므로 to smoke를 smoking으로 고쳐야 한다.

23 동사 like는 목적어로 to부정사와 동명사 모두 다 사용할 수 있다.

24 대화의 밑줄 친 부분과 ①~④는 감정의 원인을 나타내는 부사적 쓰임이고, ⑤는 주어 역할을 하는 명사적 쓰임이다.

25 「stop + to부정사」는 '~하기 위해 멈추다', 「stop + 동명사」는 '~하는 것을 멈추다'라는 의미이다.

26 to read가 앞의 명사 a book을 꾸며 주므로 '읽을 책'으로 해석하는 것이 자연스럽다.

27 ① to walking → walking[to walk] ③ are → is ④ make → making ⑤ be → is

28 of는 전치사이므로 뒤에 동명사 형태인 playing with로 써야 한다.

29 To getting은 목적을 나타내는 to부정사의 부사적 쓰임이 되어야 하므로 To get으로 고친다. keep은 목적어로 동명사를 사용하므로 to do를 doing으로 고친다.

해석 친구들과 좋은 관계를 갖는 것은 매우 중요하다. 친구들과 잘 지내기 위해서, 첫째 우리는 그들과 말하기 시작할 필요가 있다. 둘째, 친구들의 말을 주의깊게 들어라. 셋째, 그들에게 친절하려고 노력해라. 넷째, 서로 돕는 것 또한 매우 중요하다. 마지막으로, 함께 시간을 보내는 것이 필요하다. 이런 것들을 계속 실천하고 여러분의 학교생활을 즐겨라.

Recall My Memory
p. 146

01 to watch → watching **02** ○ **03** for → to **04** sends → sent **05** to hearing → to hear **06** softly → soft **07** That → It **08** drums → the drums **09** am cleaning → are cleaning **10** meet → meeting **11** ○ **12** were → was **13** ○ **14** write → writing[to write] **15** What → Which

Chapter **10** 말과 글을 살찌우는 형용사와 부사

Unit 01 Exercise
p. 149

A **1** a few **2** interesting **3** something cold **4** many

B **1** lovely / 명사 수식 **2** slow / 주어 설명 **3** popular / 주어 설명 **4** fun / 대명사 수식

C **1** a little **2** few **3** a lot of **4** little **5** a few

Unit 02 Exercise
p. 151

A **1** late **2** well **3** fast **4** sometimes listens **5** is usually

B **1** hard / study 밑줄 **2** really / good 밑줄 **3** Luckily / the firefighters put out the fire quickly 밑줄 **4** heavily / rained 밑줄 **5** nearly / always 밑줄

C **1** I often help my father in the kitchen. **2** Daniel is usually very friendly. **3** Cindy never tells a lie. **4** You should always wear a helmet.

Unit 03 Exercise
p. 153

A **1** strong **2** better **3** much **4** tallest **5** most popular

B **1** heavier **2** most expensive **3** thinner **4** good

C **1** as nice as **2** more comfortable than **3** much hotter than **4** the prettiest

Writing Practice

A 01 The new sweater is warm.
   02 She is often sick
   03 make something new
   04 I need a little help
   05 A tiger runs as fast as a lion.
   06 The school bus always arrives
   07 the funniest girl in her school
   08 Sharks are highly dangerous animals
   09 I played a few computer games
   10 Health is much more important than money.

B 01 a wonderful b the violin wonderfully
   02 a much[a lot of, lots of] money
      b He doesn't[does not] have many[a lot of, lots of] friends.
   03 a bigger
      b Watermelons are as big as basketballs.
   04 a best b Friday is better than Monday.
   05 a few eggs b There is little milk in the fridge.

Actual Test

pp. 156~159

01 ④ 02 ③ 03 ①, ③ 04 ④ 05 ④ 06 ② 07 ②
08 ⑤ 09 ③ 10 hard 11 quickly 12 ④ 13 ②
14 Dad is never late for work. 15 Tom usually comes right home after school. 16 (1) sometimes reads books (2) never plays the piano (3) usually plays soccer 17 ⑤ 18 ③ 19 ④ 20 ① 21 ④ 22 ②
23 shorter 24 Watermelon, the most expensive 25 lighter than 26 ④ 27 b most smart → smartest d most important → the most important e more healthy → healthier 28 more 29 the most exciting 30 (1) the oldest (2) the tallest (3) as heavy as (4) the heaviest

01 ④는 '명사 - 형용사', 나머지는 '형용사 - 부사'의 관계이다.

02 ③ high는 형용사(높은)와 부사(높이)의 형태가 같고, highly는 '매우' 라는 의미의 부사이다. 나머지는 '형용사 - 부사'의 관계이다.

03 「as + 형용사/부사의 원급 + as」의 형태로 쓰므로, 빈칸에는 원급인 ①, ③이 알맞다.

04 빈칸 뒤에 비교 집단을 나타내는 of all the superheroes가 있으므로, 빈칸에는 「the + 최상급」이 들어가야 한다. strong은 -est를 붙여 최상급을 만든다.

05 -thing으로 끝나는 대명사는 형용사가 뒤에서 꾸민다.

06 동사 뒤에서 주어를 설명해 주는 말은 형용사이므로, ②의 부사 kindly (친절하게)는 빈칸에 들어갈 수 없다.

07 very는 비교급 앞에 쓰여 '훨씬'의 의미를 나타낼 수 없다.

08 형용사가 동사 뒤에서 주어를 설명해 주므로, ⑤의 부사 terribly를 terrible로 고쳐야 한다.

09 (A) '늦게 잠자리에 들다'의 의미이므로 late가 알맞다. lately(최근에) (B) 동사 sleep을 수식하므로 부사 well이 알맞다. (C) 동사 뒤에서 주어를 설명해 주는 말은 형용사이므로 tired가 알맞다.

10 빈칸에는 동사 works를 수식하는 부사가 필요하므로 hard가 알맞다. hard는 형용사(열심인)와 부사(열심히)의 형태가 같다.

11 빈칸에는 동사 learns를 수식하는 부사가 필요하므로 quickly가 알맞다.

12 ④의 delicious는 명사(pie)를 수식하지만, 나머지는 주어를 보충 설명한다.

13 sometimes는 빈도부사로 조동사(can) 뒤에 위치한다.

14 빈도부사 never는 be동사 is 뒤에 써야 한다.

15 빈도부사 usually는 일반동사 comes 앞에 써야 한다.

16 빈도부사는 일반동사 앞에 쓴다. (1) sometimes(가끔) (2) never(결코 ~ 않다) (3) usually(보통, 대개)

17 셀 수 있는 명사의 복수형 books와 셀 수 없는 명사 work 앞에 쓰여 수량을 모두 나타낼 수 있는 것은 a lot of이다.

18 energy는 셀 수 없는 명사이며, 기운이 거의 없다고 하였으므로 little(거의 없는)이 알맞다.

19 movies는 셀 수 있는 명사이므로 a little을 a few로 고쳐야 한다.

20 빈도부사는 조동사 뒤에 위치하므로 never will을 will never로 고쳐 야 한다.

21 Jane이 몇 분 전에 나갔다는 대답이 자연스러우므로, 셀 수 있는 명사 의 복수형(minutes) 앞에 쓰여 '조금, 약간'의 의미를 나타내는 A few 가 알맞다.

22 cold - colder - coldest

23 키가 큰 순서는 Julie > I > Lucy이므로 short의 비교급을 이용하여 Lucy가 Julie보다 키가 작음을 나타낸다.

24 비싼 순서는 수박 > 배 > 복숭아이므로 최상급을 이용하여 수박이 가장 비쌈을 나타낸다. expensive는 3음절 이상이므로 최상급은 앞에 most를 붙인다.
해석 가게에 세 가지 종류의 과일이 있다. 복숭아는 각각 2달러이다. 배 는 각각 3달러이다. 수박은 각각 10달러이다.

25 오렌지가 사과보다 가벼우므로, light를 이용하여 「비교급 + than」으로 나타낸다.

26 too는 비교급을 강조할 수 없으므로 much, still, even, far, a lot 등으로 고쳐야 한다.

해석 나의 언니, 미나는 나보다 나이가 많다. 그녀는 나보다 키가 크고 더 날씬하다. 그리고 그녀는 나보다 더 아름답다. 하지만 나는 그녀보다 훨씬 더 똑똑하다. 그리고 나는 내 언니보다 운동을 더 잘한다.

27 b smart는 -est를 붙여서 최상급을 만든다. **d** 최상급 앞에는 the를 쓴다. **e** healthy의 비교급은 healthier이다.

28 '더 많은 책'이 되어야 하므로, many의 비교급 more가 books를 꾸며 주도록 한다.

29 「the + 최상급」 형태로 쓰며, exciting은 3음절 이상이므로 최상급은 most exciting이 된다.

30 (1), (2), (4) 최상급 표현은 「the + 최상급」으로 나타낸다. (3) 둘의 정도가 같음은 「as + 원급 + as」로 나타낸다.

해석 Tony에게는 두 명의 형제들인, Jake와 Peter가 있다. 나이에 대해 말하자면, Peter가 셋 중에서 가장 나이가 많다. 키에 대해 말하자면, Jake가 셋 중에서 가장 크다. 몸무게에 대해 말하자면, Tony는 Jake만큼 무게가 나간다. 그리고 Peter가 셋 중에서 가장 몸무게가 많이 나간다.

Recall My Memory
p. 160

01 for → to **02** fastly → fast **03** are → is **04** were going to → are going to **05** ○ **06** a little → a few **07** Is → Are **08** ○ **09** must → had to **10** sleeps often → often sleeps **11** doesn't want → don't[do not] want **12** coldest → the coldest **13** doesn't he → won't he **14** some → any **15** ○

Chapter **11** 나를 이끌어 줘,
명사의 가이드 전치사

Unit 01　Exercise
p. 163

A **1** in **2** on **3** at **4** in **5** on **6** in

B **1** for **2** during **3** until **4** before **5** after **6** by

C **1** On **2** For **3** At **4** In **5** Until

Unit 02　Exercise
p. 165

A **1** on **2** at **3** in **4** on **5** in

B **1** in front of **2** under **3** next to **4** over

C **1** behind the door
2 between Poland and France
3 across from the bookstore
4 from the airport to the hotel

Unit 03　Exercise
p. 167

A **1** by **2** about **3** with **4** of **5** for

B **1** by **2** with **3** about **4** for **5** of

C **1** by email **2** for chocolate
3 about our favorite books **4** with my friend

Writing Practice
pp. 168~169

A **01** She lived in Sydney
02 learn to swim in July
03 There is a library next to my house.
04 is across from the police station
05 is between the fire station and the hospital
06 from here to your school
07 He usually goes jogging before breakfast.
08 people eat with their hands
09 goes to the market by bike
10 have a party on Christmas Eve

B **01 a** for an hour
b He studied English grammar during the vacation.

02 a on September 15th
 b He was born in spring.
03 a by noon **b** I will wait for her until noon.
04 a in front of the bookstore
 b The bakery is behind the bookstore.
05 a on the desk
 b There is a school bag under the desk.

Actual Test

pp. 170~173

01 ④ **02** ③ **03** ② **04** during **05** ① **06** ⑤ **07** We often walk in the park after lunch. **08** ③ **09** (1) during (2) in **10** ③ **11** ⑤ **12** ④ **13** ② **14** on **15** ③ **16** ② **17** I left my umbrella at home. **18** ⑤ **19** ④ **20** ① **21** ④ **22** flying over the trees **23** ① **24** ⑤ **25** ① **26** It is open from 9 a.m. to 4 p.m.[It opens from 9 a.m. to 4 p.m.] **27** about **28** of my father → with my father, the top by the mountain → the top of the mountain, during an hour → for an hour

01 at은 '~에'의 의미로, 구체적인 시각이나 특정한 시점을 나타낼 때 쓴다.

02 for는 '~을 위해', '~ 동안'이라는 의미로 쓰인다.

03 on은 '~에'의 의미로 날짜, 요일, 특정한 날을 나타낼 때 쓴다.

04 '~ 동안'의 의미로, 특정한 기간을 나타내는 명사 앞에는 during을 쓴다.

05 your birthday는 특정한 날을 나타내므로 in을 on으로 고쳐야 한다.

06 ⑤의 in은 '~ 후에'라는 의미이지만, 나머지는 '~에'의 의미로 월, 연도, 계절, 오전, 오후, 저녁 등을 나타낼 때 쓴다.

07 '공원을 산책하다'는 walk in the park로 나타낼 수 있으며 '점심 식사 후에'는 after lunch로 나타낼 수 있다.

08 ① during → for ② on → at ④ for → during ⑤ until → by

09 (1) '~ 동안'의 의미로, 특정한 기간을 나타내는 명사(lunchtime) 앞에는 during을 쓴다. (2) '~에, ~ 안에'의 의미로, 장소 안에 있음을 나타낼 때는 in을 쓴다.

10 '너는 너의 꿈을 위해서 최선을 다해야 한다.'라는 의미가 자연스러우므로 in을 for로 고쳐야 한다.

11 ① behind: ~ 뒤에 ② in front of: ~ 앞에 ③ next to: ~ 옆에 ④ across from: ~의 맞은편에

12 '여기서 공항까지 얼마나 걸리니?'라는 의미가 자연스러우므로 'A부터 B까지'를 나타내는 from A to B가 알맞다.

13 at은 '~에'의 의미로, 버스 정류장과 같이 비교적 좁은 장소나 한 지점을 나타낼 때 쓴다. in은 '~에, ~ 안에'의 의미로, 나라와 같이 비교적 넓은 장소나 장소 안에 있음을 나타낼 때 쓴다. on은 '~에, ~ 위에'의 의미로, 벤치 위와 같이 표면에 붙어 있는 상태를 나타낼 때 쓴다.

14 책상 위에 펜이 하나 있으므로 '~에, ~ 위에'의 의미를 나타내는 on이 알맞다.

15 '우리는 건강한 치아를 갖기 위해서 식사 후에 양치를 해야 한다.'가 자연스러우므로 for를 after로 고쳐야 한다.

16 ②에는 도구를 나타내는 with(~을 가지고, ~으로)가 들어가고, ①, ③, ④에는 교통·통신수단을 나타내는 by(~으로)가, ⑤에는 시간을 나타내는 by(~까지)가 들어간다.

17 '두고 왔다'는 과거시제이므로 left로 나타내며, '집에'는 at home으로 나타낸다.

18 ⑤에는 at이 들어가고, 나머지에는 on이 들어간다.

19 '~의 맞은편에'는 across from이므로 between을 from으로 고쳐야 한다.

20 ② '너를 위해'라는 의미이므로 of를 for로 고쳐야 한다. ③ '꽃에 관한 책'이라는 의미이므로 by를 about으로 고쳐야 한다. ④ '우리 팀의 멤버'라는 의미이므로 at을 of로 고쳐야 한다. ⑤ 교통수단 앞에는 by를 쓰므로 from을 by로 고쳐야 한다.

21 첫 번째 빈칸의 문장은 그의 새 책에 대한 생각을 묻고 있으므로 '~에 대해'라는 의미의 전치사 about이 알맞다. 두 번째 빈칸의 문장은 하루 사이에 다 보았다는 의미가 자연스러우므로 전치사 in이 알맞다.

해석 A: 너는 그의 새 책에 대해서 어떻게 생각해?
 B: 그것은 너무 재미있었어. 난 하루 사이에 그것을 다 읽었어.
 A: 응, 나도 그래.

22 연이 나무들 위로 날고 있으므로 '~ 위에'라는 의미로 표면에 붙어 있지 않은 상태를 나타내는 over를 사용한다.

23 ①은 뒤에 목적지가 와서 '~을 향해'라는 의미로 쓰였고, 보기와 나머지는 '~을 위해'라는 의미로 쓰였다.

24 Mother's Day는 특정한 날이므로 in을 on으로 고쳐야 한다.

25 개 한 마리가 탁자 밑에서 잠을 자고 있으므로 전치사 under를 사용해야 한다.

26 'A부터 B까지'는 from A to B로 나타낸다.

해석 A: 은행의 영업시간은 어떻게 되나요?
 B: 그것은 오전 9시부터 오후 4시까지 열어요.
 A: 네, 고마워요.

27 '~에 대해'는 전치사 about을 사용한다.

28 '~와 함께'는 전치사 with를, '산의 정상'을 나타내는 '~의'는 전치사 of를, 시간을 나타내는 숫자의 기간 앞에서 '~ 동안'을 나타낼 때는 전치사 for를 쓴다.

해석 나는 아침에 아버지와 하이킹하러 갔다. 날씨가 하이킹하기에 아주 좋았지만, 산에 오르는 것은 힘들었다. 그러나 아버지의 도움으로 나는 오른지 두 시간 후에 마침내 산의 정상에 올랐다. 정상에서 경치가 아름다웠다. 그리고 나는 아름다운 무지개를 볼 수 있었다. 우리는 한 시간 동안 그곳에 머물고 산에서 내려왔다. 아주 멋진 경험이었다.

Recall My Memory
p. 174

01 her → hers **02** in → at **03** hardly → hard **04** tastes → tastes like **05** ○ **06** can't → couldn't [could not] **07** ○ **08** ○ **09** over → on **10** had → has **11** to winning → to win **12** What → How **13** in → on **14** the table tennis → table tennis **15** ○

Chapter **12** 너와 나를 이어 주는 오작교, 접속사

Unit 01 Exercise
p. 177

A **1** but **2** and **3** or **4** so **5** helped

B **1** but **2** and **3** or **4** so

C **1** football and baseball
2 but they are not watching
3 so I got wet
4 a jacket or a jumper

Unit 02 Exercise
p. 179

A **1** after **2** While **3** goes **4** When **5** before

B **1** while **2** before **3** When **4** after

C **1** when I arrived there
2 after she worked hard
3 while he was cooking
4 before I make a decision

Unit 03 Exercise
p. 181

A **1** If **2** that **3** because **4** that **5** don't hurry

B **1** because **2** that **3** If **4** that **5** because of

C **1** because it was raining
2 that she will win the contest
3 If you send this letter

Writing Practice
pp. 182~183

A **01** after we planted them
02 because he likes cooking
03 that I left my book
04 so I had to take the stairs
05 When she goes to the market
06 but he rides his bike
07 like to fish and play tennis
08 while she is doing the housework
09 If I find your cell phone
10 He booked a hotel room and a flight

B **01** a and she read it
b He bought a book, but he didn't[did not] read it.
02 a before you eat
b You should brush your teeth after you eat. [After you eat, you should brush your teeth.]
03 a while I was sleeping
b When my dad came home, I was sleeping.[I was sleeping when my dad came home.]
04 a so he went to the hospital
b Because he was sick, he went to the hospital. [He went to the hospital because he was sick.]
05 a When I meet her
b If I meet her, I will give her this letter.[I will give her this letter if I meet her.]

Actual Test
pp. 184~187

01 ④ **02** ② **03** ① **04** ④ **05** ③ **06** ② **07** ① **08** ④ **09** ③ **10** ③ **11** he went into the water, he did warm-up exercises **12** everyone arrived, they started the meeting **13** While mom was cooking

14 ④ see → saw **15** ⑤ **16** ④ **17** ③ **18** We were late because of the heavy traffic.[We were late because the traffic was heavy.] **19** ④ **20** When he comes back, he will call you.[He will call you when he comes back.] **21** Because I was so hungry, I ate a lot.[I ate a lot because I was so hungry.] **22** I believe that she will get well soon. **23** ③ **24** ③ **25** It, that **26** (1) it is sunny, she will ride her bike in the park (2) it rains, she will watch a movie at home **27** before you make sandwiches **28** after he took a long walk **29** c but → and g won't come → don't[do not] come

01 「A, B, and C」와 같이 비슷한 항목을 나열할 때, 맨 끝 항목 앞에 and 를 쓴다.

02 조건을 나타내는 if절에서는 미래를 나타낼 때 현재시제를 쓴다. 주어 it 이 3인칭 단수이므로 snows가 알맞다.

03 hungry(배고픈)와 tired(피곤한)는 서로 비슷한 내용이므로 and로 연결되어야 한다. (but → and)

04 know의 목적어 역할을 하는 명사절을 이끄는 접속사 that이 쓰여야 한다. (so → that)

05 빈칸 뒤의 절이 동사 heard의 목적어이므로 명사절을 이끄는 접속사 that이 알맞다.

06 만약 지금 떠난다면 늦지 않게 도착할 것이라는 내용이 적절하므로 if가 알맞다.

07 TV를 끄거나 볼륨을 줄여달라는 상황이므로 or가 알맞다.

08 빈칸 앞뒤로 상반되는 내용이 나오므로 but이 알맞다.

09 ③은 '언제'라는 뜻의 의문사이고, 나머지는 '~할 때'라는 뜻의 부사절 접속사이다.

10 ③은 '저, 저쪽의'라는 뜻의 지시형용사이고, 나머지는 명사절을 이끄는 접속사이다.

11 before(~하기 전에)가 이끄는 절에 나중에 일어난 일을 쓴다.

12 after(~한 후에)가 이끄는 절에 먼저 일어난 일을 쓴다.

13 「접속사 + 주어 + 동사」의 순서로 쓴다.

14 대등한 요소를 연결하는 and로 연결되어 있고, last night이라는 과거를 나타내는 부사구가 있으므로 시제를 과거로 써야 한다.

15 첫 번째는 빈칸 앞뒤로 서로 반대되는 내용이 연결되고 있으므로 but 이, 두 번째는 빈칸 앞뒤로 비슷한 내용이 연결되고 있으므로 and가 알맞다.

16 첫 번째는 그녀가 집에 왔을 때 그녀의 남자 형제가 간식을 먹고 있었다는 내용이므로 시간의 접속사 When이, 두 번째는 배터리가 다 되어서

그에게 전화할 수 없었다는 내용이므로 이유의 접속사 because가 알 맞다.

17 조건을 나타내는 if절에서는 미래를 나타낼 때 현재시제를 쓴다. (will eat → eat)

해석 A: 엄마, 아이스크림 더 먹어도 되나요?
B: 아니, 안 돼. 너무 많은 아이스크림을 먹으면 너는 배가 아플 거야.
A: 하지만 저는 더 먹고 싶어요. 그건 정말 맛있어요.
B: 알겠어, 하지만 아이스크림 한 스쿠프만 더 먹는 거야.

18 「because of + 명사(구)」, 「because + 주어 + 동사」

19 ④에는 after(~한 후에)가, 나머지에는 before[Before](~하기 전에) 가 들어가는 것이 적절하다.

20 '~할 때'는 접속사 when을 쓰며, 시간의 접속사가 이끄는 절에서는 미 래의 일을 나타낼 때 현재시제를 쓴다.

21 because가 이끄는 절에는 이유나 원인이 되는 내용을 쓴다.

22 that은 명사절 접속사이므로 believe 뒤에 목적어에 해당하는 내용을 that절로 쓴다.

23 a Because → Because of d will arrive → arrive

24 and로 연결되는 말들은 문법적으로 형태나 역할이 같아야 한다. 따라 서 singing and dancing 또는 to sing and (to) dance가 되어야 한다.

25 명사절 접속사 that이 이끄는 절이 주어일 때는 「It(가짜 주어) ~ that(진짜 주어) ...」의 형태로 쓴다.

26 조건을 나타내는 if절에서는 미래의 일을 현재시제로 표현하는 것에 유 의한다. 날씨를 나타낼 때는 비인칭 주어 it을 쓰고, sunny는 형용사이 므로 be동사가 필요하다.

해석 Kate는 이번 주말을 위해 계획을 세웠다. 날씨가 맑으면, 그녀는 공원에서 자전거를 탈 것이다. 비가 오면, 그녀는 집에서 영화를 볼 것이다. 그녀는 멋진 주말을 보낼 것으로 생각한다.

27 샌드위치를 만들기 전에 손을 씻으라는 의미가 되어야 하므로 before (~하기 전에)를 이용한다.

28 오래 걷고 난 후 매우 피곤했다는 의미가 되어야 하므로 after(~한 후 에)를 이용한다. 시제가 과거인 것에 주의한다.

29 c cold와 windy는 비슷한 내용이므로 접속사 and로 연결해야 한다.
g 조건의 if절에서는 미래의 일을 나타낼 때 현재시제를 쓴다.

01 There is → There are   **02** will have to → have to
03 Does → Did   **04** more heavy → heavier   **05** play
→ playing   **06** ○   **07** ○   **08** While → When   **09** to
write → to write with   **10** ○   **11** to clean →
cleaning   **12** because → so   **13** us → ourselves   **14**
after → before   **15** can't → must

수능에 꼭 나오는 중학 영문법

 기초 연습
p. 190

A **1** traveling   **2** useful   **3** much   **4** touching
  5 go

B **1** big   **2** ○   **3** receiving   **4** working   **5** ○

C ③

C ③은 접속사 and로 went와 연결되므로 trade를 과거형 traded로 고쳐야 한다.

해석 바퀴, 쟁기, 범선이라는 세 가지 중요한 발명품들이 메소포타미아에서 나왔다. 바퀴가 달린 수레는 더 많은 상품을 더 빨리 시장으로 운반했다. 동물들은 쟁기를 끌어 흙을 갈았다. 그것들은 인간들보다 훨씬 더 효율적이었다. 범선을 타고, 사람들은 바다 건너 다른 나라로 가서 그들과 무역을 했다.

 독해 적용
pp. 191~192

1 ②   **2** ⑤   **3** ⑤

1 (A) 앞에 동명사구 Eating too little이 있고, 접속사 or로 연결되므로 같은 문법적 형태인 동명사구 not eating at all이 오는 것이 적절하다. (B) '성장하기 위해서 좋은 영양이 필요하다'라는 의미가 되어야 자연스러우므로 목적을 나타내는 부사적 쓰임의 to부정사가 오는 것이 적절하다. (C) 접속사 and로 eat과 연결되므로 exercise가 알맞다.

해석 너무 적게 먹거나 전혀 먹지 않는 것은 다이어트의 좋은 방법이 아니다. 다이어트는 '안 먹는 것'을 의미하는 것이 아니다. 그것은 '올바르게 먹는 것'을 뜻한다. 다이어트를 너무 많이 하면, 체중이 아니라 건강을 잃을지도 모른다. 청소년들은 성장하기 위해서 좋은 영양이 필요하다. 정말로 좋은 몸 상태를 유지하고 싶다면, 잘 먹고 운동을 잘 할 필요가 있다. 그것이 건강을 유지하는 최선의 방법이다.

2 ⑤는 접속사 or로 painting과 연결되므로 to wash를 washing으로 고쳐야 한다.

해석 무엇이 멋진 휴가를 만드는가? 사람들은 그것에 대해 많은 다른 의견들을 갖고 있다. 어떤 사람들은 숲에서 오랜 산책을 하는 것을 좋아한다. 그들은 그곳에서 며칠 동안 아무도 보지 않을 것이다. 다른 사람들은 신나는 도시에서 그들의 휴가를 보내는 것을 좋아한다. 거기에서 그들은 박물관, 극장, 그리고 좋은 식당을 방문할 수 있다. 또 다른 사람들은 해변에서 신선한 공기를 즐긴다. 그들은 낮 시간을 해변에서 보내고 밤에는 바다의 파도 소리를 들을 수 있다. 몇몇 사람들은 집에 있으면서 몇 가지 중요한 집안일을 하기로 결심한다. 그들은 현관을 칠하거나 아파트의 모든 창문을 닦으면서 휴가를 보낼지도 모른다.

3 (A) '~만큼 …한/하게'의 「as + 원급 + as」 구문이므로 as가 알맞다. (B) 비교급 more를 강조할 수 있는 것은 much이다. (C) '~하는 것을 멈추다'라는 의미가 되어야 하므로 동명사 beating이 알맞다. 「stop + to부정사」는 '~하기 위해 멈추다'라는 의미이다.

해석 호주는 지구 상에서 가장 위험한 동물들의 서식지이다. 예를 들어, 호주 타이판은 뱀이다. 그것의 독은 단 한 번에 199명의 사람들을 죽일 수 있다. 약 300개의 이빨을 가진 백상아리도 타이판만큼 치명적이다. 그러나 호주의 들개들은 백상아리들보다 훨씬 더 많은 사람들을 죽인다. 또한 상자해파리는 강한 독을 가지고 있다. 그것의 독이 당신 몸에 들어가면 단 3분 만에 당신의 심장은 뛰는 것을 멈출 것이다.

Workbook
Answers

Chapter 1 그때그때 달라, 혼자서는 안 돼, 주어의 짝꿍 be동사

Unit 01 p.2

A 1 is, are 2 was, is 3 are, were

B 1 is 2 am 3 are 4 ○ 5 ○

C 1 He was late 2 They are kind 3 She is the writer
4 The letters were

Unit 02 p.3

A 1 is not 2 Is 3 I'm not 4 Were 5 weren't

B 1 No, I'm not 2 Was he 3 Yes, she is
4 Were they, They were

C 1 (1) The food isn't[is not] delicious.
(2) Is the food delicious?
2 (1) Nick wasn't[was not] at the party last night.
(2) Was Nick at the party last night?

Chapter 2 현재로 과거로 갑옷을 바꿔 입는, 주어의 행동대장, 일반동사

Unit 01 p.4

A 1 plays 2 brush 3 live 4 cries 5 work

B 1 a loves b love 2 a reads b read
3 a study b studies 4 a goes b go

C 1 Jenny does her homework after dinner.
2 A bird flies in the sky.
3 My parents have bread and coffee for breakfast.

Unit 02 p.5

A 1 broke 2 worked 3 swam 4 put 5 heard

B 1 ○ 2 bought 3 studied 4 ○ 5 played

C 1 She danced at the party
2 We planned a trip to Hawaii
3 Dad and I went fishing
4 He wrote a letter to his family

Unit 03 p.6

A 1 doesn't 2 ride 3 have 4 don't 5 Did

B 1 he does 2 they don't 3 Did she

C 1 Did they leave 2 don't like 3 didn't call
4 Do you do yoga

Chapter 3 이름을 불러 주면 나에게로 와서 하나의 의미가 되는 명사

Unit 01 p.7

A 1 leaves 2 babies 3 men 4 classes 5 tomatoes
6 flowers 7 pianos 8 feet 9 sheep 10 children

B 1 houses 2 knives 3 friends 4 puppies 5 ○

C 1 an apple 2 Five fish 3 potatoes 4 two boxes

Unit 02 p.8

A 1 child, egg, potato, computer, animal, friend
2 milk, cheese, love, paper, sugar, health, bread, money, water

B 1 France 2 salt 3 The meat isn't[is not] 4 ○
5 three pieces of cake

C 1 a glass of water
2 Happiness is
3 five pairs of jeans
4 three bottles of olive oil

Unit 03 p.9

A 1 a 2 × 3 an 4 × 5 the

B 1 an umbrella 2 a yellow dress 3 ○ 4 An hour
5 The sun

C 1 a a car b bike
2 a basketball b the violin
3 a The moon b A star
4 a an animal doctor b the animal

Unit 01 p.10

A 1 him 2 We 3 their 4 her 5 themselves

B 1 Ours 2 herself 3 They 4 himself 5 Its

C 1 mine 2 his 3 it 4 yourself

Unit 02 p.11

A 1 These 2 That 3 It 4 this 5 those

B 1 That 2 these 3 Those 4 this 5 It

C 1 It is five o'clock. 2 This is my sister.
3 Are those your socks? 4 These dogs are hers.

Unit 03 p.12

A 1 one 2 it 3 ones

B 1 some 2 any 3 some 4 any 5 any, some

C 1 Some people 2 have one 3 any TV 4 new ones

Chapter 5 과거부터 미래까지 시간을
품고 있는 타임머신, 시제

Unit 01 p.13

A 1 take 2 bought 3 teaches 4 Did 5 drinks

B 1 was, is 2 liked, like 3 eats, ate 4 works, worked

C 1 They were not busy yesterday.
2 The store opens at 8 every morning.
3 Water freezes at 0℃.
4 My brother studied hard last night.

Unit 02 p.14

A 1 are going to travel 2 is not going to eat
3 Are you going to watch

B 1 come 2 sell 3 ○ 4 ○ 5 is not going to

C 1 I am[I'm] going to go shopping
2 Will she see a doctor
3 They are not[They aren't, They're not] going to buy
a new computer
4 He will be a firefighter

Unit 03 p.15

A 1 raining 2 wearing 3 know 4 not singing
5 was writing

B 1 My brother is drawing a picture.
2 Were you practicing the piano?
3 I wasn't[was not] calling my friend.
4 The man isn't[is not] cutting the grass.

C 1 was studying math 2 was having lunch
3 was playing basketball 4 is watching TV

Chapter 6 함께하면 특별한 의미가 돼,
동사의 도우미 조동사

Unit 01 p.16

A 1 can't 2 may not 3 can 4 may

B 1 could 2 ○ 3 is not able to 4 may
5 Can[Could, Will, Would]

C 1 can't[cannot] ski 2 may be 3 Can she arrive
4 aren't able to come

Unit 02 p.17

A 1 must not 2 Does 3 must 4 don't have to
5 should

B 1 a Tom은 그의 전화를 받지 않았다. 그는 바쁜 것이 틀림없다.
b Cathy는 정직한 소녀이다. 그녀는 거짓말쟁이일 리 없다.
2 a 너는 너의 친구들과 싸워서는 안 된다.
b 너는 너의 신발을 벗을 필요가 없다.

C 1 should exercise every day
2 have to get some sleep
3 should not go outside
4 doesn't have to buy it

Chapter 7 의도한 바를 이렇게 전해 봐, 알아두면 유용한 문장의 종류

Unit 01   p.18

A 1 Whose   2 What   3 Who   4 Which

B 1 What did you do   2 Which fruit do you want
     3 Who can answer   4 Whose phone is ringing

C 1 Who is   2 Whose wallet   3 Which sport
     4 What time

Unit 02   p.19

A 1 How   2 When   3 Where   4 Why

B 1 b   2 d   3 a   4 c

C 1 Why are you angry
     2 How many Facebook friends does
     3 Where will they go
     4 When did she finish

Unit 03   p.20

A 1 Have   2 play   3 is   4 Don't   5 Are

B 1 makes → make
     2 Not let's → Let's not
     3 There aren't → There isn't[is not]
     4 Don't → Don't be
     5 Was there → Were there

C 1 Don't touch   2 Let's go   3 Are there cows
     4 There isn't any cheese

Unit 04   p.21

A 1 What   2 How   3 isn't he   4 What   5 did she

B 1 What interesting   2 can you   3 What a nice
     4 aren't you   5 ○

C 1 How windy
     2 likes, doesn't she
     3 What a brave boy
     4 weren't watching, were they

Chapter 8 문장의 형태를 지배하는 동사의 종류

Unit 01   p.22

A 1 thirsty   2 sounds like   3 ○   4 ○   5 wonderful

B 1 sounds   2 taste   3 smells   4 feels

C 1 smell nice   2 sounds strange   3 tastes like chicken
     4 looked tired

Unit 02   p.23

A 1 to my aunt   2 some questions of you
     3 a new computer for her

B 1 lend   2 teaches   3 tell   4 cooked

C 1 sent him the pictures
     2 show me some sneakers
     3 makes sandwiches for us
     4 write a letter to her parents

Chapter 9 동사인 듯 동사 아닌 동사 같은 너, to부정사와 동명사

Unit 01   p.24

A 1 목적어 / 사는 것을   2 주어 / 걱정하는 것은
     3 보어 / 시작하는 것(이다)   4 주어 / 보는 것은

B 1 meets → to meet   2 travel → to travel
     3 keeping → to keep   4 That → It
     5 to not buy → not to buy

C 1 to become   2 It, to drive   3 is to read

Unit 02   p.25

A 1 형용사 / 방문할   2 부사 / 타서   3 부사 / 보기 위해

B 1 d   2 e   3 c   4 a   5 b

C 1 to be a hundred   2 someone to talk to
     3 to buy a gift   4 sorry to hear your bad news

Unit 03

A 1 보어 / 찍는 것(이다) 2 목적어 / 돕는 것을
3 주어 / 걷는 것은

B 1 selling 2 watching 3 is 4 cleaning 5 writing

C 1 being late 2 mind opening 3 stop eating
4 feel like going

Chapter 10 말과 글을 살찌우는
형용사와 부사

Unit 01

A 1 friendly / 주어 설명 2 smart / 명사 수식
3 different / 주어 설명 4 wrong / 대명사 수식

B 1 a few 2 little 3 a little 4 few 5 much

C 1 Rafting is a very exciting sport.
2 She memorizes a lot of English words
3 I will tell you something important.
4 Did you buy everything necessary

Unit 02

A 1 well 2 fast 3 happily 4 carefully

B 1 Tom always makes his bed.
2 I can never hear my neighbor's TV.
3 Mina is often late for class.

C 1 finished, quickly 2 flying high 3 usually gets up
4 can hardly believe

Unit 03

A 1 best 2 hottest 3 early 4 more difficult
5 busier

B 1 as old as 2 bigger than 3 faster than

C 1 taller than 2 younger than 3 the shortest
4 heavier than

Chapter 11 나를 이끌어 줘,
명사의 가이드 전치사

Unit 01

A 1 in 2 at 3 in 4 for 5 on

B 1 until 2 in 3 for 4 on 5 at

C 1 at night 2 by next Monday 3 after dinner
4 during the weekend

Unit 02

A 1 in 2 at 3 on 4 in 5 over

B 1 next to 2 across from 3 in front of
4 between, and

C 1 behind his house 2 on the wall 3 under the tree

Unit 03

A 1 about 2 of 3 by 4 for 5 with

B 1 with 2 of 3 about 4 by 5 for

C 1 about the Korean War 2 by subway
3 with a knife 4 for Toronto

Chapter 12 너와 나를 이어 주는 오작교,
접속사

Unit 01

A 1 but 2 or 3 and 4 but 5 so

B 1 d 2 c 3 a 4 b

C 1 Is there a Disneyland in London or Paris?
2 The knife is sharp, so it is dangerous.
3 He worked hard and made a lot of money.
4 She knows the secret, but she is not telling it.

p. 34

A **1** After **2** while **3** before **4** When

B **1** b **2** c **3** d **4** a

C **1** I am studying, I always listen to music
2 you use the computer, you should turn it off
3 Cindy came home, she talked to me
4 you leave, lock all doors and windows

p. 35

A **1** if **2** because **3** that **4** wakes **5** that

B **1** He won't wash his car today because it may rain tomorrow.[Because it may rain tomorrow, he won't wash his car today.]
2 I know that Sally is studying at the library.
3 He doesn't have breakfast if he isn't hungry.[If he isn't hungry, he doesn't have breakfast.]

C **1** because the bus broke down
2 It is not true that
3 if I watch this scary movie
4 that laughing is good for our health

Overall Test

pp. 36~39

01 ③, ④   **02** (1) The students didn't[did not] study hard for the exam.   (2) Does Lily have big eyes?   **03** ①   **04** ③   **05** ①, ⑤   **06** looking at herself   **07** (1) is (2) am (3) am (4) is (5) are (6) is (7) are (8) are   **08** ③   **09** ②, ⑤   **10** ⑤   **11** (1) one (2) some   **12** ② **13** (1) must turn off (2) must not bring   **14** ③   **15** (A) much (B) were (C) many (D) was (E) any   **16** not able to   **17** ⑤   **18** ④   **19** (1) a beautiful dress (it is) (2) tall the tower is   **20** a cup of coffee, two loaves of bread   **21** (1) made some cookies for (2) gave some books to   **22** ③   **23** ④   **24** ②   **25** (1) played soccer (2) studied math (3) did my homework (4) took a walk   **26** ②   **27** the most expensive   **28** b heavier → heavy   d sadest → saddest   f very → much[still, even, far, a lot 등]   g often is → is often

01 ① is → are ② Are → Were ⑤ Were → Was

02 (1) 일반동사 과거형의 부정문: 「didn't[did not] + 동사원형」 (2) 주어가 3인칭 단수일 때 일반동사 현재형의 의문문: 「Does + 주어 + 동사원형 ~?」

03 sheep은 단·복수형이 같은 명사로 복수형도 sheep이다.

04 첫 번째 빈칸은 소유격, 두 번째 빈칸은 소유대명사의 자리로 둘의 형태가 같은 것은 his이다.

05 ① sky는 세상에 하나뿐인 자연환경으로 정관사 the가 필요하다. ⑤ 악기 이름 앞에 정관사 the를 쓴다. ② 식사 이름 앞, ③ 운동 이름 앞, ④ 장소가 본래 목적으로 사용될 때는 관사를 쓰지 않는다.

06 주어와 전치사의 목적어가 같으므로 재귀대명사 herself를 쓴다.

07 (1), (4), (6) 주어가 각각 my name, My hair, My dog Max로 3인칭 단수이므로 is를 쓴다. (2), (3) 주어가 I이므로 am을 쓴다. (5), (7), (8) 주어가 각각 my eyes, Its legs, We로 복수이므로 are를 쓴다.

해석 안녕, 내 이름은 Julie Anderson이야. 나는 14살이야. 나는 키가 약간 작아. 내 머리는 길고, 내 눈은 커. 나는 개를 한 마리 길러. 나의 개 Max는 갈색이야. 그것의 다리는 짧아. 우리는 좋은 친구야.

08 첫 번째 문장은 now로 보아 문장의 시제가 현재임을 알 수 있다. 주어가 I일 때 일반동사 현재형의 부정문은 don't를 이용해 만든다. 두 번째 문장은 last night로 보아 시제가 과거임을 알 수 있다. 일반동사 과거형의 의문문은 Did를 이용해 만든다.

09 미래에 할 일은 will이나 be going to로 나타낸다.

10 ⑤는 허락의 의미로, 나머지는 추측의 의미로 쓰였다.

11 (1) 정해지지 않은 것을 대신하는 one이 알맞다. (2) 긍정문에서 '몇몇'을 나타낼 때는 some이 알맞다.

12 b is sleeping → was sleeping e was → is f is knowing → knows

13 (1) 「must + 동사원형」: ~해야 한다 (2) 「must not + 동사원형」: ~하면 안 된다

14 b her story them → her story to them[them her story] c greatly → great

15 (A) food는 셀 수 없는 명사이므로 much로 수식한다. (B) 주어가 some cookies로 복수이므로 were가 알맞다. (C) apples는 셀 수 있는 명사의 복수형이므로 many로 수식한다. (D) bread는 셀 수 없는 명사이므로 단수 동사인 was가 알맞다. (E) 부정문이므로 any가 알맞다.

해석 우리 가족은 어제 소풍을 갔다. 엄마는 큰 바구니를 가져오셨다. 바구니에는 많은 음식이 있었다. 쿠키들이 좀 있었다. 많은 사과들이 있었다. 그리고 빵도 좀 있었다. 하지만 바구니에 음료수는 조금도 없었다.

16 couldn't(~할 수 없었다) = was/were not able to

17 don't have to: ~할 필요가 없다

18 전치사 for의 목적어로 동명사가 와야 한다. (tell → telling)

19 (1) 「What + a/an + 형용사 + 명사 (+ 주어 + 동사)!」 (2) 「How + 형용사/부사 (+ 주어 + 동사)!」

20 coffee는 a cup of, bread는 a loaf of를 이용하여 수량을 나타내며 두 개 이상일 때는 단위 명사를 복수형으로 쓴다.

21 「수여동사 + 직접목적어 + 전치사 + 간접목적어」의 순서일 때, (1) 수여동사 make는 전치사 for를, (2) 수여동사 give는 전치사 to를 쓴다.

22 ③ Reading books는 동명사 주어이므로 3인칭 단수로 취급하여 단수 동사를 쓴다. (are → is)

23 ① on → at ② in → on ③ by → until ⑤ at → in

24 머무르거나 지금 떠나는 것 중 하나를 고르는 것이므로 but이 아니라 or가 알맞다.

25 이미 지나간 일에 관해 물어보고 있으므로 각 동사의 과거형을 써서 과거시제로 답한다.
해석 미나: 지호야, 너는 어제 방과 후에 무엇을 했니?
  지호: 나는 축구를 했어. 그리고 나서 나는 수학을 공부했어. 너는 어떠니, 미나야?
  미나: 나는 숙제를 했어. 그리고 나서 산책을 했어.

26 조건을 나타내는 if절에서는 미래를 나타낼 때 현재시제를 쓴다.

27 최상급은 「the + 최상급」으로 나타내며, expensive는 3음절 이상이므로 앞에 most를 써서 최상급을 만든다.

28 **b** 동등 비교는 「as + 원급 + as」로 나타낸다. **d** sad는 「단모음 + 단자음」으로 끝나는 형용사이므로 마지막 자음을 한 번 더 쓰고 -est를 붙여서 최상급을 만든다. **f** very는 비교급(earlier)을 강조할 수 없다. **g** often은 빈도부사이므로 be동사 뒤에 쓴다.

개념 잡고 성적 올리는 필수 개념서

올리드

전과목 내신 완벽 대비!

탄탄하게! 교과서 개념을 효과적으로 정리
완벽하게! 개념과 유형의 반복 훈련
빠르게! 기출부터 신유형까지 정복
확실하게! 친절한 설명으로 오답 분석

필수 개념과 유형으로
내신을 자신있게 대비하자!

국어 1-1, 1-2, 2-1, 2-2, 3-1, 3-2
영어 1-1, 1-2, 2-1, 2-2, 3-1, 3-2
수학 1(상), 1(하), 2(상), 2(하), 3(상), 3(하)
사회 ①-1, ①-2, ②-1, ②-2
역사 ①-1, ①-2, ②-1, ②-2
과학 1-1, 1-2, 2-1, 2-2, 3-1, 3-2

*국어, 영어는 미래엔 교과서 관련 도서입니다.

구성보기

| 국어 1-1 | 영어 1-1 | 수학 1(상) | 사회 ①-1 | 과학 1-1 |

필수 유형 완성으로,
상위권 수학 실력으로 JUMP!

올리드 유형완성 시리즈
수학 1(상), 1(하), 2(상), 2(하), 3(상), 3(하)

고등학교 **개념**과 **유형**을
동시에 다지고 싶다면?

고등학교 **올리드** 시리즈

수학 고등 수학(상), 고등 수학(하), 수학Ⅰ, 수학Ⅱ, 확률과 통계, 미적분
사회 통합사회, 한국사, 한국지리, 사회·문화, 생활과 윤리, 윤리와 사상
과학 통합과학, 물리학Ⅰ, 화학Ⅰ, 생명과학Ⅰ, 지구과학Ⅰ

GRAMMAR
BITE

Chapter

1

그때그때 달라, 혼자서는 안 돼,
주어의 짝꿍

be동사

Unit 01 be동사의 현재형과 과거형

Unit 02 be동사의 부정문과 의문문

Unit 01 be동사의 현재형과 과거형

be동사는 '~이다, (~에) 있다'라는 의미로, 주어의 이름, 직업, 상태, 성격, 위치 등을 나타내는 동사이다. 동사의 원래 형태인 원형은 be이며, 주어의 인칭과 수, 현재를 나타내는지 과거를 나타내는지에 따라 형태가 달라진다.

A be동사의 현재형

수	인칭	주어	be동사	줄임말
단수	1인칭	I	am	I'm
	2인칭	You	are	You're
	3인칭	He / She / It	is	He's / She's / It's
복수	1인칭	We		We're
	2인칭	You	are	You're
	3인칭	They		They're

be동사의 현재형은 주어의 인칭과 수에 따라 am/are/is로 쓰며, '~이다, (~에) 있다'라는 의미이다. 일상 대화에서는 주로 줄임말을 쓴다.

☑ 인칭: 자신을 가리켜 1인칭, 상대방을 가리켜 2인칭, 1인칭과 2인칭을 제외한 나머지를 가리켜 3인칭이라고 한다.

a I **am** Suji. = I**'m** Suji.

b You **are** kind. = You**'re** kind.

c He **is** a teacher. = He**'s** a teacher.

d We **are** Korean. = We**'re** Korean.

e They **are** my friends. = They**'re** my friends.

cf. Mark **is** from America.
　　<u>사람 이름(3인칭 단수)</u>

　　Mark and Tyler **are** from America.
　　<u>둘 이상(복수)</u>

cf. 주어가 한 명의 사람 이름이거나 하나의 사물일 때 3인칭 단수 주어로 보아 be동사는 is를 쓴다. 주어가 둘 이상이면 be동사는 무조건 are를 쓴다.

be동사의 쓰임

be동사 혼자만은 문장의 완전한 의미를 나타낼 수 없다. be동사 뒤에 명사, 형용사, 장소를 나타내는 말 등이 함께 쓰여 주어의 이름, 직업, 상태, 성격, 위치 등을 나타낸다.

Her name **is** <u>Kelly</u>. She **is** <u>a doctor</u>. (이름, 직업 표현)
　　　　　　 명사　　　　　　　 명사

<u>It's</u> hot today. I'm <u>thirsty</u>. (상태 표현)
　형용사　　　　　　형용사

The books **are** <u>on the desk</u>. (위치 표현)
　　　　　　　 장소를 나타내는 말

B be동사의 과거형

a I **was** 13 years old last year.

　I **am** 14 years old this year.

b She **was** tired yesterday.

　She **is** fine today.

c They **were** in London last week.

　They **are** in Paris now.

am, is의 과거형은 was, are의 과거형은 were로, '~였다, (~에) 있었다'라는 의미이다.

---

vocabulary .... **A** be from ~ 출신이다　**B** tired ⑱ 피곤한

A 괄호 안에서 알맞은 말을 고르시오.

1 He [is / am] honest.

2 We [are / is] good friends.

3 I [was / were] sick last week.

4 The balls [is / are] under the table.

5 It [is / are] a cute dog.

B 빈칸에 알맞은 be동사를 쓰시오.

1 I _____ hungry now.

2 My name _____ Lisa.

3 They _____ Canadian.

4 She _____ in the library yesterday.

5 Nick and Jack _____ in the same class this year.

C 밑줄 친 부분을 괄호 안의 말로 바꾸어 문장을 다시 쓰시오.

1 A banana is on the table. (two bananas)

→ _____

2 My sisters are in the gym. (she)

→ _____

3 It is very hot today. (yesterday)

→ _____

4 The watch was expensive. (they)

→ _____

be동사의 부정문과 의문문

A be동사의 부정문

1 be동사 현재형의 부정문

주어	부정형	줄임말	
I	am not	I'm not	~~I amn't~~
You	are not	You're not	You aren't
He She It	is not	He's not She's not It's not	He isn't She isn't It isn't
We You They	are not	We're not You're not They're not	We aren't You aren't They aren't

a I **am not** hungry.

= I'**m not** hungry. *cf.* I amn't hungry.

b He **is not** at home.

= He'**s not** at home. – He **isn't** at home.

2 be동사 과거형의 부정문

a She **was not** busy yesterday.

= She **wasn't** busy yesterday.

b We **were not** in the same class last year.

= We **weren't** in the same class last year.

1 am/are/is 뒤에 not을 써서 '~이 아니다, (~에) 없다'라는 의미를 나타낸다.

cf. am not은 amn't로 줄여 쓰지 않는다.

2 was/were 뒤에 not을 써서 '~이 아니었다, (~에) 없었다'라는 의미를 나타낸다.

B be동사의 의문문

1 be동사 현재형의 의문문

a A: **Am** I right?

B: Yes, you **are**. / No, you **aren't**.

b A: **Are** you a member of the music club?

B: Yes, I **am**. / No, I'**m not**.

2 be동사 과거형의 의문문

a A: **Was** it cold last night?

B: Yes, it **was**. / No, it **wasn't**.

b A: **Were** they late for school?

B: Yes, they **were**. / No, they **weren't**.

1 주어와 am/are/is의 자리를 바꿔, '~이니?, (~에) 있니?'라는 의미를 나타낸다.

☑ 대답할 때 주의할 점
 • 문맥상 알맞은 대명사로 바꾸어 대답한다.
 • Yes라고 긍정으로 답할 때는 주어와 be동사를 줄여 쓰지 않는다.

2 주어와 was/were의 자리를 바꿔, '~이었니?, (~에) 있었니?'라는 의미를 나타낸다.

A 그림을 보고, 질문에 대한 알맞은 대답을 완성하시오.

1 A: Is he a singer?

B: _____, _____ _____.

2 A: Were you at home yesterday?

B: _____, _____ _____. I _____
at the park.

3 A: Are the cats on the sofa?

B: _____, _____ _____. The dogs
_____ on the sofa.

B 밑줄 친 부분이 어법상 맞으면 ○표, 틀리면 바르게 고치시오.

1 Ann and Emily isn't sisters. _____

2 Are Paulo from Mexico? _____

3 Were the boys in the playground after school? _____

4 My dog wasn't white. He is black. _____

C 우리말과 일치하도록 괄호 안의 말을 이용하여 문장을 완성하시오.

1 너의 삼촌은 과학자이시니? (your uncle)

→ _____ _____ _____ a scientist?

2 그 책은 도서관에 없었다. (the book)

→ _____ _____ _____ in the library.

3 너는 지난 주말에 바빴니? (busy)

→ _____ _____ _____ last weekend?

4 햄버거는 건강에 좋지 않다. (hamburgers)

→ _____ _____ good for your health.

Writing Practice

Answers p.2

A 우리말과 일치하도록 괄호 안의 말을 바르게 배열하시오. (필요하면 형태를 바꿀 것)

01 그녀는 키가 크다. (is, tall, she)

→ _____

02 우리는 중학생이다. (are, middle school students, we)

→ _____

03 많은 사람들이 거리에 있었다. (were, on the street, many people)

→ _____

04 나는 힘이 세지 않다. (strong, am, I, not)

→ _____

05 너는 어제 아팠니? (you, sick, were)

→ _____ yesterday?

06 그들은 내 남동생들이다. (be, they, my little brothers)

→ _____

07 그는 똑똑하니? (he, smart, be)

→ _____

08 어젯밤에 매우 추웠다. (be, it, very cold)

→ _____ last night.

09 Tom과 나는 같은 동아리이다. (Tom and I, in the same club, be)

→ _____

10 그 영화는 재미없었다. (be, the movie, funny, not)

→ _____

B 우리말과 일치하도록 괄호 안의 말을 이용하여 문장을 완성하시오.

01 a 나는 1학년이다. (be)

→ I ＿＿＿＿＿＿＿ in the first grade.

b 우리는 1학년이다.

→ ＿＿＿＿＿＿＿＿＿＿＿＿＿＿＿＿＿＿＿＿＿

02 a 나의 삼촌은 요리사이다. (be)

→ My uncle ＿＿＿＿＿＿＿ a cook.

b 나의 삼촌은 의사가 아니다. (a doctor)

→ ＿＿＿＿＿＿＿＿＿＿＿＿＿＿＿＿＿＿＿＿＿

03 a Mike는 지금 음악실에 있다. (be)

→ Mike ＿＿＿＿＿＿＿ in the music room now.

b Jenny는 어제 음악실에 있었다.

→ ＿＿＿＿＿＿＿＿＿＿＿＿＿＿＿＿＿＿ yesterday.

04 a 그녀는 피곤하다. (be)

→ She ＿＿＿＿＿＿＿ tired.

b 너는 피곤하니?

→ ＿＿＿＿＿＿＿＿＿＿＿＿＿＿＿＿＿＿＿＿＿

05 a Kate와 Sally는 전에 키가 작았다. (be)

→ Kate and Sally ＿＿＿＿＿＿＿ short before.

b 그들은 지금 키가 작지 않다.

→ ＿＿＿＿＿＿＿＿＿＿＿＿＿＿＿＿＿＿＿ now.

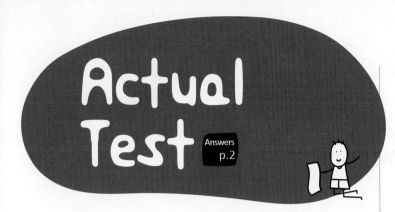

Actual Test

Answers p.2

01

빈칸에 공통으로 들어갈 말로 알맞은 것은?

> • We _____ a family.
> • You _____ very special.
> • They _____ in the cafeteria now.

① is   ② am   ③ are
④ was   ⑤ were

02

밑줄 친 부분이 어법상 틀린 것은? (바르게 고칠 것)

① You <u>are</u> so sweet.
② Mr. Han <u>is</u> a teacher.
③ We <u>are</u> very different.
④ She <u>was</u> here a minute ago.
⑤ Clara and Emma <u>is</u> from Australia.

[03~04] 빈칸에 들어갈 말로 알맞은 것을 고르시오.

03

> I _____ so busy yesterday.

① is   ② am   ③ are
④ was   ⑤ were

04

> They _____ in Japan last month.

① is   ② am   ③ are
④ was   ⑤ were

05 서술형

대화의 빈칸에 공통으로 들어갈 말을 쓰시오.

> A: _____ he your new teacher?
> B: Yes, he _____. He _____ very nice.

→ _____

06

우리말을 영어로 바르게 옮긴 것은?

> 연필들이 책상 위에 있다.

① The pencils is on the desk.
② The pencils was on the desk.
③ The pencils aren't on the desk.
④ The pencils are on the desk.
⑤ The pencils were on the desk.

07

밑줄 친 부분이 어법상 틀린 것은? (바르게 고칠 것)

> They ①<u>were</u> ②<u>no</u> ③<u>in</u> the ④<u>same</u> class last ⑤<u>year</u>.

08 서술형

우리말과 일치하도록 괄호 안의 단어 중 필요한 단어만을 바르게 배열하여 문장을 완성하시오.

> 어제는 바람이 많이 불었다.
> (was, were, it, they, windy, very, yesterday)

→ _____

09

빈칸에 들어갈 말로 알맞지 <u>않은</u> 것은?

_____ are in the computer room now.

① We
② The students
③ They
④ Ms. Kim
⑤ Lily and her brother

10 [서술형]

대화의 빈칸에 들어갈 말을 괄호 안의 말을 바르게 배열하여 쓰시오.

A: Is Jason at home now?
B: No, he isn't. _____ now.
A: Okay, thank you.

→ _____

(is, in, gym, he, the)

11

대화의 밑줄 친 부분이 어법상 <u>틀린</u> 것은? (바르게 고칠 것)

A: Alice, ①<u>is</u> that girl your little sister?
B: Yes, she is. Her name ②<u>are</u> Olivia.
A: She ③<u>is</u> so lovely. Is she an elementary school student?
B: No, she ④<u>isn't</u>. ⑤<u>She's</u> 7 years old.

12 [서술형]

우리말과 일치하도록 빈칸에 알맞은 말을 쓰시오.

그녀는 나의 담임 선생님이 아니다.

→ She _____ _____ my homeroom teacher.

13

대화의 빈칸에 들어갈 말이 순서대로 짝지어진 것은?

A: _____ it cool last night?
B: No, it _____.

① Is – is
② Is – isn't
③ Was – was
④ Was – wasn't
⑤ Were – weren't

14

괄호 안의 지시대로 바꿔 쓸 때 <u>잘못된</u> 것은? (바르게 바꿔 쓸 것)

① He is sick. (과거형으로)
→ He were sick.
② I am Minho. (축약형으로)
→ I'm Minho.
③ You are thirsty. (의문문으로)
→ Are you thirsty?
④ They were in Seoul. (현재형으로)
→ They are in Seoul.
⑤ We are good friends. (축약형으로)
→ We're good friends.

15 [서술형]

밑줄 친 단어들을 알맞은 형태로 바꿔 문장을 다시 쓰시오.

Peter <u>be</u> 13 years old last year. He <u>be</u> 14 years old this year.

→ _____

_____

16

다음 중 어법상 틀린 것은? (바르게 고칠 것)

① He's a doctor.
② It's cloudy today.
③ They're very kind.
④ You're really funny.
⑤ It wasn't not difficult.

17

밑줄 친 부분이 어법상 옳은 것은? (틀린 것들을 바르게 고칠 것)

① We wasn't there.
② It was warm today.
③ You and I are friends.
④ The balls is in the box.
⑤ She is happy yesterday.

18

밑줄 친 부분의 의미가 나머지 넷과 다른 것은?

① Is she a famous singer?
② His name is Benjamin.
③ Are you at the theater?
④ I am a good student.
⑤ Today is my mom's birthday.

19

빈칸에 들어갈 수 있는 말이 나머지 넷과 다른 것은?

① Your dogs _____ so cute.
② We _____ very hungry now.
③ James _____ my classmate.
④ _____ you ready for the test?
⑤ _____ they father and daughter?

20

대화의 빈칸에 들어갈 응답으로 알맞지 않은 것은?

A: Were you at your friend's house?
B: _____

① No, I was at the park.
② Yes, I was at school.
③ Yes, I was with Sam.
④ No, I wasn't.
⑤ Yes, I was.

21 서술형

우리말과 일치하도록 괄호 안의 말을 바르게 배열하시오.

너는 축구 동아리 회원이니?
(a, are, of, the, club, you, member, soccer)

→ _____

22

다음 중 짝지어진 대화가 어색한 것은?

① A: Am I pretty?
   B: No, I'm not.
② A: Is he your son?
   B: No, he isn't.
③ A: Are you a nurse?
   B: Yes, I am.
④ A: Is she your friend?
   B: Yes, she is.
⑤ A: Are they middle school students?
   B: Yes, they are.

23 [서술형]

다음 글에서 어법상 <u>틀린</u> 부분을 <u>모두</u> 찾아 바르게 고치시오.

Hi, my name is Suho. I'm 14 years old. I'm a Daehan Middle School student. I'm good at basketball, but I amn't good at badminton. My best friend are Chris. He's from England. We're in the same class. He and I are very close.

24

빈칸에 들어갈 말이 순서대로 짝지어진 것은?

- It _____ sunny today.
- I _____ very sad now.
- She _____ tired last night.
- The girls _____ angry at him yesterday.

① is – am – was – were
② are – am – was – are
③ is – am – is – were
④ are – was – is – were
⑤ is – was – was – are

25 [서술형]

다음 대화에서 어법상 <u>틀린</u> 부분을 <u>두 군데</u> 찾아 바르게 고치시오.

A: Hi, Ann. Is your trip good?
B: No, it wasn't. The weather were terrible. So I was at the hotel all the time.

(1) _____ → _____

(2) _____ → _____

26

각 문장을 완성할 때 빈칸에 필요하지 <u>않은</u> 것은?

- She was _____ sleepy.
- _____ we in trouble now?
- A dog _____ on the chair now.
- _____ you there three hours ago?

① is[Is]   ② are[Are]   ③ not[Not]
④ was[Was]   ⑤ were[Were]

27

표의 내용과 일치하도록 할 때 빈칸에 들어갈 말로 알맞은 것은?

this morning	now

It was rainy this morning, but now _____.

① it is rainy
② it was rainy
③ the weather is nice
④ the weather was nice
⑤ the weather is not nice

28

다음 중 어법상 옳은 것을 <u>모두</u> 고르면? (틀린 것들을 바르게 고칠 것)

① The kids was very cute.
② She isn't a good dancer.
③ Is Kevin in his room then?
④ Tennis is my favorite sport.
⑤ They's not young people.

Recall My Memory

다음 문장이 어법상 맞으면 O표, 틀리면 바르게 고치시오.

01 Kate are sad now. ⟿ p. 18

02 I were a baseball player two years ago. ⟿ p. 18

03 Are he your English teacher? ⟿ p. 20

04 We weren't at the party yesterday. ⟿ p. 20

05 The flowers are very beautiful. ⟿ p. 18

06 Is Jack and David good friends? ⟿ p. 20

07 They was in France last year. ⟿ p. 18

08 He is from New Zealand. ⟿ p. 18

09 Was you late for the club meeting? ⟿ p. 20

10 The hats were on the bed. ⟿ p. 18

11 They is my parents. ⟿ p. 18

12 Blue stars is very hot. ⟿ p. 18

13 Were he at home last night? ⟿ p. 20

14 They isn't my brothers. ⟿ p. 20

15 Brian and I was at the bookstore after school. ⟿ p. 18

Chapter

2

현재로 과거로 갑옷을 바꿔 입는,
주어의 행동대장,

일반동사

Unit 01	일반동사의 현재형
Unit 02	일반동사의 과거형
Unit 03	일반동사의 부정문과 의문문

Unit 01 일반동사의 현재형

be동사 외에 주어의 동작이나 상태를 나타내는 동사를 '일반동사'라고 한다. 일반동사도 주어의 인칭과 수, 현재를 나타내는지 과거를 나타내는지에 따라 형태가 달라진다.

A 일반동사의 현재형

a I **play** soccer after school.

b You **teach** English very well.

c We **ride** our bikes together.

d They **study** at the library.

e My sisters **have** long hair.

주어가 I/You/We/They이거나 복수일 때는 동사의 원래 형태인 동사원형을 쓴다.

B 일반동사의 3인칭 단수 현재형

a He **plays** basketball every day.

b She **teaches** math at a middle school.

c It **snows** in winter.

d Suho **studies** at home.

e My sister **has** short hair.

주어가 He/She/It이거나 3인칭 단수일 때는 대부분 동사원형에 -(e)s를 붙인다.

e have는 has로 불규칙하게 변한다.

일반동사의 3인칭 단수 현재형 만드는 법

대부분의 동사	동사원형 + -s	eat → eats play → plays speak → speaks	learn → learns read → reads visit → visits	like → likes sleep → sleeps write → writes
-o, -s, -ch, -sh, -x로 끝나는 동사	동사원형 + -es	do → does pass → passes watch → watches wish → wishes	go → goes catch → catches brush → brushes fix → fixes	miss → misses teach → teaches wash → washes mix → mixes
「자음 + y」로 끝나는 동사	y를 i로 바꾸고 + -es	carry → carries study → studies cf. 「모음 + y」로 끝나는 동사: enjoy → enjoys, buy → buys	cry → cries try → tries	fly → flies worry → worries
불규칙하게 변하는 동사	have → **has**			

자음: 알파벳 중 모음을 제외한 나머지(b, c, d, f ...) 모음: a, e, i, o, u

vocabulary ············ A after school 방과 후에 B miss ⑧ 놓치다; 그리워하다 wish ⑧ 원하다, 바라다 fix ⑧ 수리하다, 고치다 mix ⑧ 섞다

Exercise

Answers p.3

 A Daniel이 방과 후에 하는 일을 보고, 빈칸에 알맞은 말을 쓰시오.

MON	TUE	WED	THU	FRI
study	play	wash	have	see

1 Daniel _____ at the library on Mondays.

2 He _____ badminton on Tuesdays.

3 He _____ his pet dog on Wednesdays.

4 He _____ a swimming lesson on Thursdays.

5 He _____ a movie on Fridays.

B 밑줄 친 부분이 어법상 맞으면 O표, 틀리면 바르게 고치시오.

1 My father <u>fixs</u> computers.   _____

2 The kites <u>flies</u> high.   _____

3 Emily <u>miss</u> her grandparents.   _____

4 We <u>wear</u> school uniforms.   _____

5 Yumi and her sister <u>goes</u> hiking.   _____

C 밑줄 친 부분을 괄호 안의 말로 바꾸어 문장을 다시 쓰시오.

1 <u>I</u> have brown eyes. (Mike)

→ _____

2 <u>They</u> watch TV every evening. (my mom)

→ _____

3 <u>The boy</u> wakes up at 7 in the morning. (the children)

→ _____

Unit 02 일반동사의 과거형

A 일반동사의 과거형

a I **cleaned** my room yesterday.

b He **lived** in Busan a year ago.

c The baby **cried** all night.

d The bus driver **stopped** suddenly.

주어의 인칭과 수에 관계없이, 대부분 동사원형에 -(e)d를 붙인다.

일반동사의 과거형 만드는 법

대부분의 동사	동사원형 + -ed	clean → clean**ed** look → look**ed** want → want**ed**	end → end**ed** play → play**ed** wash → wash**ed**	learn → learn**ed** start → start**ed** watch → watch**ed**
-e로 끝나는 동사	동사원형 + -d	arrive → arrive**d** live → live**d**	dance → dance**d** love → love**d**	like → like**d** move → move**d**
「자음 + **y**」로 끝나는 동사	y를 i로 바꾸고 + -ed	carry → carr**ied** study → stud**ied** cf. 「모음 + y」로 끝나는 동사: enjoy → enjoy**ed**, stay → stay**ed**	cry → cr**ied** try → tr**ied**	hurry → hurr**ied** worry → worr**ied**
「단모음 + 단자음」으로 끝나는 동사	마지막 자음을 한 번 더 쓰고 + -ed	drop → drop**ped** cf. 강세가 앞에 오는 2음절 동사: visit → visit**ed**, enter → enter**ed**	plan → plan**ned**	stop → stop**ped**

단모음: 하나의 모음으로 이루어진 짧은 모음   단자음: 자음 하나
강세: 단어에서 강하게 발음하는 부분(음절), 강세 표시는 강하게 발음하는 부분의 모음에 표시함(vísit, énter)
음절: 자음과 모음이 합쳐져서 하나의 소리를 이루는 단위(visit → vi/sit(2음절), enter → en/ter(2음절))

B 불규칙하게 변하는 일반동사의 과거형

a She **cut** her finger with a knife.

b My uncle **came** to my house.

c I **sent** text messages to my friends.

d Mina **ate** fried chicken for dinner.

e We **went** to the BTS concert last night.

일반동사의 과거형 중에는 과거형이 동사원형과 같거나 불규칙하게 다른 형태로 바뀌는 동사들이 있다.

불규칙 변화의 과거형

동사원형과 과거형이 같은 동사	cut → **cut** read[ri:d] → **read**[red]	hit → **hit**	hurt → **hurt**	put → **put**	set → **set**
동사원형과 과거형이 다른 동사	build → **built** eat → **ate** go → **went** make → **made** send → **sent** swim → **swam**	buy → **bought** feel → **felt** have → **had** meet → **met** shine → **shone** take → **took**	come → **came** fly → **flew** hear → **heard** ride → **rode** sing → **sang** teach → **taught**	do → **did** get → **got** leave → **left** run → **ran** sleep → **slept** tell → **told**	drink → **drank** give → **gave** lose → **lost** see → **saw** speak → **spoke** write → **wrote**

vocabulary ----------- **A** all night 밤새도록   suddenly ⑨ 갑자기   **B** text message 문자 메시지   hurt ⑧ 다치게 하다(-hurt-hurt)   set ⑧ 놓다(-set-set)   leave ⑧ 떠나다(-left-left)   lose ⑧ 잃어버리다; 지다(-lost-lost)   shine ⑧ 빛나다(-shone-shone)

A 괄호 안에서 알맞은 말을 고르시오.

1 I [losed / lost] my bag yesterday.

2 The horses [runned / ran] very fast.

3 They [drank / drunk] coffee after lunch.

4 He [visited / visitted] Russia ten years ago.

5 My mom [maked / made] these cookies.

B 빈칸에 알맞은 말을 보기에서 골라 과거형으로 쓰시오.

보기	play	mix	stop	ride	win

1 The soccer team _____ the final game.

2 I _____ the flute very well.

3 His car _____ suddenly.

4 She _____ the yogurt, fruit, and nuts.

5 They _____ their bikes along the lake.

C 밑줄 친 부분을 괄호 안의 말로 바꾸어 문장을 완성하시오.

1 She sees a movie <u>every Sunday</u>. (a week ago)

→ She _____.

2 They eat cereal <u>in the morning</u>. (this morning)

→ They _____.

3 He goes swimming <u>on weekends</u>. (last weekend)

→ He _____.

4 I have a piano lesson <u>after school</u>. (yesterday)

→ I _____.

일반동사의 부정문과 의문문

A 일반동사의 부정문

1 일반동사 현재형의 부정문

a I **do not watch** horror movies.

= I **don't watch** horror movies.

b You **don't need** much money.

c He **does not tell** lies.

= He **doesn't tell** lies.

d Lilly **doesn't drink** coffee.

1 주어가 I/You/We/They이거나 복수일 때는 동사원형 앞에 do not(= don't)을, 주어가 He/She/It이거나 3인칭 단수일 때는 동사원형 앞에 does not(= doesn't)을 쓴다.

2 일반동사 과거형의 부정문

a I **did not bring** an umbrella.

= I **didn't bring** an umbrella.

b They **didn't sleep** well last night.

2 주어의 인칭과 수에 관계없이, 동사원형 앞에 did not(= didn't)을 쓴다.

B 일반동사의 의문문

1 일반동사 현재형의 의문문

a A: **Do** you **like** Daniel?

B: Yes, I **do**. / No, I **don't**.

b A: **Do** you and your brother **get** along?

B: Yes, we **do**. / No, we **don't**.

c A: **Does** Suji **know** Minho?

B: Yes, she **does**. / No, she **doesn't**.

d A: **Does** Sam **eat** cheonggukjang?

B: Yes, he **does**. / No, he **doesn't**.

1 주어가 I/You/We/They이거나 복수일 때는 「Do + 주어 + 동사원형 ~?」, 주어가 He/She/It이거나 3인칭 단수일 때는 「Does + 주어 + 동사원형 ~?」 형태로 쓴다.

2 일반동사 과거형의 의문문

a A: **Did** you **do** your homework?

B: Yes, I **did**. / No, I **didn't**.

b A: **Did** they **win** the game?

B: Yes, they **did**. / No, they **didn't**.

2 주어의 인칭과 수에 관계없이, 「Did + 주어 + 동사원형 ~?」 형태로 쓴다.

vocabulary ·············· **A** horror 몡 공포   tell a lie 거짓말하다   **B** get along 사이좋게 지내다   homework 몡 숙제, 과제

Exercise

Answers p.3

A 주어진 문장을 괄호 안의 지시대로 바꿔 쓰시오.

1 My mother has a car. (부정문으로)

→ _____

2 Mr. Smith lives in Seoul. (의문문으로)

→ _____

3 They got up early this morning. (부정문으로)

→ _____

4 She went to the beach last summer. (의문문으로)

→ _____

B 밑줄 친 부분이 어법상 맞으면 ○표, 틀리면 바르게 고치시오.

1 <u>Does</u> they finish their work?　　　　　　　_____

2 Emily <u>don't has</u> classes on Saturdays.　　　_____

3 Does the man <u>exercises</u> every day?　　　　_____

4 Jiho and I <u>don't play</u> table tennis yesterday.　_____

5 <u>Did he teach</u> music two years ago?　　　　_____

C 괄호 안의 말을 이용하여 대화를 완성하시오.

1 A: _____ _____ _____ the piano? (play)

B: Yes, she does.

2 A: I like soccer.

B: I _____ _____ soccer. I like baseball. (like)

3 A: _____ _____ _____ dinner? (cook)

B: No, he didn't. He washed the dishes.

4 A: Tom got a bad grade on the exam.

B: Yeah, he _____ _____ hard. (study)

Writing Practice

Answers p.3

A 우리말과 일치하도록 괄호 안의 말을 바르게 배열하시오. (필요하면 형태를 바꿀 것)

01 우리는 방과 후에 농구를 한다. (play, we, basketball)

→ _____ after school.

02 아빠가 어제 피자를 만드셨다. (Dad, a pizza, made)

→ _____ yesterday.

03 나는 매일 조깅을 하러 가지 않는다. (I, jogging, do, go, not)

→ _____ every day.

04 그가 이 그림을 그렸니? (he, did, draw, this picture)

→ _____

05 그들은 지난 주말에 캠핑하러 갔다. (they, camping, went)

→ _____ last weekend.

06 나는 어제 흰색 운동화를 샀다. (I, white sneakers, buy)

→ _____ yesterday.

07 그는 저녁 식사 전에 숙제를 한다. (he, his homework, do)

→ _____ before dinner.

08 너의 여동생은 바이올린을 연주하니? (your sister, play, do, the violin)

→ _____

09 나는 어젯밤에 TV를 보지 않았다. (I, watch, not, TV, do)

→ _____ last night.

10 그녀는 제주도에 집을 가지고 있다. (a house, she, have)

→ _____ on Jeju Island.

B 우리말과 일치하도록 괄호 안의 말을 이용하여 문장을 완성하시오.

01 a 나는 버스로 학교에 간다. (go)

→ I _____ to school by bus.

b 그는 지하철로 학교에 간다.

→ _____ by subway.

02 a 그녀는 아침에 일찍 일어난다. (get up)

→ She _____ early in the morning.

b 나는 오늘 아침에 일찍 일어났다.

→ _____ this morning.

03 a 너는 아침으로 샌드위치를 먹니? (eat)

→ _____ a sandwich for breakfast?

b 그녀는 점심으로 샌드위치를 먹니?

→ _____ for lunch?

04 a 그는 야구를 좋아한다. (like)

→ He _____ baseball.

b 그녀는 야구를 좋아하지 않는다.

→ _____

05 a 우리는 도서관에서 영어를 공부했다. (study)

→ We _____ English at the library.

b 그들은 도서관에서 영어를 공부했니?

→ _____ at the library?

Actual Test

Answers p.4

01

동사의 3인칭 단수 현재형이 잘못된 것은? (바르게 고칠 것)

① carry → carrys
② miss → misses
③ hope → hopes
④ enjoy → enjoys
⑤ teach → teaches

02

동사의 과거형이 잘못된 것은? (바르게 고칠 것)

① ask → asked
② plan → planed
③ worry → worried
④ visit → visited
⑤ play → played

03

빈칸에 들어갈 말로 알맞은 것은?

_____ potatoes grow in the ground?

① Is
② Do
③ Am
④ Are
⑤ Does

04

빈칸에 들어갈 말로 알맞지 않은 것은?

_____ walks the dog every day.

① Mr. Wilson
② My son
③ His neighbor
④ The girls
⑤ My friend Jenny

05

빈칸에 들어갈 말로 알맞은 것을 모두 고르면?

I went to the movies _____.

① on Saturdays
② yesterday
③ tomorrow
④ last Sunday
⑤ a week ago

[06~07] 빈칸에 들어갈 말이 순서대로 짝지어진 것을 고르시오.

06

• I _____ need your help now.
• She _____ answer my call yesterday.

① don't – don't
② don't – didn't
③ don't – doesn't
④ didn't – didn't
⑤ didn't – doesn't

07

Many children _____ sweets, but this child _____ sweets.

① like – likes
② like – doesn't like
③ like – don't like
④ likes – don't like
⑤ likes – doesn't like

08

다음 중 빈칸에 Does가 들어가는 것은?

① _____ his parents watch TV?
② _____ their son like sports?
③ _____ your sister always kind?
④ _____ Brian and Tom often fight?
⑤ _____ we have homework today?

[09~10] 대화의 빈칸에 들어갈 말로 알맞은 것을 고르시오.

09

A: Did he walk to school yesterday?
B: _____ He rode his bike to school.

① Yes, he do. ② Yes, he did.
③ Yes, he does. ④ No, he doesn't.
⑤ No, he didn't.

10

A: Do you live near the school?
B: _____ I live far from the school.

① Yes, I am. ② No, I do.
③ Yes, I do. ④ No, I'm not.
⑤ No, I don't.

11

대화의 빈칸에 들어갈 말이 순서대로 짝지어진 것은?

A: _____ she go shopping last weekend?
B: Yes, she _____. She _____ a skirt.

① Do – do – bought
② Does – does – buys
③ Does – does – bought
④ Did – did – buys
⑤ Did – did – bought

12

다음 중 어법상 틀린 것은? (바르게 고칠 것)

① Does she often cook?
② My cat sleeps a lot.
③ Do the boys like badminton?
④ He doesn't gets enough sleep.
⑤ I don't need your advice.

13 서술형

우리말과 일치하도록 괄호 안의 말을 이용하여 문장을 완성하시오.

너의 여동생은 스파게티를 좋아하니? (like)

→ _____ your sister _____ spaghetti?

14

다음 중 어법상 옳은 것은? (틀린 것들을 바르게 고칠 것)

① Are they speak Japanese?
② They doesn't travel by bus.
③ The children don't like mice.
④ Sue doesn't has any brothers.
⑤ Bob and Judy don't knows each other.

15 서술형

다음 글에서 어법상 틀린 부분을 세 군데 찾아 바르게 고치시오.

Peter has some good habits. He gets up early. He exercise every day. But he also has some bad habits. He don't goes to bed early. He use his cell phone too much.

(1) _____ → _____
(2) _____ → _____
(3) _____ → _____

16

다음 문장을 의문문으로 바르게 바꿔 쓴 것은?

Ms. Green teaches science.

① Do Ms. Green teach science?
② Do Ms. Green teaches science?
③ Is Ms. Green teaches science?
④ Does Ms. Green teach science?
⑤ Does Ms. Green teaches science?

17

다음 문장을 부정문으로 바르게 바꿔 쓴 것은?

Eric does the dishes after dinner.

① Eric don't the dishes after dinner.
② Eric doesn't do the dishes after dinner.
③ Eric not does the dishes after dinner.
④ Eric doesn't the dishes after dinner.
⑤ Eric doesn't does the dishes after dinner.

18

우리말을 영어로 바르게 옮긴 것은?

네 형이 방과 후에 숙제를 했니?

① Does your brother did his homework after school?
② Does your brother do his homework after school?
③ Did your brother do his homework after school?
④ Did your brother did his homework after school?
⑤ Did your brother does his homework after school?

[19~20] 다음 문장을 부정문으로 바꿔 쓰시오.

19 서술형

His friends play tennis on Sundays.

→ _____

20 서술형

He told the truth to me.

→ _____

[21~22] 다음 문장을 의문문으로 바꿔 쓰시오.

21 서술형

He takes care of sick animals.

→ _____

22 서술형

She found the money.

→ _____

23

밑줄 친 do의 쓰임이 나머지 넷과 다른 것은?

① I do not remember her name.
② Do you do any housework?
③ James doesn't do his homework.
④ I do taekwondo in the afternoon.
⑤ We do the laundry every weekend.

24 서술형

친구들이 방과 후에 하는 일을 보고, 빈칸에 알맞은 말을 쓰시오.

Jinsu	Mina	Seho
play	watch	have

Jinsu usually (1)_____ basketball after school. Seho (2)_____ a snack, and Mina (3)_____ TV.

25

다음 중 어법상 옳은 것은 모두 몇 개인가? (틀린 것들을 바르게 고칠 것)

a. Do the boys know you?
b. Does your brother nice?
c. He doesn't likes vegetables.
d. My sister play the cello every day.
e. Do you drink milk before bed?
f. Do your cousins speaks English?

① 1개 ② 2개 ③ 3개 ④ 4개 ⑤ 5개

26 서술형

그림을 보고, 대화의 빈칸에 알맞은 말을 쓰시오.

cry   sleep

A: (1) _____ Sally cry?
B: Yes, she did. She (2) _____ at the
   end of the movie.
A: (3) _____ Fred enjoy the movie?
B: No, he (4) _____. He (5) _____
   through the movie.

27 서술형

수지가 지난 주말에 한 일을 보고, 빈칸에 알맞은 말을 쓰시오.

| ride her bike | ○ | read books | ○ |
| make lunch | ○ | go shopping | × |

Last weekend, Suji (1)_____ her bike. And
she (2)_____ lunch. She (3)_____
books, too. But she (4)_____ _____
shopping.

28

다음 중 어법상 옳은 것으로 바르게 짝지어진 것은? (틀린 것들을 바르게 고칠 것)

a. He taught history at school.
b. I waked up early this morning.
c. Mia wore a sweater yesterday.
d. He sended a letter to his mom.
e. My dad caught a big fish last Saturday.
f. She read a newspaper last night.

① a, b, e   ② a, d, e
③ b, d, e   ④ a, c, d, f
⑤ a, c, e, f

29 서술형

괄호 안의 동사를 빈칸에 알맞은 형태로 써서 글을 완성하시오.

Yesterday was a great day. My friend Katie
came to Seoul. We (1) _____ (go) to
Insa-dong. It is a very famous place in
Korea. We (2) _____ (shop) for nice
clothes. And we (3) _____ (eat) Korean
street food. Katie (4) _____ (like) the
food very much. We (5) _____ (have)
a lot of fun. We were very happy.

30 서술형

다음 중 어법상 틀린 것을 모두 골라 바르게 고치시오.

a. Jack studied science in the classroom.
b. She losed her textbook.
c. Did your brother buy a camera?
d. The boy didn't broke the window.
e. He built a house last year.
f. Did they ate lunch with you?
g. Bob swimmed in the river.

Recall My Memory

다음 문장이 어법상 맞으면 O표, 틀리면 바르게 고치시오.

01 She watchs TV after dinner. ➘ p. 30

02 I don't go to school on Sunday. ➘ p. 34

03 Are your sister tall? ➘ p. 20

04 They buyed new bikes last weekend. ➘ p. 32

05 I am sick last night. ➘ p. 18

06 John and Bill plays basketball. ➘ p. 30

07 My brothers are twins. ➘ p. 18

08 Daniel have a nice watch. ➘ p. 30

09 I were in Jeju Island last week. ➘ p. 18

10 Do your father work at a bank? ➘ p. 34

11 He got up early this morning. ➘ p. 32

12 Did you wrote the report? ➘ p. 34

13 He wasn't hungry now. ➘ p. 20

14 Jane didn't finished her homework. ➘ p. 34

15 I readed the book yesterday. ➘ p. 32

이름을 불러 주면 나에게로 와서
하나의 의미가 되는

명사

Unit
01   셀 수 있는 명사

Unit
02   셀 수 없는 명사

Unit
03   관사

셀 수 있는 명사

명사란 사람, 사물, 개념 등의 이름을 나타내는 말로, 셀 수 있는 명사와 셀 수 없는 명사로 나뉜다.

A 셀 수 있는 명사의 종류

일정한 형태가 있거나 서로 확실히 구분되는 것을 나타내는 명사는 개수를 셀 수 있다.

a friend, dog, flower, apple, book, house ...

b family, class, team, club, group ...

a 사람이나 사물을 나타내는 명사

b 사람이나 사물이 모여 집합체를 나타내는 명사

B 셀 수 있는 명사의 수

1 셀 수 있는 명사가 하나일 때

a I ate **a banana**.

b She ate **an apple**.
　　　　　첫 발음이 모음으로 시작

2 셀 수 있는 명사가 둘 이상일 때

a He studied for four **hours**.

b I need three **boxes**.

c We grow **tomatoes** at home.

d She has two **babies**.

e **Leaves** change color in fall.

f Janghun's **feet** are 320mm long.

g The fisherman caught many **fish**.

1 명사가 하나일 때는 명사 앞에 a를 쓴다.

b 명사의 첫 발음이 모음으로 시작하면 an 을 쓴다.

2 명사가 둘 이상일 때는 대부분 명사에 -(e)s를 붙여 복수형으로 쓴다.

f 불규칙하게 변하는 복수형도 있다.

g 단수형과 복수형이 같은 명사도 있다.

셀 수 있는 명사의 복수형 만드는 법

대부분의 명사	명사 + -s	apple → apples friend → friends	book → books hour → hours	dog → dogs pen → pens
-s, -ch, -sh, -x로 끝나는 명사	명사 + -es	bus → bus**es** watch → watch**es**	class → class**es** dish → dish**es**	bench → bench**es** box → box**es**
「자음 + o」로 끝나는 명사	명사 + -es	potato → potato**es** tomato → tomato**es** 예외: photo → photos, piano → pianos *cf.* 「모음 + o」로 끝나는 명사: video → videos, radio → radios		
「자음 + y」로 끝나는 명사	y를 i로 바꾸고 + -es	baby → bab**ies** family → famil**ies** *cf.* 「모음 + y」로 끝나는 명사: boy → boys, day → days	city → cit**ies** lady → lad**ies**	country → countr**ies** story → stor**ies**
-f, -fe로 끝나는 명사	f, fe를 v로 바꾸고 + -es	knife → kni**ves** 예외: roof → roofs	leaf → lea**ves**	life → li**ves**
불규칙하게 변하는 명사	foot → **feet** child → **children**	tooth → **teeth** mouse → **mice**	man → **men** goose → **geese**	woman → **women** ox → **oxen**
단·복수형이 같은 명사	deer → **deer**	fish → **fish**	sheep → **sheep**	

vocabulary　　　B change ⑧ 바꾸다, 변화시키다 fisherman ⑲ 어부

Exercise

Answers p.5

A 괄호 안에서 알맞은 말을 고르시오.

1 They are [a dog / dogs].

2 I ate three [tomatos / tomatoes].

3 Kate visited many [citys / cities].

4 [Deer / Deers] live in the forest.

5 I really hate [mouses / mice].

B 괄호 안의 말을 빈칸에 알맞은 형태로 쓰시오.

1 I saw two _____ in the zoo. (fox)

2 We traveled to three _____ in Europe. (country)

3 The tree has many _____. (leaf)

4 Old _____ are in the album. (photo)

5 I brush my _____ after meals. (tooth)

C 우리말과 일치하도록 괄호 안의 말을 이용하여 문장을 완성하시오.

1 영국 숙녀들은 결혼식에 모자를 쓴다. (lady)

→ British _____ wear hats to weddings.

2 원숭이들은 바나나를 좋아한다. (monkey)

→ _____ like bananas.

3 요리사는 좋은 칼들이 필요하다. (knife)

→ A cook needs good _____.

4 그는 다섯 마리 소와 열 마리 양을 기른다. (ox, sheep)

→ He keeps five _____ and ten _____.

Unit 02 셀 수 없는 명사

A 셀 수 없는 명사의 종류

일정한 형태가 없거나 눈에 보이지 않는 것, 세상에 하나밖에 없는 고유한 것을 나타내는 명사는 개수를 셀 수 없다.

a water, milk, butter, bread, paper, air, salt, sugar, rice, furniture, money ...	**a** 형태가 일정하지 않거나 나누어 셀 수 없는 물질, 비슷한 종류의 것들 전체를 말하는 개념을 나타내는 명사
b health, news, advice, love, happiness ...	**b** 추상적인 개념, 감정을 나타내는 명사
c Sam, America, London, Mt. Everest ...	**c** 사람 이름, 지명 등 고유한 이름을 나타내는 명사

B 셀 수 없는 명사의 수

1 셀 수 없는 명사의 형태

a This soup needs **salt**.

b **Health** is very important.

c I'm from **Korea**.

1 항상 단수 형태로 쓰며, 앞에 a/an을 쓰지 않는다.

2 셀 수 없는 명사의 수량 표현

a I want **a glass of juice**.
They want **two glasses of milk**.

b Sugeun ate **a piece of cake**.
Hodong ate **three pieces of pizza**.

2 cup, glass, bottle, bowl처럼 담는 그릇이나 piece, slice, loaf처럼 모양을 나타내는 말을 이용하여 수량을 표현한다.

☑ 여러 개의 수량을 나타낼 때, 셀 수 없는 명사는 그대로 두고 단위를 나타내는 명사를 복수형으로 쓴다.

a cup of	~ 한 잔	(주로 따뜻한 음료) tea, coffee, hot chocolate	two cups of coffee (커피 두 잔)
a glass of	~ 한 잔	(주로 차가운 음료) water, milk, juice, soda	two glasses of water (물 두 잔)
a bottle of	~ 한 병	water, juice, milk, soda	two bottles of soda (소다 두 병)
a bowl of	~ 한 그릇	rice, soup, cereal	two bowls of rice (밥 두 그릇)
a piece of	~ 한 부분[조각] ~ 하나	bread, pizza, cake, cheese, meat paper, furniture, advice, information, news	two pieces of cake (케이크 두 조각) two pieces of furniture (가구 두 점)
a slice of	~ (얇은) 한 조각	bread, pizza, cake, cheese, ham, meat	two slices of pizza (피자 두 조각)
a loaf of	~ 한 덩어리	bread	two loaves of bread (빵 두 덩어리)
a sheet of	~ 한 장	paper	two sheets of paper (종이 두 장)

항상 복수형으로 쓰는 명사

pants, shorts, jeans, glasses, scissors와 같이 모양이 같은 두 부분으로 이루어진 사물은 항상 복수형으로 쓰며, a pair of, two pairs of ...로 수를 나타낸다.

I bought **a pair of jeans** and **two pairs of shorts**.
　　　　　　　　복수형　　　　　복수형

cf. I bought **two bottles of juice**.
　　　　　　　　복수형　　　단수형

vocabulary ----- **A** rice 몡 쌀; 밥　furniture 몡 가구　health 몡 건강　advice 몡 조언　happiness 몡 행복　**B** information 몡 정보

A 괄호 안에서 알맞은 말을 고르시오.

1 Cheese [is / are] good for children.

2 Elena gives great [advice / advices].

3 Do they want [two cup of / two cups of] tea?

4 My aunt lives in [New York / a New York].

5 Many people wear [a sunglass / sunglasses] in summer.

B 보기에서 알맞은 말을 골라 그림에 맞는 수량 표현을 쓰시오. (한 번씩만 쓸 것)

| 보기 | bottle | pair | sheet | bowl | loaf | piece |

1

_____ soup

2

_____ water

3

_____ socks

4

_____ cake

5

_____ bread

6

_____ paper

C 우리말과 일치하도록 괄호 안의 말을 이용하여 문장을 완성하시오.

1 나는 우유 두 잔을 마셨다. (milk)

→ I drank _____ _____ _____ _____.

2 엄마는 항상 음식에 너무 많은 소금을 넣는다. (salt)

→ Mom always puts too much _____ in the food.

3 물은 강으로 흐른다. (water, flow)

→ _____ _____ into the river.

Unit 03 관사

관사는 명사 앞에 쓰여 명사의 수와 성격을 나타내는 말로, 부정관사 a/an과 정관사 the가 있다.

A 부정관사 a/an을 쓰는 경우

'정해지지 않은, 특정하지 않은 어떤 하나'를 의미한다고 해서 a/an을 '부정관사'라고 한다. a나 an은 셀 수 있는 명사의 단수형 앞에 쓰며, 명사의 첫 발음이 자음으로 시작하면 a, 모음으로 시작하면 an을 쓴다.

a	Bogeom is **an** actor.	a	막연한 어떤 하나를 나타낼 때
b	**A** week has seven days.	b	'한 개(= one)'의 의미를 나타낼 때
c	We have music class twice **a** week.	c	'~마다(= per, every)'의 의미를 나타낼 때
d	**A** dog is a useful animal.	d	종류나 종족 전체를 대표할 때

a vs. an

명사의 첫 알파벳이 자음이든 모음이든 상관없이 첫 발음이 자음이면 a, 첫 발음이 모음이면 an을 쓴다. 형용사가 명사를 앞에서 꾸며 줄 때는 형용사의 첫 발음에 따라 a나 an을 쓴다.

a uniform, **a** university, **a** European (첫 알파벳은 모음이지만 첫 발음이 자음이므로 a)

an hour, **an** MP3 file, **an** X-ray, **an** honest man (첫 알파벳은 자음이지만 첫 발음이 모음이므로 an)

B 정관사 the를 쓰는 경우

'정해진 것, 특정한 것'을 의미한다고 해서 the를 '정관사'라고 한다. the는 셀 수 있는 명사의 단수형과 복수형, 셀 수 없는 명사 앞에 모두 쓸 수 있다.

a	Jiyong has a cat. **The** cat is gray.	a	앞에서 말한 명사를 다시 말할 때
b	Did you turn off **the** computer?	b	상황상 무엇을 가리키는지 알 수 있을 때
c	**The** room over there is a restroom.	c	명사 뒤에 꾸며 주는 말이 있어서 가리키는 것이 분명할 때
d	**The** earth is round like a ball.	d	세상에 하나뿐인 것을 말할 때: the sun, the moon, the earth, the sky 등

☑ earth처럼 명사의 첫 발음이 모음일 때는 the를 '디[ði]'로 읽는다.

C 관사를 쓰지 않는 경우

a	I had **breakfast**.	a	식사 이름 앞
b	Stephen Curry plays **basketball** every day.	b	운동 이름 앞
cf.	Seongjin plays **the piano** very well.	*cf.*	악기 이름 앞에는 the를 쓴다.
c	My family went to Gyeongju **by train**.	c	by + 교통·통신수단: ~로
d	I go to **bed** at 11.	d	장소가 본래의 목적으로 쓰일 때
cf.	Don't jump on **the bed**.		go to bed: 잠자리에 들다 go to school: (공부하러) 학교에 가다 go to church: (예배 보러) 교회에 가다
		cf.	다른 목적으로 쓰일 때는 관사를 쓴다.

Exercise

Answers p.5

A 괄호 안에서 알맞은 말을 고르시오.

1 I don't understand [a / an / the] question.

2 We ate [a / an / the] orange and two pears.

3 Mom goes swimming three times [a / an / the] week.

4 He read a book. [A / An / The] book was funny.

5 Spain is [a / an / the] European country.

B 빈칸에 a, an, the 중 알맞은 말을 쓰시오. (필요 없으면 ×로 표시할 것)

1 Justin is _____ honest boy.

2 She played _____ tennis yesterday.

3 He always goes to _____ bed at 10.

4 _____ year has 365 days.

5 I like _____ blue T-shirt over there.

C 우리말과 일치하도록 괄호 안의 말을 이용하여 문장을 완성하시오.

1 너는 교복을 입니? (uniform)

→ Do you wear _____ _____ ?

2 나는 학교 밴드에서 기타를 연주한다. (play, guitar)

→ I _____ _____ _____ in the school band.

3 코끼리는 코가 길다. (elephant, long nose)

→ _____ _____ has _____ _____ _____ .

4 달은 한 달에 한 번 보름달이 된다. (moon, month)

→ _____ _____ is full once _____ _____ .

Writing Practice **Answers p.5**

Answers p.5

A 　우리말과 일치하도록 괄호 안의 말을 바르게 배열하시오. (필요하면 형태를 바꾸거나 관사를 추가할 것)

01 TV 속 남자는 코미디언이다. (man, is, on, the, TV)

→ _____ a comedian.

02 개미는 다리가 여섯 개다. (ant, six, has, an, legs)

→ _____

03 나는 매일 아침 빵 한 조각을 먹는다. (a, bread, have, slice, of)

→ I _____ every morning.

04 그들은 버스를 타고 박물관에 갔다. (went, the, bus, by, museum, to)

→ They _____ .

05 우리 가족은 일 년에 두 번 치과를 방문한다. (dentist, the, visits, a, twice, year)

→ My family _____ .

06 나의 삼촌은 밭에서 감자들을 재배한다. (my, potato, uncle, grows)

→ _____ in his field.

07 여자 두 명이 내 옆에 앉았다. (woman, sat, two)

→ _____ next to me.

08 태양은 동쪽에서 뜬다. (rises, sun, in, east, the)

→ _____

09 그는 어제 주스 세 병을 샀다. (he, bottle, bought, three, juice, of)

→ _____ yesterday.

10 나는 자기 전에 이를 닦는다. (I, tooth, brush, my)

→ _____ before bed.

B 우리말과 일치하도록 괄호 안의 말을 이용하여 문장을 완성하시오. (필요하면 관사를 추가할 것)

01 a 나는 토끼 한 마리를 기른다. (rabbit)

→ I keep _____.

b 그는 물고기 네 마리를 기른다. (fish)

→ He _____ ˙ _____.

02 a 나는 우유 한 잔을 마셨다. (milk)

→ I drank _____.

b 그녀는 물 두 잔을 마셨다. (water)

→ She _____.

03 a 우리는 케이크 하나를 샀다. (cake)

→ We bought _____.

b 나는 케이크 세 조각을 샀다.

→ _____

04 a 그 아이는 피아노를 잘 친다. (piano)

→ The child plays _____ well.

b 그 아이들은 축구를 잘한다. (soccer)

→ _____

05 a 새 한 마리가 나무에 있다. 그 새는 노란색이다. (bird)

→ _____ is in the tree. _____ is yellow.

b 부엉이 한 마리가 나무에 있다. 그 부엉이는 갈색이다. (owl, brown)

→ _____

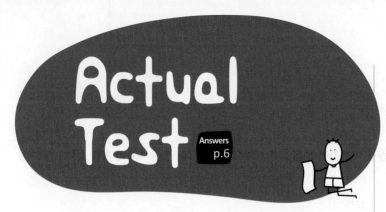

Actual Test

Answers p.6

01

빈칸에 들어갈 말로 알맞지 <u>않은</u> 것은?

Susan has two _____.

① sisters ② papers
③ babies ④ jobs
⑤ cats

[02~03] 빈칸에 들어갈 말로 알맞은 것을 고르시오.

02

Did you eat an _____?

① cake ② apple
③ banana ④ sandwich
⑤ hamburger

03

John's father caught many _____ in the river.

① fish ② fishs
③ fishves ④ fishies
⑤ fishees

04

명사의 복수형이 잘못 연결된 것은? (바르게 고칠 것)

① roof – roofs ② knife – knives
③ house – houses ④ country – countrys
⑤ tomato – tomatoes

05

빈칸에 들어갈 말이 순서대로 짝지어진 것은?

• I have six _____ a day.
• Giraffes eat _____ from tall trees.

① class – leaf ② class – leafs
③ class – leaves ④ classes – leafs
⑤ classes – leaves

[06~07] 우리말과 일치하도록 괄호 안의 말을 이용하여 문장을 완성하시오.

06 서술형

나는 상자 다섯 개가 필요하다. (need, box)

→ I _____ _____ _____.

07 서술형

그들은 우유 두 잔을 원한다. (glass, milk)

→ They want _____ _____ _____
_____.

08

밑줄 친 부분이 어법상 틀린 것은? (바르게 고칠 것)

① He has <u>a big feet</u>.
② You have <u>nine pens</u>.
③ Do you need <u>a hand</u>?
④ I play <u>the violin</u> very well.
⑤ She grows <u>many flowers</u> at home.

09 서술형

우리말과 일치하도록 괄호 안의 단어 중 필요한 단어만을 바르게 배열하여 문장을 완성하시오.

> 많은 어린이들이 단것들을 좋아한다.
> (like, things, many, child, childs, children, likes, sweet)

→ _____

10

대화의 밑줄 부분이 어법상 틀린 것은? (바르게 고칠 것)

> A: How is the ① soup?
> B: It has too much ② salts.
> A: Do you want a ③ drink?
> B: Yes, please. I want a ④ glass of ⑤ water.

11 서술형

그림의 내용과 일치하도록 괄호 안의 말을 이용하여 문장을 완성하시오.

→ _____ _____ _____ in the basket. (mouse, be)

12

밑줄 친 부분이 어법상 틀린 것은? (바르게 고칠 것)

> She ① bought a ② pair of ③ short and two ④ pairs of ⑤ jeans yesterday.

13

다음 중 셀 수 없는 명사로 바르게 짝지어진 것은?

> **a.** air   **b.** love   **c.** group
> **d.** bread   **e.** butter   **f.** London

① a, b, c
② a, b, c, e
③ a, c, d, f
④ b, c, d, e, f
⑤ a, b, d, e, f

14

우리말을 영어로 바르게 옮긴 것은?

> 거위들은 물 근처에서 산다.

① Geese lives near water.
② Gooses lives near water.
③ Geese live near water.
④ Gooses live near water.
⑤ Geeses live near water.

15

밑줄 친 부분이 어법상 옳은 것은? (틀린 것들을 바르게 고칠 것)

① It is good for healths.
② I took many photoes.
③ Boyes like soccer very much.
④ Look at the oxen over there.
⑤ Mt. Everest are 8,848 meters high.

16 서술형

우리말과 일치하도록 괄호 안의 말을 바르게 배열하시오.

> 그들은 주스 세 병을 마셨다.
> (three, of, they, drank, juice, bottles)

→ _____

17

우리말을 영어로 바르게 표현한 것은? (틀린 것들을 바르게 고칠 것)

① 밥 한 그릇 → a bowl of rices
② 피자 한 조각 → a sheet of pizza
③ 빵 두 덩어리 → two loafs of bread
④ 커피 세 잔 → three cups of coffees
⑤ 가구 네 점 → four pieces of furniture

18

다음 중 어법상 틀린 것은? (바르게 고칠 것)

① A day has twenty-four hours.
② The scissor is under the table.
③ I need two sheets of paper.
④ It is a piece of cake.
⑤ James is an actor.

19

우리말을 영어로 옮길 때 필요하지 않은 것은?

나는 매주 일요일에 교회로 예배 보러 간다.

① I
② go
③ to
④ the
⑤ church

20

빈칸에 부정관사 a가 들어갈 수 없는 것은?

① I saw _____ UFO last night.
② He went to _____ university.
③ She didn't bring _____ umbrella.
④ Do you work for _____ U.S. company?
⑤ A high school student wears _____ uniform.

21 서술형

다음 대화에서 어법상 틀린 부분을 찾아 바르게 고치시오.

A: Do you have breakfast?
B: No, I don't. How about you?
A: I eat two bowls of cereals every morning.

_____ → _____

22

빈칸에 정관사 The[the]가 필요한 것은?

① _____ earth is our home.
② I had _____ lunch with my friends.
③ We went to Incheon by _____ bus.
④ Do you play _____ baseball very well?
⑤ Claire went to _____ bed at 10 last night.

23 서술형

다음 글에서 어법상 틀린 부분을 모두 찾아 바르게 고치시오.

I went to Tom's birthday party yesterday. Many people were at a party. The food was delicious. I ate three pieces of cakes and two slices of pizza. Tom got many presents. Among them, he liked a pair of shoe very much. Everyone had fun.

24

밑줄 친 부분의 쓰임이 보기와 같은 것은?

> 보기　　He goes to the gym twice <u>a</u> week.

① I take a shower once <u>a</u> day.
② <u>A</u> computer is a useful tool.
③ <u>A</u> year has twelve months.
④ I need <u>a</u> glass of water.
⑤ She is <u>a</u> writer.

25

빈칸에 a/an[A/An]이 들어갈 수 없는 것은?

① Let's take _____ X-ray.
② That clock is _____ hour slow.
③ Do you have _____ boyfriend?
④ Mina is _____ smart student.
⑤ _____ deer eat grass and wild fruits.

26 서술형

그림을 보고, 괄호 안의 말을 바르게 배열하여 문장을 완성하시오.

→ _____

(go, the, school, students, by, to, school bus)

27

(A), (B), (C)의 각 네모 안에서 어법에 맞는 표현으로 순서대로 짝지어진 것은?

> A: Did you have a good weekend?
> B: Yes, I went to (A)[Jeju Island / the Jeju Island] with my family.
> A: Great. Was the weather good?
> B: Yes, it was very nice. (B)[A sun / The sun] shone all day. We rented a car and visited many famous places by (C)[car / the car].

① Jeju Island – A sun – car
② Jeju Island – The sun – car
③ Jeju Island – The sun – the car
④ the Jeju Island – A sun – car
⑤ the Jeju Island – The sun – the car

28 서술형

빈칸에 공통으로 들어갈 말을 쓰시오.

> • Did you turn on _____ fan?
> • _____ man over there is my uncle.
> • Jennifer has a dog. _____ dog is very big.

→ _____

29

다음 중 어법상 옳은 것은? (틀린 것들을 바르게 고칠 것)

① Don't jump on bed.
② I have a piece of advice for you.
③ He plays drums very well.
④ The books on the table is mine.
⑤ They went on an European tour.

Recall My Memory

Answers p.7

다음 문장이 어법상 맞으면 O표, **틀리면** 바르게 고치시오.

01 I want some waters. p. 46

02 Judy don't like math. p. 34

03 My mother were in the kitchen ten minutes ago. p. 18

04 The leafs are red and yellow. p. 44

05 Peter takes a walk in the morning. p. 30

06 We isn't 14 years old. p. 20

07 I drink three glass of milk a day. p. 46

08 Did you ate a hamburger for lunch? p. 34

09 This is a interesting film. p. 48

10 My nickname is Little Deer. p. 18

11 Three childs swim in the pool. p. 44

12 My dad and I go fishing last weekend. p. 32

13 They played the badminton after school. p. 48

14 Was your parents happy at that time? p. 20

15 She bought a pair of pants. p. 46

Chapter

4

명사의 대리인

대명사

Unit 01   인칭대명사, 재귀대명사

Unit 02   this, that, it

Unit 03   one, some, any

인칭대명사, 재귀대명사

Unit 01

대명사는 명사를 대신하는 말로, 사람이나 사물 이름 대신 쓰여 말과 글을 간단하고 깔끔하게 만들어 준다.

A 인칭대명사

1 인칭대명사의 형태

수	인칭	주격 (~은/는, ~이/가)	목적격 (~을/를)	소유격 (~의)	소유대명사 (~의 것)
단수	1인칭	I	me	my	mine
	2인칭	you	you	your	yours
	3인칭	he	him	his	his
		she	her	her	hers
		it	it	its	-
복수	1인칭	we	us	our	ours
	2인칭	you	you	your	yours
	3인칭	they	them	their	theirs

1 인칭대명사는 사람이나 사물을 대신하는 대명사로, 단수와 복수, 인칭과 격에 따라 형태가 다르다.

☑ its는 it의 소유격이고, it's는 it is의 줄임말임에 주의한다.

2 인칭대명사의 격

a Eric is a firefighter. **He** is brave.

b We saw the movie *The Avengers*. We liked **it**.
  I met Jun and Hani. I had fun with **them**.

c Suji bought a smartphone. **Its** color is pink.

d Your birthday is in March. **Mine** is in April.
  = My birthday

2 문장에서의 역할에 따라 격이 달라진다.

a 주격(~은/는, ~이/가): 문장에서 주어로 쓰인다.

b 목적격(~을/를): 동사나 전치사의 목적어로 쓰인다.

c 소유격(~의): 명사 앞에 쓰여 그 명사가 누구의 것인지를 나타낸다.

d 소유대명사(~의 것): 「소유격 + 명사」를 대신한다.

명사의 소유격과 소유대명사

명사의 소유격과 소유대명사는 명사 뒤에 's를 붙인다. 명사가 -s로 끝나는 복수형일 때는 뒤에 아포스트로피(')만 붙인다.
Henry's sister studies in Canada.   The **teachers'** room is on the first floor.

B 재귀대명사

1 재귀대명사의 형태

인칭	단수(-self)	복수(-selves)
1인칭	myself	ourselves
2인칭	yourself	yourselves
3인칭	himself / herself / itself	themselves

1 재귀대명사는 '~ 자신'이라는 의미로, 인칭대명사의 소유격이나 목적격에 -self / -selves를 붙인 형태이다. 자기 자신을 다시 가리키는 대명사라고 해서 '재귀대명사'라고 한다.

2 재귀대명사의 쓰임

a I introduced **myself** to the class.
  They are proud of **themselves**.

b My father (**himself**) fixed the car.
  Did you make it (**yourself**)?

2 목적어로 쓰이거나 강조할 때 쓰인다.

a 동사나 전치사의 목적어가 주어 자신일 때 목적어로 쓴다. '~ 자신'의 의미이며, 생략할 수 없다.

b 주어가 '직접' 했다는 것을 강조할 때 주어 바로 뒤나 문장 끝에 쓴다. 강조하기 위해 덧붙인 말이므로 생략할 수 있다.

Answers p.7

A 밑줄 친 부분을 알맞은 형태로 쓰시오.

1 Tina met <u>they</u> yesterday. _____

2 <u>We</u> garden is very beautiful. _____

3 The soccer ball is <u>he</u>. _____

4 I looked at <u>I</u> in the mirror. _____

5 He takes care of <u>she</u> dog on Sundays. _____

B 빈칸에 밑줄 친 부분을 대신하는 알맞은 대명사를 쓰시오.

1 This is <u>my uncle</u>. _____ is a pilot.

2 <u>Nancy</u> is kind and honest. I like _____.

3 <u>That car</u> doesn't need a driver. It drives _____.

4 He has <u>two cats</u>. _____ color is white.

5 <u>Your textbook</u> is right here. This is _____.

6 <u>The students</u> made the robot _____. They are very smart.

C 우리말과 일치하도록 괄호 안의 말을 이용하여 문장을 완성하시오.

1 많은 사람들이 그의 영화를 좋아한다. (movies)

　　→ Many people like _____ _____.

2 내 친구들은 매일 나에게 전화한다. (call)

　　→ My friends _____ _____ every day.

3 탁자 위의 지갑은 그녀의 것이다. (be)

　　→ The wallet on the table _____ _____.

4 그 남자는 심하게 다쳤다. (hurt)

　　→ The man _____ _____ badly.

Unit 02 this, that, it

this와 that은 가까이 또는 멀리 있는 사람이나 사물을 가리킬 때 쓰는 대명사로, '지시대명사'라고 한다. it은 인칭대명사로 쓰일 뿐만 아니라 시간, 날짜, 요일, 날씨, 계절 등을 나타낼 때 문장의 주어로도 쓰인다. 이때의 it은 '그것'을 가리키는 것이 아니므로 '비인칭 주어'라고 한다.

A this, that

1 this

a **This** is my bag.

b **This** is my friend, Yuna.

c **These** are nice jeans.

2 that

a **That** is the Seoul Tower.

b **That**'s my teacher, Ms. Kim.

c Are **those** your shoes?

1 '이것, 이 사람'이라는 의미로, 가까이 있는 사물이나 사람을 가리킨다. 복수형은 these(이것들, 이 사람들)이다.

2 '저것, 저 사람'이라는 의미로, 멀리 있는 사물이나 사람을 가리킨다. 복수형은 those(저것들, 저 사람들)이다.

☑ That is는 That's로 줄여 쓸 수 있다. This is는 This's로 줄여 쓸 수 없다.

형용사로 쓰이는 this와 that

this와 that은 단수 명사 앞에서 '이 ~', '저 ~'라는 의미의 형용사로 쓰여 명사를 꾸며 줄 수 있다. 명사가 복수일 때는 these와 those를 쓴다.

This skirt is mine. **That** shirt is yours. (this/that + 단수 명사)

These cars are cheap. **Those** cars are expensive. (these/those + 복수 명사)

B it

1 인칭대명사 it

a I love Jeju Island. **It** has beautiful beaches.

b Look at that dog. **It**'s so cute.

2 비인칭 주어 it

a **It** is nine o'clock.

b **It** is October 11th. **It** is Thursday.

c **It** is summer now. **It** is very hot.

d **It** is 300 meters to the bus stop.

e **It** is dark outside.

1 '그것'이라는 의미로, 앞에서 말한 사물이나 동물을 대신할 때 쓴다.

2 시간, 날짜, 요일, 계절, 날씨, 거리, 명암 등을 나타낼 때 문장의 주어로 쓴다. 특별한 의미가 없으므로 해석하지 않는다.

a 시간

b 날짜, 요일

c 계절, 날씨

d 거리

e 명암

vocabulary .... A cheap 형 값싼 expensive 형 비싼   B island 명 섬 outside 부 밖에

Exercise

Answers p.7

A 괄호 안에서 알맞은 말을 고르시오.

1 [That / Those] is not my pencil case.

2 I like [this / these] pink socks.

3 [This / It] is two kilometers to the station.

4 [This / That] pencil in my hand is red.

5 [These / Those] people over there are my friends.

B 빈칸에 알맞은 말을 보기에서 골라 쓰시오. (한 번씩만 쓸 것)

보기	this	that	it	these	those

1 _____ jeans here are cheap and nice.

2 _____ building across the street is City Hall.

3 _____ is January 20th today.

4 Do you see _____ lions over there?

5 We have a new classmate today. _____ is Minji.

C 우리말과 일치하도록 괄호 안의 말을 이용하여 문장을 완성하시오.

1 이 소녀가 1등을 했다. (girl)

   → _____ _____ won first prize.

2 이 꽃들은 Kelly를 위한 것이다. (flowers)

   → _____ _____ are for Kelly.

3 저분이 네 할아버지시니? (your grandfather)

   → _____ _____ _____ _____?

4 지금 10시 30분이다. (ten thirty)

   → _____ _____ _____ _____ now.

Unit 03 one, some, any

one, some, any는 정해지지 않은 불특정한 사람이나 사물, 수나 양을 가리키는 대명사이다. 특정하지 않은 막연한 대상을 가리키므로 '부정대명사'라고 한다.

A one

a My computer is too slow. I need a new **one**.

b These pants are small. Do you have big **ones**?

앞에서 말한 명사와 종류는 같지만 특정하지 않은 아무거나 하나를 가리킬 때 쓴다. 복수형은 ones이다.

one vs. it

one은 앞에서 말한 단수 명사와 같은 종류의 것으로 어느 것이든 하나를 가리키지만, it은 앞에서 말한 단수 명사 바로 그것을 가리킨다.

My camera is too old. I want a new **one**.
= camera

My camera is too old. I don't use **it**.
= my camera

B some, any

some과 any는 '조금, 몇 개[사람]'이라는 의미로, 정해지지 않은 막연한 수나 양을 가리킨다. 명사 앞에서는 형용사로 쓰여 '조금의, 몇 개[사람]의'라는 의미를 나타내며, 셀 수 있는 명사와 셀 수 없는 명사 둘 다에 쓸 수 있다.

1 some

a Dad bought a box of doughnuts.

I brought **some** for you.
= some doughnuts

b She put **some** sugar in her coffee.

cf. A: Do you want **some** milk?

B: Yes, please.

1 some은 주로 긍정문에 쓰인다.

cf. 긍정적인 대답을 예상하는 권유나 부탁을 나타내는 의문문에도 쓰인다.

2 any

a I took a lot of pictures.

Tom didn't take **any**.
= any pictures

b Do you have **any** plans for the weekend?

cf. We welcome **any** questions.

2 any는 주로 부정문과 의문문에 쓰인다.

cf. 긍정문에도 쓰이는데, '어느 것이든, 누구든' 또는 '어떤 ~라도'의 의미를 나타낸다.

vocabulary ┈┈┈┈┈ **B** a box of ~ 한 상자   a lot of 많은   welcome ⑧ 환영하다

Exercise

Answers p.7

A 괄호 안에서 알맞은 말을 고르시오.

1 She made [some / any] cookies.

2 He didn't buy [any / some] tomatoes.

3 I need a pen. Do you have [it / one]?

4 Do you know [some / any] good hotels in Seoul?

5 These jackets are stylish. I want one of these [one / ones].

B 빈칸에 알맞은 말을 보기에서 골라 쓰시오. (한 번씩만 쓸 것)

보기	one	ones	it	some	any

1 I got _____ nice presents for my birthday.

2 This bag is very old. I need a new _____ .

3 They didn't make _____ mistakes.

4 Do you like this T-shirt? I bought _____ yesterday.

5 I want some flowers. I like yellow _____ .

C 우리말과 일치하도록 괄호 안의 말을 이용하여 문장을 완성하시오.

1 너는 애완동물을 기르니? (pets)

→ Do you have _____ _____ ?

2 나는 안경을 부러뜨려서 새것을 샀다. (new)

→ I broke my glasses, so I bought _____ _____ .

3 그녀는 빵에 버터를 조금 발랐다. (butter)

→ She put _____ _____ on the bread.

4 그는 노트북이 없지만 일을 위해 한 대 필요하다. (need)

→ He doesn't have a laptop, but he _____ _____ for work.

Writing Practice

Answers p.7

A 우리말과 일치하도록 괄호 안의 말을 바르게 배열하시오. (필요하면 형태를 바꿀 것)

01 저 자전거가 그의 것이니? (is, bike, that, his)

→ _____

02 집안이 어둡다. (is, dark, it)

→ _____ in the house.

03 나는 매주 약간의 용돈을 저축한다. (pocket money, I, some, save)

→ _____ every week.

04 너는 너 자신에 대해 잘 아니? (yourself, do, you, know)

→ _____ well?

05 이것은 그녀의 신발이 아니다. (these, her, shoes, are, not)

→ _____

06 그는 하루 종일 아무 음식도 먹지 않았다. (food, eat, he, any, not, did)

→ _____ all day.

07 Mary는 초록색 키위를 좋아하고, 나는 노란색 키위를 좋아한다. (yellow, I, one, like)

→ Mary likes green kiwis, and _____.

08 그녀는 물에 비친 자기 자신을 보았다. (saw, she, her)

→ _____ in the water.

09 그들의 조부모님은 그들을 사랑하신다. (they, their, love, grandparents)

→ _____

10 이 티셔츠는 저 청바지와 잘 어울린다. (jeans, T-shirt, that, this, goes well with)

→ _____

B 우리말과 일치하도록 괄호 안의 말을 이용하여 문장을 완성하시오.

01 a 이것은 네 우산이다. (umbrella)

→ _____ is _____ .

b 저것은 내 우산이다.

→ _____

02 a 그녀는 토끼 한 마리를 기른다. 그것은 매우 귀엽다.

→ _____ has a rabbit. _____ is so cute.

b 그는 토끼 두 마리를 기른다. 그것들은 매우 귀엽다.

→ _____

03 a 우리는 주스를 좀 마셨다. (juice)

→ We drank _____ .

b 그들은 주스를 조금도 마시지 않았다.

→ _____

04 a 저 장갑은 나의 것이다. (gloves)

→ _____ are _____ .

b 이 장갑은 너의 것이다.

→ _____

05 a 나는 종종 혼잣말을 한다.

→ I often talk to _____ .

b 그는 종종 혼잣말을 한다.

→ _____

Actual Test

Answers p.7

01

짝지어진 두 단어의 관계가 나머지 넷과 다른 것은?

① I – me
② you – your
③ he – him
④ she – her
⑤ they – them

[02~04] 빈칸에 들어갈 말로 알맞은 것을 고르시오.

02

I have a beautiful dress. _____ color is green.

① It
② They
③ Its
④ Their
⑤ It's

03

You and Fred are good friends. _____ never fight each other.

① I
② You
③ We
④ He
⑤ They

04

Cathy has a cat. _____ is 6 months old.

① This
② That
③ It
④ These
⑤ Those

[05~06] 빈칸에 들어갈 말로 알맞지 <u>않은</u> 것을 고르시오.

05

Grandma called _____ in the garden.

① me
② you
③ her
④ our
⑤ them

06

The glasses on the desk are _____.

① his
② her
③ John's
④ mine
⑤ my brother's

07

대화의 빈칸에 들어갈 말로 알맞은 것은?

A: Are _____ your socks over there?
B: Yes, they are.

① this
② that
③ it
④ these
⑤ those

08

대화의 빈칸에 공통으로 들어갈 말로 알맞은 것을 <u>모두</u> 고르면?

A: Is this _____ pen?
B: Yes. It's _____.

① my
② your
③ his
④ her
⑤ Katie's

09

① Tom is not my brother. He is my cousin.
② This is my watch. It is not very expensive.
③ Henry and I were tired. They were sleepy, too.
④ The cookies smell good. They are very delicious, too.
⑤ Kevin and his dog are not at home. They are out in the park.

10

① This ring is mine.
② This book is Lisa's.
③ These shoes are you.
④ That backpack is his.
⑤ That doll is my sister's.

11 서술형

그림을 보고, 대화의 빈칸에 공통으로 들어갈 말을 쓰시오.

A: Did the boy look at _____ in the mirror?
B: Yes, he did. He talked to _____, too.

→ _____

12 서술형

다음 문장을 복수형 문장으로 다시 쓰시오.

This is a white wolf.

→ _____

13 서술형

대화의 빈칸에 들어갈 대명사를 각각 쓰시오.

A: Brian, is this your bike?
B: No, it's not (1) _____.
A: Is that yours?
B: Yes, it's (2) _____ bike.

14

대명사와 재귀대명사가 잘못 짝지어진 것은? (바르게 고칠 것)
① it – itself
② we – ourselves
③ she – herself
④ you – yourselves
⑤ they – theirselves

15 서술형

밑줄 친 부분이 어법상 틀린 것을 골라 바르게 고치시오.

You ①take care of ②your little ③brothers, but you ④don't take care of ⑤you.

→ _____

16

① Do you like this?
② This is my pet dog.
③ That are my pants.
④ Is that your car?
⑤ This is my friend, Joe.

17

① I saw them last night.
② I spoke to her myself.
③ I took her to the hospital.
④ I helped him with his homework.
⑤ I fell down the stairs and I hurt me.

18

빈칸에 알맞은 말이 순서대로 짝지어진 것은?

> • Do you have _____ brothers or sisters?
> • I don't want _____ cheese on my burger.
> • He bought _____ flowers for his girlfriend.

① any – any – some
② some – any – any
③ any – some – some
④ some – some – any
⑤ any – some – any

19

밑줄 친 부분의 쓰임이 보기와 같은 것은?

| 보기 | Some people don't like <u>themselves</u>. |

① They did it <u>themselves</u>.
② He will go there <u>himself</u>.
③ I fixed the computer <u>myself</u>.
④ Socrates said, "Know <u>yourself</u>."
⑤ She <u>herself</u> made this scarf.

20 서술형

다음 글에서 밑줄 친 부분이 어법상 <u>틀린</u> 것을 골라 바르게 고치시오.

> ① <u>My</u> dad is a vet and ② <u>my</u> mom is a teacher. ③ <u>I</u> have two little sisters. ④ <u>Her</u> names are Lily and Alice. Lily is tall and thin. Alice is short and fat. ⑤ <u>They</u> are very cute.

_____ → _____

21

다음 중 밑줄 친 부분을 생략할 수 있는 것은?

① Did you enjoy <u>yourself</u> at the party?
② I grew these flowers <u>myself</u>.
③ She cut <u>herself</u> by mistake.
④ He wrote a story about <u>himself</u>.
⑤ The girl loved <u>herself</u> so much.

22

① I like his story.

② His eyes are blue.

③ That's not his painting.

④ The phone on the table is his.

⑤ I found his book under the desk.

23

① Is this your aunt?

② This isn't my watch.

③ This box is too heavy.

④ This is the school gym.

⑤ This was my teacher, Ms. Lee.

24

① It is Friday today.

② It is spring now.

③ Is it inside the car?

④ What time is it now?

⑤ Is it dark in the room?

[25~26] 대화의 빈칸에 들어갈 말을 보기에서 골라 쓰시오.

25 서술형

보기	it	one	any	some

A: I need a red pen. Do you have (1) _____?

B: Yes, I do. I have (2) _____ red pens in my pencil case.

26 서술형

보기	it	one	ones	them

A: These shoes are too old. I don't like (1) _____.

B: You want new (2) _____. Let's go shopping.

27 서술형

다음 중 어법상 틀린 것을 모두 골라 바르게 고치시오.

a. Did you bring any money with you?

b. He didn't have some friends.

c. Any day is fine with me.

d. Do you want some hot tea?

e. I introduced me to the class.

f. Sam himself solved the problem.

g. I bought a new umbrella, but I lost one.

28 서술형

보기를 이용하여 대화를 완성하시오. (중복 가능, 필요하면 형태를 바꿀 것)

보기	this	that	it

A: (1) _____ is my house right here.

B: Wow, (2) _____ is very nice. Is (3) _____ your horse across the field?

A: Yes, (4) _____ name is Jet.

다음 문장이 어법상 맞으면 ○표, 틀리면 바르게 고치시오.

01 I want that black jeans. ➲ p. 60

02 We have a good time last week. ➲ p. 32

03 That rains a lot in summer. ➲ p. 60

04 Jones finishs work at 5:30. ➲ p. 30

05 Did you go there by the bus? ➲ p. 48

06 I don't need some help. ➲ p. 62

07 Your eyes are beautiful. ➲ p. 18

08 We enjoyed ourself on the stage. ➲ p. 58

09 He had bread and two glass of milk for breakfast. ➲ p. 46

10 I have a camera. Do you have one? ➲ p. 62

11 Were she in the kitchen? ➲ p. 20

12 My father don't cook well. ➲ p. 34

13 She exercises for a hour every day. ➲ p. 48

14 The book on the table is his. ➲ p. 58

15 They saw many sheeps in New Zealand. ➲ p. 44

point 1 — 주어의 인칭과 수에 따른 단수 동사 vs. 복수 동사

🔗 Chapter 1, 2, 3

The skin around her eyes make(→ **makes**) small and thin lines. › 고2 연합
그녀의 눈 주변의 피부에는 작고 가는 선들이 생긴다.

- 주어는 핵심 주어와 이것을 꾸며 주는 수식어(구)들로 이루어진다. 핵심 주어의 수를 파악한 후, 단수 동사가 맞는지 복수 동사가 맞는지를 결정한다.
- 핵심 주어가 명사일 때 보통 명사 끝에 -(e)s가 붙으면 셀 수 있는 명사의 복수형을 나타내지만, 불규칙하게 변하거나 단수와 복수의 형태가 같은 경우도 있으므로 주의해야 한다.

불규칙하게 변하는 명사	foot → **feet**	tooth → **teeth**	man → **men**	woman → **women**
	child → **children**	mouse → **mice**	goose → **geese**	ox → **oxen**
단·복수형이 같은 명사	fish → **fish**	deer → **deer**	sheep → **sheep**	

- 핵심 주어가 셀 수 있는 명사의 단수형 또는 셀 수 없는 명사일 때 동사의 현재형은 3인칭 단수여야 한다. 일반동사의 3인칭 단수형은 보통 동사원형에 -(e)s를 붙인다.

point 2 — 대명사의 수와 격

🔗 Chapter 4

What is beauty? Different cultures explain [**it** / them] differently. › 고1 연합
아름다움이란 무엇인가? 각각의 문화는 그것을 다르게 설명한다.

- 대명사는 앞에 나온 명사를 다시 말할 때 쓰므로, 앞에 나온 명사 중 어느 것을 가리키는지를 먼저 파악한다.
- 앞에 나온 명사가 단수인지 복수인지를 확인하고, 인칭대명사의 경우에는 해당 문장에서 주격, 목적격, 소유격 등 어느 격으로 쓰여야 하는지를 판단한다.

point 3 — 재귀대명사 vs. 인칭대명사

🔗 Chapter 4

Know you(→ **yourself**) and learn your weak points. › 고1 연합
당신 자신에 대해 알고 당신의 약점을 파악하라.

- 동사나 전치사의 목적어가 주어 자신일 때는 재귀대명사를 쓴다. 앞뒤 문맥상 대명사 목적어가 주어와 같은 것을 가리키는지 앞에 언급된 다른 것을 가리키는지 파악한다.
- 주어가 직접 했음을 강조할 때는 주어 바로 뒤나 문장 끝에 재귀대명사를 쓸 수 있다. 이때의 재귀대명사는 문장을 구성하는 데 꼭 필요한 요소가 아니므로 생략할 수 있으며, 재귀대명사를 생략했을 때 문장에는 필수 구성 요소들이 모두 있어야 한다.

	단수(-self)		복수(-selves)	
1인칭	I	myself	we	ourselves
2인칭	you	yourself	you	yourselves
3인칭	he / she / it	himself / herself / itself	they	themselves

---

thin 웹 얇은, 가는 explain 동 설명하다 weak point 약점

수능 기초 연습 ^{Answers p.8}

중학 영문법으로

A 괄호 안에서 알맞은 말을 고르시오.

1 I see [me / myself] in her eyes. › 고2 연합

2 The old buildings of the farm [surround / surrounds] us. › 고1 연합

3 Americans often tell guests, "Make [you / yourself] at home." › 고1 연합

4 Every wrong try is another step forward. The important events on the road to success [is / are] always the failures. › 고1 연합

5 These days, many products are much the same in [its / their] quality and price. › 고1 연합

B 밑줄 친 부분이 어법상 맞으면 O표, 틀리면 바르게 고치시오.

1 Buildings all over the city <u>was</u> on fire. › 고1 연합

2 I wrote a note about my worries, and put <u>them</u> on the seat. › 고1 연합

3 Do you compete against <u>yourself</u>? That competition is healthy. › 고2 연합

4 Canberra, with under half a million people, <u>are</u> the capital city of Australia. › 고2 연합

5 Louise Wilkinson works at a library. At night, she transforms <u>her</u> into a vampire. › 고2 연합

C 다음 글의 밑줄 친 부분 중, 어법상 <u>틀린</u> 것은? (바르게 고칠 것) › 고1 연합

A guy and a big dog ① <u>runs</u> into a field. The dog chases the guy. The guy sees a bathtub in the field. He runs to the bathtub and pulls it over ② <u>himself</u>. The dog just barks and barks. Finally, ③ <u>it</u> goes away. Then the guy comes out of the bathtub, and goes home.

A surround ⑧ 둘러싸다 guest ⑨ 손님 try ⑨ 시도 forward ⑨ 앞으로 success ⑨ 성공 failure ⑨ 실패 product ⑨ 상품 quality ⑨ 질　B compete against ~와 경쟁하다 competition ⑨ 경쟁 million ⑨ 100만 capital city 수도 transform A into B A를 B로 바꾸다　C chase ⑧ 뒤쫓다 bathtub ⑨ 욕조 pull A over B A를 B 위로 뒤집어쓰다 bark ⑧ 짖다 go away 가버리다 come out of ~에서 나오다

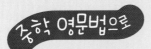

수능 독해 적용 Answers p.9

1 (A), (B), (C)의 각 네모 안에서 어법에 맞는 표현으로 가장 적절한 것은? › 고1 연합

Once upon a time, a king put a big rock on a road. Then he hid (A)itself / himself and watched it. Most people came by and just walked around (B)it / them. They said, "The roads aren't clear. The king doesn't do his work." Then a farmer came along and found the stone. He moved the stone to the side of the road. The king became very happy and gave a lot of (C)gold / golds to the farmer.

	(A)		(B)		(C)
①	itself	·····	it	·····	gold
②	itself	·····	them	·····	golds
③	himself	·····	it	·····	gold
④	himself	·····	them	·····	gold
⑤	himself	·····	it	·····	golds

2 다음 글의 밑줄 친 부분 중, 어법상 틀린 것은? (바르게 고칠 것) › 고1 연합

My grandmother is seventy years old. She has ① an interest in computers, so she learned about ② it at the public library. In class, she ③ was a good student. She listened to the teacher and asked many ④ questions. She learned a lot. I am very proud of ⑤ her.

3 (A), (B), (C)의 각 네모 안에서 어법에 맞는 표현으로 가장 적절한 것은? › 고2 연합

Right-handed people easily push buttons on the right through holes on the left. Most people are right-handed, so men's clothes (A)[have / has] buttons on the right. But what about women? At first, buttons were very expensive, and only rich people's clothes had them. Long ago rich women did not usually dress (B)[them / themselves]. Maids dressed them. So dressmakers put the buttons on the maid's right, and this put (C)[it / them] on the woman's left.

	(A)		(B)		(C)
①	have	······	them	······	it
②	has	······	them	······	it
③	have	······	themselves	······	it
④	has	······	themselves	······	them
⑤	have	······	themselves	······	them

---

1 once upon a time 옛날에 hide ⑧ 숨기다(-hid-hidden) come by 다가오다 walk around 돌아 지나가다 come along 나타나다

2 have (an) interest in ~에 관심을 갖다 public library 공립 도서관 a lot 많이 be proud of ~을 자랑스러워하다

3 right-handed ⑩ 오른손잡이인 through ⑳ ~을 통해 hole ⑳ 구멍 at first 처음에 dress ⑧ 옷을 입다[입히다] maid ⑳ 하녀 dressmaker ⑳ (여성복) 양재사

Chapter

5

과거부터 미래까지
시간을 품고 있는 타임머신,

시제

Unit 01 현재시제, 과거시제

Unit 02 미래시제

Unit 03 진행시제

Unit 01 현재시제, 과거시제

시제란 어떤 일이 언제 일어난 것인지를 동사의 형태를 바꿔서 나타내는 것을 말한다. 시제에는 기본적으로 현재시제, 과거시제, 미래시제가 있다.

A 현재시제

동사의 현재형을 쓰며, 현재의 상태나 성질, 반복되는 일이나 습관, 일반적인 사실이나 변하지 않는 진리 등을 나타낸다.

a Lisa **is** a teacher.
　　She **teaches** English.
b Suho **goes** jogging every morning.
　　_{얼마나 자주 일어나는지를 나타내는 부사구}
c The sun **rises** in the east.
d Time **is** money.

a 현재의 상태

b 반복되는 일

c 변하지 않는 진리

d 속담·격언

현재시제와 함께 쓰이는 부사(구)

현재시제가 반복되는 일이나 습관을 나타낼 때는 주로 every day, always, usually, often, sometimes, never 등 얼마나 자주 일어나는지를 나타내는 부사(구)와 함께 쓰인다.
My mom *often* **changes** her hair style.

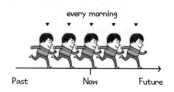

B 과거시제

동사의 과거형을 쓰며, 과거에 일어난 일이나 과거의 상태, 역사적 사실을 나타낸다.

a Daniel **ate** ramen last night.
　　　　　　　　_{과거의 시간을 나타내는 부사구}
　　He **was** full.
b Bell **didn't invent** the telephone.
　　Antonio Meucci **invented** it.

a 과거의 일이나 상태

b 역사적 사실

과거시제와 함께 쓰이는 부사(구)

과거시제는 주로 yesterday, last night, a year ago, in 2010 등 과거의 시간을 나타내는 부사(구)와 함께 쓰인다.
I **went** skating with my friends *yesterday*.

vocabulary ┈┈┈┈┈ **A** go jogging 조깅하러 가다　rise ⑧ 떠오르다(-rose-risen)　**B** full ⑱ 배가 부른　invent ⑧ 발명하다

A 주어진 동사를 빈칸에 알맞은 형태로 쓰시오.

1 be

    a Ms. Lee _____ a student in 2015.

    b She _____ a teacher now.

2 play

    a Harry _____ basketball every day.

    b He _____ basketball yesterday.

3 live

    a My grandparents _____ in Seoul last year.

    b They _____ in Busan now.

B 밑줄 친 부분이 어법상 맞으면 ○표, 틀리면 바르게 고치시오.

1 She always <u>walked</u> to school.   _____

2 <u>Does</u> Alex write this book two years ago?   _____

3 My mother <u>don't drink</u> coffee at night.   _____

4 He <u>washed</u> the dishes this morning.   _____

5 Brian <u>rode</u> a bike once a week.   _____

C 우리말과 일치하도록 괄호 안의 말을 이용하여 문장을 완성하시오.

1 레오나르도 다 빈치가 「모나리자」를 그렸다. (paint)

    → Leonardo da Vinci _____ *Mona Lisa*.

2 태양은 서쪽으로 진다. (set)

    → The sun _____ in the west.

3 우리는 지난 일요일에 낚시하러 가지 않았다. (go fishing)

    → We _____ _____ _____ last Sunday.

4 그녀는 매일 공원에서 운동하니? (exercise)

    → _____ _____ _____ in the park every day?

Unit 02 미래시제

미래시제는 앞으로 일어날 일을 나타낼 때 쓰며, will이나 be going to를 써서 표현한다.

A will

1 형태와 의미

a It **will** rain tomorrow.
<u>미래의 시간을 나타내는 부사</u>

b I **will**(= I**'ll**) go camping this weekend.

2 부정문

He **will not**(= **won't**) go camping this weekend.

3 의문문

A: **Will** you go camping this weekend?

B: Yes, I **will**. / No, I **won't**.

1 주어의 인칭과 수에 상관없이 「will + 동사원형」으로 미래의 일을 나타낸다. 주어가 인칭대명사일 때 will을 'll로 줄여 쓸 수 있다.

a 미래에 대한 예측: ~일[할] 것이다

b 주어의 의지: ~하겠다

2 will 뒤에 not을 쓰며, won't로 줄여 쓸 수 있다.

3 주어와 will의 자리를 바꾼다.

미래시제와 함께 쓰이는 부사(구)

미래시제는 주로 tomorrow, tonight, this weekend, next year, soon 등 미래의 시간을 나타내는 부사(구)와 함께 쓰인다.

You **will** hear good news *soon*.

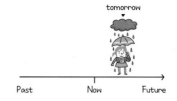

B be going to

1 형태와 의미

a I **am going to** be 15 years old next year.

= I **will** be 15 years old next year.

b We **are going to** see a movie tonight.

2 부정문

She **is not going to** see a movie tonight.

3 의문문

A: **Are** you **going to** see a movie tonight?

B: Yes, I **am**. / No, I**'m not**.

1 「be going to + 동사원형」으로 미래의 일을 나타낸다. be동사는 주어의 인칭과 수에 따라 am/are/is로 바꿔 쓴다.

a 미래에 대한 예측: ~일[할] 것이다 (= will)

b 이미 정해 놓은 미래의 계획: ~할 예정이다

2 be동사 뒤에 not을 쓴다.

3 주어와 be동사의 자리를 바꾼다.

---

vocabulary ---------- A go camping 캠핑하러 가다 soon (뷰) 곧

A 괄호 안에서 알맞은 말을 고르시오.

1 It will [be / is] sunny tomorrow.

2 He [be going to / is going to] meet Minji at 5 p.m.

3 Will Suho [stay / stays] at home tonight?

4 I [am not going to / am going not to] make that mistake again.

5 Are they going [join / to join] the photo club?

B 지호의 다음 주 계획표를 보고, 괄호 안의 말을 이용하여 문장을 완성하시오.

Mon	Tue	Wed	Thur	Fri	Sat & Sun
clean my room	ride my bike	play tennis	school holiday	go to a concert	travel to Gyeongju

1 Jiho _____ next Monday. (will)

2 He _____ next Wednesday. (be going to)

3 He _____ to school next Thursday. (will, go)

4 A: _____ to a concert next weekend? (he, be going to)

   B: No, _____. He _____ to Gyeongju. (will)

C 우리말과 일치하도록 괄호 안의 말을 이용하여 문장을 완성하시오.

1 그는 그녀에게 편지를 쓸 것이다. (write)

   → He _____ _____ a letter to her.

2 나는 오늘 밤에 TV를 보지 않을 것이다. (watch)

   → I _____ _____ TV tonight.

3 Lisa가 너를 도와줄 것이다. (help)

   → Lisa _____ _____ _____ _____ you.

4 너는 내일 그를 방문할 거니? (visit)

   → _____ _____ _____ _____ _____ him tomorrow?

Unit 03 진행시제

진행시제는 어떤 순간에 일어나고 있는 일을 나타내며, be동사 뒤에 동사의 -ing형을 쓴다.

A 현재진행시제

1 형태와 의미

a I **am reading** a book now.

b She **is reading** a book now.

2 부정문

He **is not reading** a book now.

3 의문문

A: **Are** you **reading** a book now?

B: Yes, I **am**. / No, I**'m not**.

1 「am/are/is + 동사원형-ing」로 바로 지금 진행되고 있는 일을 나타내며 '~하고 있다, ~하는 중이다'의 의미이다.

2 be동사 뒤에 not을 쓴다.

3 주어와 be동사의 자리를 바꾼다.

동사의 -ing형 만드는 법

대부분의 동사	동사원형 + -ing	do → do**ing** play → play**ing**	eat → eat**ing** read → read**ing**	go → go**ing** study → study**ing**
「자음 + **e**」로 끝나는 동사	e를 빼고 + -ing	come → com**ing** write → writ**ing**	make → mak**ing** cf. 「모음 + e」로 끝나는 동사: see → see**ing**	ride → rid**ing**
-ie로 끝나는 동사	ie를 y로 바꾸고 + -ing	die → d**ying**	lie → l**ying**	tie → t**ying**
「단모음 + 단자음」으로 끝나는 동사	마지막 자음을 한 번 더 쓰고 + -ing	cut → cut**ting** run → run**ning**	put → put**ting** cf. 강세가 앞에 오는 2음절 동사: visit → visit**ing**	swim → swim**ming**

B 과거진행시제

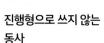

1 형태와 의미

a I **was making** dinner then.

b They **were making** dinner then.

2 부정문

She **was not making** dinner then.

3 의문문

A: **Were** you **making** dinner then?

B: Yes, I **was**. / No, I **wasn't**.

1 「was/were + 동사원형-ing」로 과거의 어떤 순간에 진행되고 있었던 일을 나타내며 '~하고 있었다, ~하는 중이었다'의 의미이다.

2 be동사 뒤에 not을 쓴다.

3 주어와 be동사의 자리를 바꾼다.

진행형으로 쓰지 않는 동사

have(가지다), like, want, know 등 동작이 아닌 소유나 감정, 상태를 나타내는 동사는 진행형으로 쓰지 않는다.

I **have**[~~am having~~] a cat.

cf. I **am having** lunch. (동작의 의미일 때는 진행형으로 쓸 수 있다.)

A 현재시제 문장은 현재진행시제로, 과거시제 문장은 과거진행시제로 바꿔 쓰시오.

1 I make blueberry pancakes every weekend.

→ I _____ _____ blueberry pancakes now.

2 He read the newspaper this morning.

→ He _____ _____ the newspaper this morning.

3 Linda doesn't drive in the snow.

→ Linda _____ _____ in the snow now.

4 Do you fish on the boat?

→ _____ _____ _____ on the boat?

B 밑줄 친 부분을 어법상 바르게 고치시오.

1 The horses are runing fast now.   _____

2 I am liking my friend, Max.   _____

3 Was he fix the computer now?   _____

4 John and Kate isn't cooking then.   _____

C 우리말과 일치하도록 괄호 안의 말을 이용하여 문장을 완성하시오.

1 아이들이 간식을 먹고 있다. (have)

→ The children _____ _____ a snack.

2 나는 소파에 누워 있었다. (lie)

→ I _____ _____ on the sofa.

3 너희들은 수영장에서 수영하고 있었니? (swim)

→ _____ _____ _____ in the pool?

4 비가 오지 않고 해가 빛나고 있다. (rain, shine)

→ It _____ _____ and the sun _____ _____.

Writing Practice Answers p.9

A
우리말과 일치하도록 괄호 안의 말을 바르게 배열하시오. (필요하면 형태를 바꿀 것)

01 그들은 공원에서 산책하고 있다. (taking, they, a walk, are)

→ _____ in the park.

02 그녀는 주말에 늦게 잠자리에 든다. (she, bed, goes, to)

→ _____ late on weekends.

03 나는 과학 경시대회에 최선을 다할 것이다. (will, I, my best, do)

→ _____ at the science contest?

04 그는 모자를 쓰고 있지 않았다. (a hat, he, not, wearing, was)

→ _____

05 나는 이번 주 일요일에 등산하지 않을 것이다. (will, a mountain, not, I, climb)

→ _____ this Sunday.

06 그녀는 새 운동화를 살 거니? (going, be, she, buy, to)

→ _____ new sneakers?

07 소년들이 길거리에서 춤을 추고 있었다. (the boys, dance)

→ _____ in the street.

08 그 가수는 어제 한국에 왔다. (Korea, come, the singer, to)

→ _____ yesterday.

09 그녀는 벤치에 앉아 있니? (sit, she, the bench, on)

→ _____

10 우리는 내일 그의 생일 파티를 할 예정이다. (going, his birthday party, be, we, to, have)

→ _____ tomorrow.

B 우리말과 일치하도록 괄호 안의 말을 이용하여 문장을 완성하시오.

01 a 나는 어제 스케이트보드를 탔다. (ride)

→ I _____ my skateboard yesterday.

b 그는 내일 스케이트보드를 탈 것이다. (will)

→ _____ tomorrow.

02 a 그는 선생님에게 거짓말을 하고 있다. (lie)

→ He _____ to the teacher.

b 그녀는 선생님에게 거짓말을 하고 있지 않다.

→ _____

03 a 너는 그때 스파게티를 만들고 있었다. (make)

→ You _____ spaghetti at that time.

b 나는 지금 스파게티를 만들고 있다.

→ _____ now.

04 a 우리는 도서관에 갈 예정이다. (be going to, go)

→ We _____ to the library.

b 그들은 도서관에 갈 예정이니?

→ _____

05 a 런던은 오늘 날씨가 맑지 않다. (sunny)

→ It _____ in London today.

b 런던은 다음 주에 날씨가 맑지 않을 것이다. (will)

→ _____ next week.

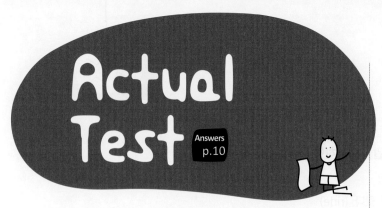

Actual Test
Answers p.10

01

빈칸에 들어갈 말로 알맞은 것은?

> The sun doesn't rise in the west. It _____ in the east.

① rise   ② rose   ③ rises
④ is rising   ⑤ will rise

[02~03] 빈칸에 들어갈 말로 알맞지 <u>않은</u> 것을 고르시오.

02

> They will arrive here _____.

① soon   ② tonight
③ next week   ④ a year ago
⑤ two days later

03

> Ted _____ become a middle school student next year.

① will   ② will not
③ is going to   ④ was going to
⑤ is not going to

04 [서술형]

대화의 빈칸에 공통으로 들어갈 말을 쓰시오.

> A: _____ your dad a teacher?
> B: Yes, he _____. He teaches science.

→ _____

[05~06] 밑줄 친 부분이 어법상 <u>틀린</u> 것을 고르시오. (바르게 고칠 것)

05

① He <u>plays</u> soccer yesterday.
② She <u>lives</u> in New York now.
③ We all <u>have</u> 24 hours a day.
④ I usually <u>watch</u> TV on weekends.
⑤ The Wright brothers <u>invented</u> the airplane.

06

① I <u>won't say</u> anything.
② Kelly <u>is going to do</u> the dishes.
③ <u>Will you eat</u> out tonight?
④ He <u>is going not to return</u> the book.
⑤ <u>Are the children going to help</u> their mother?

07

빈칸에 들어갈 말이 순서대로 짝지어진 것은?

> • It _____ snow tomorrow.
> • The train _____ every morning at 8 a.m.

① is – leave   ② is – leaves
③ was – left   ④ will – left
⑤ will – leaves

08 [서술형]

우리말과 일치하도록 괄호 안의 단어 중 필요한 단어만을 바르게 배열하여 문장을 완성하시오.

> 너는 음악을 듣는 중이니?
> (you, do, are, listen, listens, listening, to, music, were)?

→ _____

09

다음 중 어법상 <u>틀린</u> 것은? (바르게 고칠 것)

① She is having a house.
② It will be sunny this Friday.
③ I was updating my blog then.
④ Columbus discovered America in 1492.
⑤ We are going to move next week.

10

다음 중 짝지어진 대화가 <u>어색한</u> 것은?

① A: Did you finish the report?
　 B: Yes, I did.
② A: Will she come to the party?
　 B: No, she won't.
③ A: Do you like baseball?
　 B: Yes, I do. It's my favorite sport.
④ A: Are you going to the bookstore now?
　 B: No, I'm going to go shopping.
⑤ A: Were you watching TV then?
　 B: Yes, we were.

11 　서술형

그림을 보고, 괄호 안의 말을 이용하여 문장을 완성하시오.

→ A man and a woman _____ _____
　 now. (run)

12

우리말을 영어로 바르게 옮긴 것은?

> 그녀는 그때 숙제하고 있었다.

① She did her homework then.
② She is doing her homework then.
③ She does her homework at that time.
④ She is doing her homework at that time.
⑤ She was doing her homework at that time.

13

대화의 빈칸에 공통으로 들어갈 말로 알맞은 것은?

> A: _____ you have good time in Paris last week?
> B: Yes, I _____. I will visit there again.

① Are[are]　　　　② Were[were]
③ Will[will]　　　　④ Do[do]
⑤ Did[did]

14

다음 중 어법상 옳은 것으로 바르게 짝지어진 것은? (틀린 것들을 바르게 고칠 것)

> a. Korea has four seasons.
> b. Did you ate pizza yesterday?
> c. She is a high school student.
> d. Will you go hiking this weekend?
> e. The earth moved around the sun.
> f. I will go to Jeju Island every summer.

① a, b, c　　　　② a, b, e
③ a, c, d　　　　④ b, d, e, f
⑤ c, d, e, f

15 서술형

우리말과 일치하도록 괄호 안의 말을 이용하여 문장을 완성하시오.

> 그녀는 지금 잠을 자고 있지 않다. (sleep)

→ She _____ _____ _____ now.

16

밑줄 친 부분이 어법상 틀린 것은? (바르게 고칠 것)

> Mina ① and I ② meet for ③ the first time ④ about five ⑤ years ago.

17

밑줄 친 부분이 어법상 옳은 것은? (틀린 것들을 바르게 고칠 것)

① She is dancing an hour ago.
② We stayed at home last night.
③ I am wanting a glass of water.
④ I will eat lunch at noon every day.
⑤ He was walking on the street now.

18 서술형

밑줄 친 단어들을 알맞은 형태로 바꿔 문장을 다시 쓰시오.

> Mike go hiking yesterday. He see some beautiful flowers.

→ _____
_____

19

괄호 안의 지시대로 바꿔 쓸 때 잘못된 것은? (바르게 바꿔 쓸 것)

① They are tall. (부정문으로)
   → They are not tall.
② I will tell you later. (부정문으로)
   → I will not tell you later.
③ She was watching a movie. (의문문으로)
   → Did she watching a movie?
④ He draws a picture. (현재진행형으로)
   → He is drawing a picture.
⑤ You are going to join us. (의문문으로)
   → Are you going to join us?

20

대화의 빈칸에 들어갈 말이 순서대로 짝지어진 것은?

> A: Hi, Jisu. _____ you have any plans for this afternoon?
> B: Yes, I'm going to walk my dog in the park. How about you?
> A: My cousin _____ from Canada last night. So we're going to look around the city.

① Do – arrived   ② Do – will arrive
③ Will – arrived   ④ Will – will arrive
⑤ Did – arrived

21

빈칸에 들어갈 말이 나머지 넷과 다른 것은?

① _____ the baby smiling now?
② I _____ talking to Amy at 10 p.m.
③ _____ Claire making cookies then?
④ He _____ studying at that time.
⑤ She _____ cleaning her house an hour ago.

07:20~07:40

07:40~07:50

22 서술형

He _____ _____ a shower at 7:30 a.m. (take)

23 서술형

He _____ _____ _____ his clothes at 7:45 a.m. (put on)

24

빈칸에 들어갈 말이 순서대로 짝지어진 것은?

• The baby is _____ now.
• It _____ be cloudy tomorrow.
• She _____ riding her bicycle then.
• I _____ a ticket three days ago.

① cried – is – was – bought
② cried – will – was – buy
③ crying – is – is – buy
④ crying – will – is – buy
⑤ crying – will – was – bought

25 서술형

다음 글에서 어법상 틀린 부분을 모두 찾아 바르게 고치시오.

I like table tennis and basketball. Every Saturday, I play table tennis with Sam. He does not like table tennis before, but now he enjoys it. Every Sunday, I will go to the gym and play basketball with James. He is really good at basketball. Tomorrow is Saturday. So Sam and I are going to playing table tennis together.

26

대화의 밑줄 친 부분이 어법상 틀린 것은? (바르게 고칠 것)

A: Congratulations! You ① got first prize in the English speech contest.
B: Thanks. I ② win it because of you. You ③ helped me a lot.
A: ④ You're welcome. You ⑤ did your best.

27

각 문장을 완성할 때 빈칸에 필요하지 않은 것은?

• I _____ busy last week.
• The game is going to start _____.
• We _____ P.E. class every Monday.
• _____ you brushing your teeth now?

① are[Are]   ② was[Was]
③ soon[Soon]   ④ have[Have]
⑤ were[Were]

Recall My Memory

다음 문장이 어법상 맞으면 O표, <u>틀리면</u> 바르게 고치시오.

01 This is Wednesday today. ⟳ p. 60

02 Deers live in the woods. ⟳ p. 44

03 He goes bowling once a week. ⟳ p. 76

04 Do you want some orange juice? ⟳ p. 62

05 Does they like Chinese food? ⟳ p. 34

06 I will be not late for school again. ⟳ p. 78

07 She was in her office yesterday. ⟳ p. 76

08 My grandfather was watering the flowers now. ⟳ p. 80

09 A sugar is on the table. ⟳ p. 46

10 I studied English every day. ⟳ p. 76

11 He watches a drama last night. ⟳ p. 76

12 I got birthday presents. I like it. ⟳ p. 58

13 Are you washing the dishes then? ⟳ p. 80

14 This is not her shoes. ⟳ p. 60

15 We're going to make sandwiches. ⟳ p. 78

Chapter

6

함께하면 특별한 의미가 돼,
동사의 도우미

조동사

Unit
01   can, may

Unit
02   must, have to, should

can, may

조동사는 동사 앞에 쓰여 능력, 추측, 의무 등의 의미를 더해 주는 말이다. 조동사는 주어의 인칭과 수에 따라 형태가 바뀌지 않으며, 뒤에 동사원형을 쓴다.

A can

1 능력

a I **can** swim. = I **am able to** swim.

b He **can't**(= **cannot**) swim.
  = He **isn't able to** swim.

c A: **Can** you swim?
  B: Yes, I **can**. / No, I **can't**.
  = A: **Are** you **able to** swim?
    B: Yes, I **am**. / No, I**'m not**.

d I **couldn't**(= **could not**) swim last year.
  = I **wasn't able to** swim last year.

2 허가

a You **can** sit here.

b She **can't** sit here.

c A: **Can**[**Could**] I sit here?
  B: Sure. / Sorry, you can't.

3 요청

  A: **Can**[**Could**] you open the door?
  B: Of course. / Sorry, I can't.
cf. **Will**[**Would**] you open the door?

---

1 '~할 수 있다'라는 의미로, be able to로 바꿔 쓸 수 있다. 이때 be동사는 주어의 인칭과 수, 시제에 맞게 바꿔 쓴다.

b can't(= cannot)는 '~할 수 없다'라는 의미이다.

c 조동사 의문문은 주어와 조동사의 자리를 바꾼다.

d could는 can의 과거형으로, '~할 수 있었다'라는 의미이고, couldn't(= could not)는 '~할 수 없었다'라는 의미이다.

2 '~해도 된다'라는 의미이다.

b can't(= cannot)는 '~하면 안 된다'라는 의미로, 금지를 나타낸다.

c Can I ~?보다 Could I ~?가 더 공손한 표현이다.

3 Can[Could] you ~?를 써서 '~해 주겠니?'라는 의미를 나타낸다. Could가 더 공손한 표현이다.

cf. Will[Would] you ~?로 바꿔 쓸 수 있으며, Would가 더 공손한 표현이다.

B may

1 추측

a It **may** rain tonight.

b It **may not** rain tonight.

2 허가

a You **may** use my phone.
  = You **can** use my phone.

b He **may not** use my phone.

c A: **May** I use your phone?
  B: Yes, you **may**. / No, you **may not**.

---

1 '~일지도 모른다'라는 의미로, 확신이 없는 추측을 나타낸다.

b may not은 '~이 아닐지도 모른다'라는 의미이다.

2 '~해도 된다'라는 의미로, can으로 바꿔 쓸 수 있다.

b may not은 '~하면 안 된다'라는 의미로, 금지를 나타낸다.

Exercise

Answers p.11

A 밑줄 친 부분의 의미로 알맞은 것을 보기에서 골라 기호를 쓰시오.

보기	**a** ~할 수 있다	**b** ~해도 된다	**c** ~일지도 모른다	**d** ~해 주겠니?

1 You <u>can</u> call me anytime. _____

2 She <u>can</u> ride a bike very well. _____

3 <u>May</u> I speak to Daniel? _____

4 Our answer <u>may</u> be wrong. _____

5 <u>Can</u> you help me? _____

B 빈칸에 알맞은 말을 보기에서 골라 쓰시오. (한 번씩만 쓸 것)

보기	can	can't	may	may not

1 I'm cold. _____ you close the window?

2 Suho is absent today. He _____ be sick.

3 I don't know his phone number. I _____ call him now.

4 You _____ talk loudly here. Students are studying.

C 우리말과 일치하도록 괄호 안의 말을 이용하여 문장을 완성하시오.

1 나는 오늘 너를 만날 수 없다. (see)

→ _____ _____ _____ you today.

2 이 코트를 입어 봐도 되나요? (try on)

→ _____ _____ _____ _____ this coat?

3 우리 모두가 그 시험에 통과할 수 있었다. (pass)

→ We all _____ _____ the test.

4 그 가수는 5개 국어를 할 수 있다. (speak)

→ The singer _____ _____ _____ five languages.

Unit 02 must, have to, should

A must

1 의무

a I **must** leave now.

b You **must not** leave now.

2 추측

a The baby is crying. He **must** be hungry.

b The baby is smiling. He **can't**[~~must not~~] be hungry.

1 '~해야 한다'라는 의미로, 매우 중요하거나 반드시 해야 하는 일을 나타낸다.

b must not은 '~하면 안 된다'라는 의미로, 금지를 나타낸다.

2 '~임이 틀림없다'라는 의미로, 확신이 강한 추측을 나타낸다.

b '~일 리 없다'라는 의미의 강한 부정의 추측을 나타낼 때는 must not이 아니라 can't (= cannot)를 쓴다.

B have to

a I **have to** go to school. = I **must** go to school.

b She **has to** go to school.

c We **had to** go to school last Saturday.

d I **don't have to** go to school today.
   ≠ I **must not** go to school today.

e They **didn't have to** go to school yesterday.

f A: **Do** I **have to** go to school today?
   B: Yes, you **do**[have to]. / No, you **don't have to**.

a '~해야 한다'라는 의미로, must로 바꿔 쓸 수 있다.

b 주어의 인칭과 수에 따라 have/has to로 쓴다.

c 과거형은 had to로, '~해야 했다'라는 의미이다. must는 과거형이 없으므로 과거의 의무를 나타낼 때는 **had to**를 쓴다.

d don't/doesn't have to는 '~할 필요가 없다'라는 의미로, must not(~하면 안된다)과 의미가 다르다.

e didn't have to는 '~할 필요가 없었다'라는 의미이다.

f 의문문은 「Do/Does/Did + 주어 + have to ~?」로 쓴다.

주의해야 할 조동사의 쓰임

조동사는 두 개를 연달아 쓸 수 없다. 둘 중 하나를 조동사를 대신하는 말로 바꿔 써야 한다.
You **will have to**[~~will must~~] take a taxi.   He **will be able to**[~~will can~~] get a job.

C should

a You **should** be honest.

b You **shouldn't**(= **should not**) lie to me.

a '~해야 한다, ~하는 것이 좋겠다'라는 의미로, 어떤 일을 하는 것이 옳은 일임을 나타내거나 충고할 때 쓴다.

b shouldn't(= should not)는 '~하지 말아야 한다, ~하지 않는 것이 좋겠다'라는 의미이다.

Exercise

A 괄호 안에서 알맞은 말을 고르시오.

1 Yuna helps old people. She [must / should] be kind.

2 Hurry up! We [can't / must not] miss the plane.

3 You [have to / don't have to] make dinner. Let's eat out.

4 I have a bad cold. I [should / shouldn't] see a doctor.

5 You [must not / don't have to] cheat on the exam.

B 밑줄 친 부분이 어법상 맞으면 O표, 틀리면 바르게 고치시오.

1 She <u>have to</u> take a rest at home. _____

2 He <u>must</u> work last weekend. _____

3 You <u>will must</u> take a level test first. _____

4 Students <u>should</u> listen to their teachers. _____

5 Morris <u>don't have to</u> stay here. _____

C 보기와 괄호 안의 말을 이용하여 대화를 완성하시오. (필요하면 형태를 바꿀 것)

보기	must	have to	don't have to	shouldn't

1 A: Did Tyler solve the difficult problems?

   B: Yes, he did. He _____ smart. (be)

2 A: Can Suji go shopping this afternoon?

   B: No, she can't. She _____ her sister. (take care of)

3 A: I like chocolate very much.

   B: But you _____ too much chocolate. (eat)

4 A: Thank you for dinner. I'll do the dishes.

   B: Oh, no. You _____ that. I have a dishwasher. (do)

Writing Practice

Answers p.11

A 우리말과 일치하도록 괄호 안의 말을 바르게 배열하시오. (필요하면 형태를 바꿀 것)

01 너는 노래를 잘할 수 있니? (you, sing, can)

→ _____ well?

02 우리는 도서관에서 조용히 해야 한다. (be, should, we, quiet)

→ _____ in the library.

03 그 이야기는 사실임이 틀림없다. (the story, be, true, must)

→ _____

04 학생들은 규칙을 지켜야 한다. (have, students, keep, the rules, to)

→ _____

05 오늘 밤에 눈이 올지도 모른다. (it, snow, may, tonight)

→ _____

06 개들은 빨간색을 볼 수 없다. (cannot, dogs, red, see)

→ _____

07 사람들은 학교 근처에서 빨리 운전해서는 안 된다. (drive, not, people, fast, should)

→ _____ near schools.

08 그녀는 8시까지 집에 와야 한다. (come, have, she, to, home)

→ _____ by 8.

09 Sam은 한국어를 잘 말할 수 있다. (be, Sam, speak, able, Korean, to)

→ _____ well.

10 Amy는 내일 학교에 갈 필요가 없다. (go, don't, to, Amy, have, school, to)

→ _____ tomorrow.

B 우리말과 일치하도록 괄호 안의 말을 이용하여 문장을 완성하시오.

01 **a** 그는 오늘 숙제를 끝내야 한다. (have to, finish)

→ He _____ his homework today.

b 그녀는 오늘 숙제를 끝낼 필요가 없다.

→ _____

02 **a** 그는 수업에 늦을지도 모른다. (be)

→ He _____ late for class.

b 그는 수업에 늦는 것이 틀림없다.

→ _____

03 **a** 우리는 길거리에 쓰레기를 버리면 안 된다. (should, throw)

→ We _____ trash on the street.

b 우리는 쓰레기통에 쓰레기를 버려야 한다. (in the trash can)

→ _____

04 **a** 그녀는 지금 너를 도와줄 수 없다. (can, help)

→ She _____ you now.

b 그녀는 나중에 너를 도와줄 수 있을 것이다. (will, later)

→ _____

05 **a** Jenny는 일찍 일어나야 한다. (must, get up)

→ Jenny _____ early.

b Jack은 어제 일찍 일어나야 했다.

→ _____ yesterday.

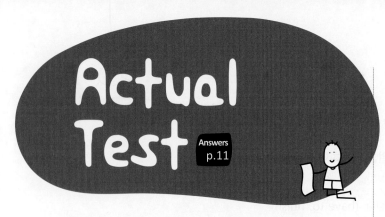

Actual Test

Answers p.11

[01~02] 빈칸에 들어갈 말로 알맞은 것을 고르시오.

01

> Shhh, you're speaking too loud. You _____ wake the baby.

① won't   ② have to   ③ may
④ should   ⑤ may not

02

> Sam stayed up all night. He _____ be very tired.

① must   ② cannot   ③ may not
④ is able to ⑤ doesn't have to

03

다음 중 빈칸에 can[Can]이 들어갈 수 <u>없는</u> 것은?

① Penguins _____ swim.
② _____ you jump high?
③ He _____ fixing the bike.
④ You _____ feed the animals.
⑤ My little sister _____ write her name.

04

대화의 빈칸에 들어갈 응답으로 알맞은 것은?

> A: Can you dance well?
> B: _____ I'm not good at dancing.

① Yes, I do.   ② No, I don't.
③ Yes, I can.   ④ No, I can't.
⑤ Yes, I am.

[05~06] 대화의 빈칸에 들어갈 말로 알맞은 것을 고르시오.

05

> A: _____ I open the window? It's very hot in here.
> B: Of course. Go ahead.

① Do   ② Can   ③ Will
④ Must   ⑤ Should

06

> A: Let's play outside.
> B: Sorry, I _____ study for the exam.

① won't   ② should   ③ can't
④ may   ⑤ am not able to

07

우리말을 영어로 바르게 옮긴 것은?

> 네가 다음번에는 운전해야 할 것이다.

① You had to drive next time.
② You may not drive next time.
③ You should not drive next time.
④ You are able to drive next time.
⑤ You will have to drive next time.

08

우리말과 일치하도록 빈칸에 들어갈 말로 알맞은 것은?

> 승강기가 저기에 있다. 우리는 계단으로 올라갈 필요가 없다.
> → The elevator is over there. We _____ climb the stairs.

① cannot   ② may not
③ must not   ④ should not
⑤ don't have to

09

대화의 밑줄 친 문장과 의미가 같은 것은?

> A: Can you fix my computer?
> B: Of course. I can fix it.

① I am fixing it.
② I enjoy fixing it.
③ I am able to fix it.
④ I am going to fix it.
⑤ I am not good at fixing.

10

다음 중 짝지어진 대화가 <u>어색한</u> 것은?

① A: May I try on this shirt?
  B: Yes, you can.
② A: Can I borrow your book?
  B: Sure, here you go.
③ A: Do I have to do the work now?
  B: No, you can do it later.
④ A Should I wear sunblock every day?
  B: Yes, you should.
⑤ A: Must I go to the gym three times a week?
  B: No, you must not. Twice a week is OK.

11

대화의 빈칸에 공통으로 들어갈 말로 알맞지 <u>않은</u> 것은?

> A: _____ you help me?
> B: Sure. What is it?
> A: We're going to go on a family trip. _____ you please take care of our dog?
> B: Okay. No problem.

① Can   ② Could   ③ Will
④ Would   ⑤ Should

12 서술형

대화의 밑줄 친 문장을 may를 이용하여 다시 쓰시오.

> A: Judy doesn't answer her phone.
> B: Don't worry. Perhaps she is sleeping.

→ _____

13 서술형

다음 표지판의 의미를 must와 괄호 안의 말을 이용하여 완성하시오.

→ You _____ pictures. (take)

[14~15] 밑줄 친 부분과 바꿔 쓸 수 있는 것을 고르시오.

14

> <u>May</u> I go home now?

① Can   ② Should   ③ Must
④ Will   ⑤ Would

15

> You <u>must</u> keep your promise.

① can   ② could   ③ may
④ have to   ⑤ are able to

16

① Can I see your photo?
② Can you hear this sound?
③ I can make delicious pies.
④ Monkeys can climb trees.
⑤ He can run very fast.

17

① Ted may be hungry.
② You may need this money.
③ She may be in her room.
④ You may go home early today.
⑤ They may like your food.

18

① We must be on time.
② You must listen to your parents.
③ He must be tired after the long trip.
④ They must keep quiet in the museum.
⑤ We must finish the work by tomorrow.

19 서술형

우리말과 일치하도록 빈칸에 알맞은 말을 쓰시오.

> 그는 하나의 동아리만 선택해야 했다.

→ He _____ _____ choose only one club.

20 서술형

대화의 밑줄 친 부분을 어법상 바르게 고치시오.

A: Look! It's raining outside.
B: Oh, my! We won't can have our picnic this afternoon.

→ _____

21

짝지어진 문장의 의미가 서로 다른 것은?

① May I use your pen?
  = Can I use your pen?
② You must not hurry.
  = You don't have to hurry.
③ Maybe he is very rich.
  = He may be very rich.
④ Can you skate?
  = Are you able to skate?
⑤ You can't park here.
  = You must not park here.

22 서술형

대화의 빈칸에 들어갈 말을 괄호 안의 말을 바르게 배열하여 쓰시오.

A: Don't tell the secret to Jenny.
B: Why not?
A: She has a big mouth. She _____.
B: Oh, I didn't know that. Okay, I won't tell it to her.

→ _____

(keep, secret, not, the, may)

23

다음 중 어법상 옳은 것으로 바르게 짝지어진 것은? (틀린 것들을 바르게 고칠 것)

> a. She don't have to do that.
> b. Jack have to go back now.
> c. He didn't have to say sorry.
> d. She has to take her son to the hospital yesterday.
> e. Do I have to wear a seat belt?

① a, b   ② b, c   ③ c, e
④ a, c, d   ⑤ b, c, e

24 (서술형)

우리말과 일치하도록 주어진 조건을 이용하여 영어로 쓰시오.

> 조건   1. be able to와 the English words를 이용할 것
>   2. 총 8단어로 쓸 것

> 그는 영어 단어를 읽을 수 없었다.

→ _____

25 (서술형)

다음 중 어법상 틀린 것을 모두 골라 바르게 고치시오.

> a. You may catch a cold.
> b. The rumor cannot be true.
> c. You should always is careful.
> d. Do I have to go to bed now?
> e. He didn't have to buy the book.
> f. She had to cook dinner that night.
> g. You will must change trains at the next station.

26

다음 중 어법상 옳은 것은? (틀린 것들을 바르게 고칠 것)

① Can we are friends again?
② Can he plays badminton?
③ You cannot eat food here.
④ Does your mom can drive a car?
⑤ He cans cook tomato spaghetti.

27 (서술형)

다음은 Tony가 할 수 있는 일과 할 수 없는 일을 나타낸 표이다. 표를 보고, can을 이용하여 문장을 완성하시오.

do 20 push-ups	○
make pasta	×
play the violin	×
ride a bike	○

[할 수 있는 것]

(1) Tony _____ .

(2) Tony _____ .

[할 수 없는 것]

(3) Tony _____ .

(4) Tony _____ .

28 (서술형)

주어진 조건과 괄호 안의 말을 이용하여 도서관에서 지켜야 할 예절을 완성하시오.

> 조건   should 또는 should not을 이용할 것

(1) You _____ loudly. (talk)

(2) You _____ your cell phone. (turn off)

(3) You _____ your books in two weeks. (return)

Recall My Memory

Answers
p.12

다음 문장이 어법상 맞으면 ○표, 틀리면 바르게 고치시오.

01 It's very hot. The dog has to be thirsty. ⊙ p. 92

02 Those chickens and ducks are theirs. ⊙ p. 58

03 Cindy have to go to see a dentist today. ⊙ p. 92

04 Money can't buy a happiness. ⊙ p. 46

05 Water freezes at 0℃. ⊙ p. 76

06 My uncle may not come on Friday. ⊙ p. 90

07 Did you washed your hands before dinner? ⊙ p. 34

08 Kim Yuna wins a gold medal at the 2010 Vancouver Winter Olympics. ⊙ p. 76

09 I heard the news. They were really surprising. ⊙ p. 58

10 I was busy yesterday. I can't play with my friends. ⊙ p. 90

11 He will is a police officer in the future. ⊙ p. 78

12 You should study hard for the final exam. ⊙ p. 92

13 Jihun and I wasn't in the science room then. ⊙ p. 20

14 A dog is runing on the street now. ⊙ p. 80

15 The student didn't wear an uniform. ⊙ p. 48

Chapter

7

의도한 바를 이렇게 전해 봐,
알아두면 유용한

문장의 종류

Unit 01 who, what, which 의문문

Unit 02 when, where, why, how 의문문

Unit 03 명령문, Let's ~, There is/are ~

Unit 04 감탄문, 부가의문문

who, what, which 의문문

'누가, 언제, 어디서, 무엇을, 어떻게, 왜'처럼 구체적인 내용을 물어볼 때 쓰는 말을 '의문사'라고 하며, 영어의 의문사에는 who, what, which, when, where, why, how가 있다. 의문문을 만들 때는 의문사를 의문문의 맨 앞에 쓰고, 대답할 때는 Yes/No가 아니라 구체적인 내용으로 답한다.

A who

a A: **Who** is your favorite comedian?
B: It's Yu Jaeseok.

b A: **Who** wants an ice cream?
B: I want an ice cream.

c A: **Who[Whom]** will you go with?
B: I'll go with Yuna.

d A: **Whose** pen is this? / **Whose** is this pen?
B: It's my pen. / It's mine.

'누구'라는 의미로, 사람에 관해 물을 때 쓴다.

b 의문사가 문장의 주어일 때는 「의문사 + (조)동사 ~?」의 형태로 쓴다. 이때 의문사는 3인칭 단수로 취급한다.

c 의문사가 문장의 목적어일 때는 who나 whom을 쓴다.

d 누구의 것인지를 물을 때는 whose(누구의, 누구의 것)를 쓴다.
whose + 명사: 누구의(소유격)
whose: 누구의 것(소유대명사)

B what

a A: **What** is your name?
B: My name is Jiyong.

b A: **What** did you do yesterday?
B: I went to the museum.

c A: **What** time is it now?
B: It's four thirty.

'무엇'이라는 의미로, 사물에 관해 물을 때 쓴다.

c what 뒤에 명사가 오면 '무슨 ~, 어떤 ~'이라는 의미이다.

C which

a A: **Which** would you like, juice or soda?
B: Juice, please.

b A: **Which** color do you want, green or blue?
B: I want blue.

'어느 것'이라는 의미로, 몇 가지 중에서 선택을 물을 때 쓴다.

b which 뒤에 명사가 오면 '어느 ~'라는 의미이다.

의문문의 형태

	의문사가 없는 의문문	의문사로 시작하는 의문문
be동사가 쓰인 경우	Be동사 + 주어 ~?	의문사 + be동사 + 주어 ~?
일반동사가 쓰인 경우	Do/Does/Did + 주어 + 동사원형 ~?	의문사 + do/does/did + 주어 + 동사원형 ~?
조동사가 쓰인 경우	조동사 + 주어 + 동사원형 ~?	의문사 + 조동사 + 주어 + 동사원형 ~?
의문사가 문장의 주어인 경우	—	의문사 + (조)동사 ~?

Exercise

Answers p.12

A 괄호 안에서 알맞은 말을 고르시오.

1 [What / Who] did you eat for lunch?

2 [Whose / Who] bag is this?

3 [What / Which] day is it today?

4 [Who / Whose] is that girl over there?

5 [Which / What] subject does she teach, art or music?

B 빈칸에 알맞은 말을 보기에서 골라 대화를 완성하시오.

보기	who	whose	what	which

1 A: _____ did David call? B: He called his father.

2 A: _____ are they doing now? B: They're studying.

3 A: _____ turn is it next? B: It's Jenny's.

4 A: _____ did you buy, a book or a magazine?

   B: I bought a book.

C 우리말과 일치하도록 괄호 안의 말을 이용하여 문장을 완성하시오.

1 너는 어제 누구를 만났니? (meet)

   → _____ _____ _____ _____ yesterday?

2 이것과 저것 중 어느 것이 네 컵이니? (your cup)

   → _____ _____ _____, this one or that one?

3 너는 이번 주말에 뭐 할 거니? (will, do)

   → _____ _____ _____ this weekend?

4 그는 누구의 차를 운전하고 있니? (car)

   → _____ _____ _____ driving?

when, where, why, how 의문문

A when

a A: **When** is your birthday?

B: It's October 11th.

b A: **When** will the movie come out?

B: It will come out next week.

'언제'라는 의미로, 시간이나 날짜, 때를 물을 때 쓴다.

B where

a A: **Where** are you going now?

B: I'm going to the library.

b A: **Where** does Mr. Park live?

B: He lives near the school.

'어디에'라는 의미로, 장소나 위치를 물을 때 쓴다.

C why

a A: **Why** is she absent today?

B: Because she is very sick.

b A: **Why** did Ted leave?

B: Because he had a meeting.

'왜'라는 의미로, 이유를 물을 때 쓴다. 대답할 때는 because(왜냐하면)를 사용하여 답한다.

D how

a A: **How** was your vacation?

B: It was great.

b A: **How** can I get to the hotel from the airport?

B: You can take a bus or a taxi.

c A: **How tall** is Janghun?

B: He's 207cm tall.

'어떻게'라는 의미로, 상태나 방법을 물을 때 쓴다.

c how 뒤에 형용사나 부사가 오면 '얼마나 ~한/하게'라는 의미이다.

• how old: 몇 살의	• how tall: 얼마나 키가 큰, 얼마나 높은
• how long: 얼마나 긴, 얼마나 오래	• how far: 얼마나 먼
• how often: 얼마나 자주	• how much: 얼마
• how many + 셀 수 있는 명사의 복수형: 얼마나 많은 수의	• how much + 셀 수 없는 명사: 얼마나 많은 양의

vocabulary ·············· **A** come out 개봉하다   **C** absent 휑 결석한   **D** vacation 몡 방학 get to ~에 도착하다

A 괄호 안에서 알맞은 말을 고르시오.

1 A: [Why / How] are you today?   B: I'm fine, thanks.

2 A: [When / Where] do banks open?   B: They open at nine.

3 A: [Where / How] is Robin from?   B: He's from France.

4 A: [How / Why] do you like that movie?   B: Because it's funny.

5 A: [How long / How far] is your holiday?   B: It's five days.

B 빈칸에 알맞은 말을 보기에서 골라 대화를 완성하시오.

보기	when	where	why	how

1 A: _____ do you go to school?   B: I walk to school.

2 A: _____ will you be home?   B: I'll be home in an hour.

3 A: _____ is Suho so happy?   B: Because he won first prize.

4 A: _____ did you go yesterday?   B: I went to a water park.

C 우리말과 일치하도록 빈칸에 알맞은 말을 쓰시오.

1 내 신발이 어디에 있니?

→ _____ _____ my shoes?

2 너는 언제 야구를 하니?

→ _____ _____ _____ play baseball?

3 너는 얼마나 자주 조부모님을 방문하니?

→ _____ _____ _____ _____ visit your grandparents?

4 그녀는 왜 울고 있니?

→ _____ _____ _____ crying?

명령문, Let's ~, There is/are ~

A 명령문

1 긍정 명령문

a **Close** the door.

b **Be** careful.

cf. **Please** sit here. / Sit here, **please**.

2 부정 명령문

a **Don't speak** loudly.

b **Don't be** late.

1 상대방에게 '~해라'라고 명령, 지시, 충고, 부탁 등을 하는 말로, 상대방인 주어 You 를 생략하고 동사원형으로 시작한다.

cf. 명령문의 앞이나 뒤에 please를 붙이면 좀 더 공손한 표현이 된다.

2 「Don't + 동사원형」으로 '~하지 마라'의 의미를 나타낸다.

B Let's ~

a **Let's eat** something.

b **Let's be** friends.

c **Let's not go** out.

Let's ~는 '~하자'라고 상대방에게 제안이나 권유를 하는 말로, 뒤에 동사원형을 쓴다. 「Let's not + 동사원형」은 '~하지 말자'라는 의미이다.

C There is/are ~

1 There is/are의 쓰임

a **There is** a book on the desk.

b **There are** many books on the desk.

c **There is** some milk in the fridge.

1 '~이 있다'라는 의미로, 바로 뒤에 주어가 오며, 주어의 수에 따라 is나 are를 쓴다. There는 해석하지 않는다.

a There is + 셀 수 있는 명사의 단수형

b There are + 셀 수 있는 명사의 복수형

c There is + 셀 수 없는 명사

2 There is/are의 부정문과 의문문

a **There aren't** any books on the desk.

b A: **Is there** any milk in the fridge?

B: Yes, **there is**. / No, **there isn't**.

2 부정문은 be동사 뒤에 not을 쓰고, 의문 문은 There와 be동사의 자리를 바꾼다.

a There is/are not ~: ~이 없다

b Is/Are there ~?: ~이 있니?

3 There is/are의 과거형

a **There was** a book on the desk.

b **There were** many books on the desk.

3 '~이 있었다'는 There was/were ~로 나타낸다.

---

vocabulary ---------- **A** loudly ⊕ 큰 소리로 **C** fridge ⑲ 냉장고(= refrigerator)

Exercise

Answers
p.12

A 괄호 안에서 알맞은 말을 고르시오.

1 [Turn / Turns] off your cell phones.

2 Let's [go / going] on a picnic.

3 [Not / Don't] touch the paintings.

4 [Let's not / Don't let's] play computer games.

5 [Do / Be] quiet in the library.

B 그림을 보고, 빈칸에 알맞은 말을 쓰시오. (현재시제로 쓸 것)

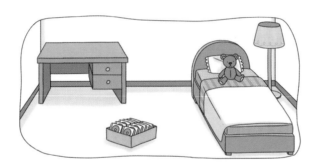

1 _____ _____ a teddy bear on the bed.

2 _____ _____ some CDs in the box.

3 _____ _____ a computer on the desk.

4 A: _____ _____ a lamp near the bed?   B: Yes, there is.

C 우리말과 일치하도록 괄호 안의 말을 이용하여 문장을 완성하시오.

1 산책하러 가자. (take)

→ _____ _____ a walk.

2 수업 중에 떠들지 마라. (talk)

→ _____ _____ during class.

3 쇼핑몰에는 많은 사람들이 있었다. (many people)

→ _____ _____ _____ _____ at the shopping mall.

A 감탄문

'정말 ~구나!'라고 자신의 느낌을 표현할 때 쓰는 말이다. How나 What으로 시작하며 문장 끝에 느낌표(!)를 붙인다.

1 How로 시작하는 감탄문

a You are very kind.

   → **How** kind (you are)!

b He runs very fast.

   → **How** fast (he runs)!

1 형용사나 부사를 강조할 때 쓰며, 「How + 형용사/부사 (+ 주어 + 동사)」의 형태이다. 주어와 동사는 생략할 수 있다.

2 What으로 시작하는 감탄문

a She has a very nice house.

   → **What** a nice house (she has)!

b These are very beautiful flowers.

   → **What** beautiful flowers (these are)!

2 명사를 강조할 때 쓰며, 「What + a/an + 형용사 + 명사 (+ 주어 + 동사)」의 형태이다. 주어와 동사는 생략할 수 있다.

b 명사가 복수이거나 셀 수 없는 명사일 때는 a/an을 쓰지 않는다.

B 부가의문문

자신이 말하는 내용에 대해 '그렇지?', '그렇지 않니?'라고 상대방에게 확인하거나 동의를 구하기 위해 평서문 뒤에 짧게 덧붙이는 의문문이다.

1 긍정문 + 부정 부가의문문

a She is a teacher, **isn't she?**

b You play the guitar, **don't you?**

c He likes tennis, **doesn't he?**

d Yeona can speak English, **can't she?**

1 긍정문 뒤에는 부정의 부가의문문이 온다. 이때 부정형은 축약형으로 쓴다.

☑ 부가의문문 만들 때 주의할 점
   • 동사의 수와 시제는 앞 문장에 맞춘다. (be동사/조동사는 그대로, 일반동사는 do/does/did로 쓴다.)
   • 주어는 앞 문장의 주어를 대명사로 바꾼다.

2 부정문 + 긍정 부가의문문

a You aren't tired, **are you?**

b We don't have to go now, **do we?**

c The test won't be difficult, **will it?**

2 부정문 뒤에는 긍정의 부가의문문이 온다.

부가의문문의 대답

부가의문문의 내용이 긍정이든 부정이든 상관없이 대답하는 내용이 긍정이면 Yes, 부정이면 No로 답한다.

A: They went to the cinema, didn't they? / They didn't go to the cinema, did they?

B: (영화 보러 갔으면) **Yes, they did.** / (영화 보러 가지 않았으면) **No, they didn't.**

vocabulary ········· B tired 톙 피곤한 difficult 톙 어려운

A 주어진 문장을 감탄문으로 바꿔 쓰시오.

1 It is a very hot day. → What _____ !

2 The final game was very exciting. → How _____ !

3 Those are very tall buildings. → What _____ !

4 Daniel dances very well. → How _____ !

B 빈칸에 알맞은 부가의문문을 쓰시오.

1 You're hungry, _____ _____ ?

2 He often goes hiking, _____ _____ ?

3 We shouldn't enter this room, _____ _____ ?

4 Your sister studied hard last night, _____ _____ ?

5 Tim and Jake don't know each other, _____ _____ ?

C 우리말과 일치하도록 괄호 안의 말을 이용하여 문장을 완성하시오.

1 이 음식은 정말 맛있구나! (delicious)

→ _____ _____ this food is!

2 정말 긴 다리구나! (long, bridge)

→ _____ _____ _____ _____ it is!

3 Lisa는 숙제를 하지 않았어, 그렇지? (do)

→ Lisa _____ _____ her homework, _____ _____ ?

4 John은 내일 올 거지, 그렇지 않니? (will, come)

→ John _____ _____ tomorrow, _____ _____ ?

Writing Practice

Answers p.13

A 우리말과 일치하도록 괄호 안의 말을 바르게 배열하시오.

01 너의 가장 친한 친구는 누구니? (your, who, best, is, friend)

→ _____

02 그는 정말 높이 뛰어오르는구나! (high, jumps, he, how)

→ _____

03 회의는 언제 시작하니? (the meeting, will, when, begin)

→ _____

04 그 여자는 무엇을 하고 있니? (the woman, is, what, doing)

→ _____

05 시험에 대해서는 걱정하지 마. (worry, don't, the exam, about)

→ _____

06 그 영화는 상영 시간이 얼마나 되니? (how, last, the movie, does, long)

→ _____

07 너는 정말 귀여운 강아지를 기르는구나! (you, what, have, puppy, a, cute)

→ _____

08 그녀는 해물피자와 해물파스타 중에 어느 요리를 주문했니? (dish, she, order, which, did)

→ _____, the seafood pizza or the seafood pasta?

09 호수에 오리가 다섯 마리 있었다. (ducks, were, five, there)

→ _____ on the lake.

10 어제는 추웠어, 그렇지 않았니? (wasn't, cold, was, yesterday, it)

→ It _____, _____?

B 우리말과 일치하도록 괄호 안의 말을 이용하여 문장을 완성하시오.

01 a 동물원에 호랑이가 한 마리 있다. (tiger)

→ There _____ in the zoo.

b 동물원에 코끼리가 네 마리 있다. (elephant)

→ _____

02 a 그 사고는 어디에서 일어났니? (the accident)

→ _____ happen?

b 그 사고는 왜 일어났니?

→ _____

03 a 네 친구들에게 잘 대해 줘라. (nice)

→ _____ to your friends.

b 네 친구들에게 무례하게 대하지 마라. (rude)

→ _____

04 a 너는 연필이 얼마나 필요하니? (pencil)

→ _____ do you need?

b 너는 종이가 얼마나 필요하니? (paper)

→ _____

05 a 너는 당근을 먹지, 그렇지 않니?

→ You eat carrots, _____ ?

b Sam은 당근을 먹지 않지, 그렇지?

→ _____

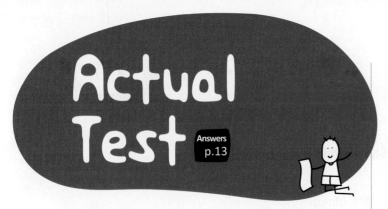

Actual Test

Answers p.13

[01~02] 대화의 빈칸에 들어갈 말로 알맞은 것을 고르시오.

01

A: _____ is your favorite subject?
B: It's English.

① What   ② When   ③ Who
④ Why   ⑤ How

02

A: _____ notebook is this?
B: It's mine.

① Who   ② What   ③ When
④ Where   ⑤ Whose

03

빈칸에 들어갈 말로 알맞지 <u>않은</u> 것은?

There is _____ on the table.

① an apple   ② a banana
③ some milk   ④ lots of pens
⑤ a cup of juice

04

밑줄 친 부분이 어법상 <u>틀린</u> 것은? (바르게 고칠 것)

① <u>What</u> time is it now?
② <u>Whose</u> pencil is this?
③ <u>Where</u> is your mom's birthday?
④ <u>Whom</u> are you going to dance with?
⑤ <u>Which</u> would you like, coffee or tea?

05 서술형

우리말과 일치하도록 괄호 안의 말을 이용하여 문장을 완성하시오.

수업 시간에 누가 네 옆에 앉니? (sit)

→ _____ _____ next to you in class?

06

밑줄 친 부분이 어법상 <u>틀린</u> 것은? (바르게 고칠 것)

①<u>Which</u> ②<u>color</u> ③<u>do</u> you ④<u>want</u>, yellow ⑤<u>and</u> green?

[07~08] 우리말을 영어로 바르게 옮긴 것을 고르시오.

07

너는 파티에 누구를 초대할 거야?

① Who will invite to the party?
② Whom will invite to the party?
③ Who will you invite to the party?
④ Which will you invite to the party?
⑤ What will you invite to the party?

08

그는 훌륭한 친구들을 가지고 있구나!

① What great friend he is!
② How great friends he is!
③ How a great friend he has!
④ What great friends he has!
⑤ What a great friends he has!

09 서술형

빈칸에 공통으로 들어갈 말을 쓰시오.

- _____ was your trip?
- _____ can I get to the post office?

→ _____

10

빈칸에 들어갈 말이 나머지 넷과 다른 것은?

① _____ tall is your dad?
② _____ should we hurry?
③ _____ was he so angry?
④ _____ does she have to go?
⑤ _____ did you go to bed late?

11

대화의 빈칸에 들어갈 말이 순서대로 짝지어진 것은?

A: You are tired, _____ you?
B: Actually, _____. I stayed up late last night. I had to finish my report.

① aren't – yes   ② aren't – not
③ aren't – no   ④ are – yes
⑤ are – no

12 서술형

우리말과 일치하도록 괄호 안의 말을 바르게 배열하시오.

집 안에 개 한 마리가 있었다.
(a, in, house, there, dog, was, the)

→ _____

13

다음 중 짝지어진 대화가 어색한 것은?

① A: Who did the dishes?
   B: I did.
② A: Why is Chris in the hospital?
   B: Because he caught the flu.
③ A: Where are you going now?
   B: Right now.
④ A: When did you hear about it?
   B: About three hours ago.
⑤ A: What did you do last weekend?
   B: I saw a movie.

14 서술형

대화의 빈칸에 들어갈 말을 괄호 안의 말을 바르게 배열하여 쓰시오.

A: _____?
B: I go to Daehan Middle School.

→ _____

(do, go, where, you, to, school)

15

괄호 안의 지시대로 바꿔 쓸 때 잘못된 것은? (바르게 바꿔 쓸 것)

① Be quiet. (부정문으로)
   → Don't be quiet.
② Help me. (공손한 표현으로)
   → Please help me.
③ There is a bird. (부정문으로)
   → There is not a bird.
④ You are very smart. (감탄문으로)
   → How smart you are!
⑤ Let's play outside. (부정문으로)
   → Let's don't play outside.

16

A: When does the next bus arrive?
B: _____

① Because it's an hour late.
② It will arrive in 5 minutes.
③ It's not far from here.
④ You can take a taxi.
⑤ It's 7 o'clock now.

17

A: You like badminton, don't you?
B: _____

① Yes, it's my favorite sport.
② No, you don't like badminton.
③ Sure, I usually play table tennis.
④ No, I like badminton very much.
⑤ Yes, you sometimes play badminton.

18

빈칸에 들어갈 말이 순서대로 짝지어진 것은?

• How _____ is this skirt?
• How _____ is your cousin?
• How _____ does he exercise?
• How _____ will you stay here?

① much – old – far – long
② much – old – often – long
③ much – long – often – tall
④ many – old – often – long
⑤ many – long – far – tall

19

A: Hi, Daniel. ① Did you see Robert today?
B: No, he ② didn't come ③ to school.
A: Oh, ④ when was he absent today?
B: ⑤ Because he hurt his leg.

20

A: We don't ① have to go now, ② do we?
B: ③ No, we should go ④ now.
A: Okay. Then ⑤ let's hurry.

21 서술형

밑줄 친 단어들을 알맞은 형태로 바꿔 문장을 다시 쓰시오.

There be many student in the playground now.

→ _____
_____

22

각 문장을 완성할 때 빈칸에 필요하지 않은 것은?

• _____ run in the classroom.
• _____ a wonderful story it is!
• Let's _____ kind to our friends.
• Is _____ any cake in the fridge?

① Be[be]   ② How[how]
③ What[what]   ④ Don't[don't]
⑤ There[there]

23 서술형

다음 대화에서 어법상 틀린 부분을 찾아 바르게 고치시오.

A: Jenny, it's so cold. Please closed the door.
B: Okay, I will.

_____ → _____

24

다음 중 어법상 틀린 것은? (바르게 고칠 것)

① Who can cook well?
② What an interesting trip!
③ You play the drums, don't you?
④ He can't speak Chinese, can he?
⑤ How many brother do you have?

25

대화의 빈칸에 들어갈 질문으로 알맞은 것은?

A: _____
B: I need five minutes.

① What time do you have?
② Why do you need time?
③ How much time do you need?
④ When do you need time?
⑤ Where do you spend your time?

26 서술형

우리말과 일치하도록 괄호 안의 말을 이용하여 영어로 쓰시오.

너는 다시는 늦지 않을 거야, 그렇지?
(won't, late, again)

→ _____

[27~28] 다음 문장을 감탄문으로 바꿔 쓰시오.

27 서술형

She talks very fast.

→ How _____ !

28 서술형

It is a very beautiful day.

→ What _____ !

29

밑줄 친 부분이 어법상 옳은 것은? (틀린 것들을 바르게 고칠 것)

① Be watch out for cars!
② Don't afraid of the spider.
③ Let's playing soccer outside.
④ What pretty flowers these are!
⑤ There were some bread on the table.

30 서술형

다음 글에서 어법상 틀린 부분을 모두 찾아 바르게 고치시오.

Many students use the library every day. So there is some rules in the library. First, don't make any noise. Second, being nice to other people. Third, don't eat or drink in the library. Fourth, put each book back in the right place. Let's be follow these rules and have fun in the library.

Recall My Memory

 **Answers** p.14

다음 문장이 어법상 맞으면 ○표, <u>틀리면</u> 바르게 고치시오.

01 There are some beef in the soup. ⊛ p. 106

02 The sun rose every morning. ⊛ p. 76

03 The black shoes are mine. The white one are my sister's. ⊛ p. 62

04 Was she in Guam last winter? ⊛ p. 20

05 Don't do upset about it. ⊛ p. 106

06 May I talk to Cindy? ⊛ p. 90

07 Where do you go to bed? – At 10:30. ⊛ p. 104

08 These children grew some vegetables himself. ⊛ p. 58

09 Let's cleaning the house. ⊛ p. 106

10 Two knifes are on the table. ⊛ p. 44

11 Paul had a haircut, wasn't he? ⊛ p. 108

12 Lisa is going leave for Prague next week. ⊛ p. 78

13 What does your father do after work? ⊛ p. 102

14 What big her eyes are! ⊛ p. 108

15 She visitted her aunt last Sunday. ⊛ p. 32

Chapter

8

문장의 형태를 지배하는

동사의 종류

Unit
01   감각동사

Unit
02   수여동사

Unit 01 감각동사

감각동사란 눈, 코, 귀, 혀, 피부 등을 통해 느끼는 감각을 나타내는 동사를 말한다. 감각동사에는 look, smell, sound, taste, feel이 있다.

A 감각동사 + 형용사

감각동사 뒤에는 형용사가 온다. 이때 형용사는 주어의 상태나 성질을 보충 설명해 준다. 감각동사 뒤에 부사는 올 수 없음에 주의한다.

a You **look** happy[~~happily~~].
　　　　　형용사
b These flowers **smell** good.
c Your plan **sounds** great.
d This cake **tastes** sweet.
e I **feel** hungry.

a look + 형용사: ~해 보이다
b smell + 형용사: ~한 냄새가 나다
c sound + 형용사: ~하게 들리다
d taste + 형용사: ~한 맛이 나다
e feel + 형용사: ~하게 느끼다

B 감각동사 + like + 명사

감각동사 뒤에 명사가 올 때는 전치사 like와 함께 쓴다. 이때 like는 '~처럼, ~ 같은'이라는 뜻이다.

a Suho **looks like** his father.
　　　　　　　　명사
b Your hands **smell like** soap.
c His voice **sounds like** a robot.
d This tofu **tastes like** meat.
e Her skin **feels like** silk.

a look like + 명사: ~처럼 보이다
b smell like + 명사: ~ 같은 냄새가 나다
c sound like + 명사: ~처럼 들리다
d taste like + 명사: ~ 같은 맛이 나다
e feel like + 명사: ~처럼 느끼다

주격보어와 함께 쓰이는 동사

감각동사 뒤에 오는 형용사처럼 주어의 상태나 성질을 보충 설명해 주는 말을 '주격보어'라고 한다. 주격보어와 함께 쓰이는 동사에는 감각동사 외에 be동사, '~이 되다, ~해지다'라는 의미의 become, get, turn 등이 있다. 주격보어로는 명사와 형용사가 온다.

She **is** a doctor.
주어　동사　주격보어(명사)

Daniel **became** famous.
주어　　동사　　주격보어(형용사)

cf. 동사 혼자만으로도 완전한 의미를 전달하는 동사도 있다. 주로 부사나 전치사를 포함한 부사구가 함께 쓰여 동사를 꾸며 준다.

He **dances** well.
주어　동사　수식어(부사)

My uncle **lives** in Daegu.
주어　　동사　수식어(부사구)

vocabulary ·········· A sweet 혱 달콤한, 단　　B soap 몡 비누　voice 몡 목소리　tofu 몡 두부　silk 몡 실크, 비단

Exercise

Answers p.14

A 괄호 안에서 알맞은 말을 고르시오.

1 This soup tastes [salt / salty].

2 The players [feel / feel like] winners tonight.

3 Your hair looks [love / lovely].

4 Dinner smells [good / well].

5 A Halloween party sounds like [fun / funny].

B 빈칸에 알맞은 말을 보기에서 골라 현재형으로 쓰시오. (한 번씩만 쓸 것)

보기	look	feel	taste	smell	sound

1 Her perfume _____ nice.

2 You _____ beautiful in that dress.

3 Honey _____ very sweet.

4 The story _____ interesting.

5 We all _____ tired after a long run.

C 우리말과 일치하도록 괄호 안의 말을 이용하여 문장을 완성하시오.

1 이 치즈는 고약한 냄새가 난다. (bad)

→ This cheese _____ _____.

2 모든 아기들은 천사처럼 보인다. (angels)

→ All babies _____ _____ _____.

3 그 의자는 편안하게 느껴진다. (comfortable)

→ The chair _____ _____.

4 이 음료는 딸기 같은 맛이 난다. (strawberries)

→ This drink _____ _____ _____.

Unit 02 수여동사

수여동사란 '~에게 …을 (해)주다'라는 의미를 가진 동사로, '주다'라는 의미가 있다고 해서 '수여동사'라고 한다. 수여동사에는 give, send, teach, tell, show, buy, make, ask 등이 있다.

A 수여동사 + 간접목적어 + 직접목적어

a Carol **gave** her dog some food.
　　　　　　간접목적어(~에게)　직접목적어(…을)

b Mom **bought** me a new smartphone.

c The teacher **asks** us many questions.

수여동사는 뒤에 '~에게'에 해당하는 간접목적어와 '…을'에 해당하는 직접목적어가 온다.

수여동사와 다른 주의해야 할 동사

수여동사의 문장 형태와 비슷하게 call, name, make, elect 등의 동사는 「동사 + 목적어 + 명사」의 형태를 이룬다. 이때의 명사는 직접목적어가 아니라 목적격보어이다. 목적격보어란 목적어의 상태나 성질, 이름이나 신분 등을 보충 설명해 주는 말이다.

Dad **calls** me princess.
주어　동사　목적어　목적격보어(명사)

We **elected** Daniel class president.
주어　　동사　　목적어　　　목적격보어(명사)

B 수여동사 + 직접목적어 + 전치사 + 간접목적어

간접목적어가 직접목적어 뒤에 올 수도 있는데, 이때 동사에 따라 간접목적어 앞에 전치사 to, for, of 중 하나를 쓴다.

a I **sent** her a text message.

→ I **sent** a text message **to** her.

b We **made** John a birthday cake.

→ We **made** a birthday cake **for** John.

c She **asked** him a favor.

→ She **asked** a favor **of** him.
　주어　동사　목적어　　수식어(부사구)

a 전치사 to를 쓰는 동사: give, send, show, tell, teach, lend, write, read, pass, bring 등

b 전치사 for를 쓰는 동사: buy, make, cook, get, find 등

c 전치사 of를 쓰는 동사: ask 등

☑ 「전치사 + 간접목적어」는 부사구이다. 부사구는 수식어로, 문장의 필수 성분이 아니므로 「주어 + 동사 + 목적어」의 문장 형태가 된다.

목적어와 함께 쓰이는 동사

'~을'에 해당하는 목적어와 함께 쓰이는 동사에는 like, love, want, watch, meet 등이 있다.

My brother **loves** cartoons.
　　　주어　　　동사　　목적어

I **want** a bike for Christmas.
주어 동사　목적어　　수식어(부사구)

---

vocabulary ---------- A name ⑧ 이름을 지어 주다, 명명하다 elect ⑧ 선출하다 princess ⑲ 공주 class president 반장
B favor ⑲ 부탁 cartoon ⑲ 만화

A

빈칸에 알맞은 전치사를 쓰시오. (필요 없으면 X표 할 것)

1 He bought some ice cream _____ us.

2 She gave some money _____ the poor man.

3 Could you make me _____ some tea?

4 Mina sent her friends _____ Christmas cards.

5 I asked a question _____ him.

B

밑줄 친 부분이 어법상 맞으면 ○표, 틀리면 바르게 고치시오.

1 They showed to me their new car.　　　　　　_____

2 I'll get you for some snacks.　　　　　　_____

3 Ms. Smith told a story her students.　　　　　　_____

4 He cooked a delicious meal to his parents.　　　　　　_____

5 She teaches kids English.　　　　　　_____

C

두 문장의 의미가 같도록 빈칸에 알맞은 말을 쓰시오.

1 I wrote a letter to her.

　→ I wrote _____ _____ _____ .

2 The little boy asked a favor of me.

　→ The little boy asked _____ _____ _____ .

3 He bought his teacher a carnation.

　→ He bought _____ _____ _____ _____ _____ .

4 She lent him her dictionary.

　→ She lent _____ _____ _____ _____ .

Writing Practice

Answers p.14

A 우리말과 일치하도록 괄호 안의 말을 바르게 배열하시오. (필요하면 형태를 바꿀 것)

01 이 방은 춥다. (feel, I, cold)

→ _____ in this room.

02 당신에게 질문을 하나 해도 될까요? (you, a question, ask, of)

→ Can I _____ ?

03 꽃들은 좋은 향기가 난다. (good, smell, flowers)

→ _____

04 저에게 여권을 보여 주시겠어요? (me, show, your passport)

→ Can you _____ ?

05 오렌지들은 달콤하고 새콤한 맛이 난다. (sour, and, taste, sweet, oranges)

→ _____

06 그는 어둠 속에서 나무처럼 보였다. (like, look, a tree)

→ He _____ in the dark.

07 삼촌은 내게 선물을 보내 주셨다. (me, a present, send, to)

→ My uncle _____ .

08 그녀의 목소리는 매우 아름답게 들린다. (very, sound, beautiful)

→ Her voice _____ .

09 Sally는 그에게 초콜릿을 좀 주었다. (some chocolate, him, give, to)

→ Sally _____ .

10 Tom은 그의 개에게 멋진 집을 만들어 주었다. (make, his dog, a nice house)

→ Tom _____ .

B 우리말과 일치하도록 괄호 안의 말을 이용하여 문장을 완성하시오.

01 a 이 음식은 맛있는 냄새가 난다. (smell)

→ This food _____ delicious.

b 저 음식은 짠 맛이 난다. (salty)

→ _____

02 a 그녀는 우리에게 책을 한 권 읽어 주었다. (read)

→ She _____ a book.

b 그녀는 그들에게 편지를 한 통 썼다. (write, a letter)

→ _____

03 a 그는 배우처럼 보인다. (look)

→ He _____ an actor.

b 그는 영웅이 된 것처럼 느낀다. (a hero)

→ _____

04 a 엄마는 그에게 가방을 사 주셨다. (buy, a bag)

→ Mom _____ him.

b 엄마는 내게 가방을 만들어 주셨다. (make)

→ _____

05 a Harry는 그녀에게 마술을 가르쳐 주었다. (teach, magic)

→ Harry _____ her.

b Harry는 그에게 마술을 보여 주었다. (show)

→ _____

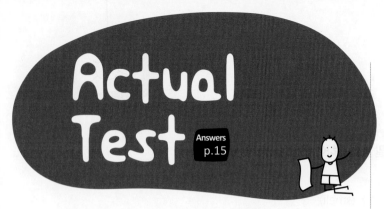

Actual Test

Answers p.15

01

빈칸에 들어갈 말로 알맞은 것은?

Your sister looks _____ today.

① differently
② smart girl
③ so angry
④ really sadly
⑤ very beautifully

[02~03] 빈칸에 들어갈 말로 알맞지 <u>않은</u> 것을 고르시오.

02

The teacher _____ a book to me.

① gave
② showed
③ lent
④ bought
⑤ brought

03

He _____ me a map.

① gave
② sent
③ showed
④ brought
⑤ explained

04

빈칸에 공통으로 들어갈 말로 알맞은 것은?

• Mr. Anderson teaches history _____ us.
• Eric sends a text message _____ me every morning.

① to
② of
③ in
④ for
⑤ with

[05~06] 대화의 빈칸에 들어갈 말로 알맞지 <u>않은</u> 것을 고르시오.

05

A: How does the cake taste?
B: It tastes _____.

① bad
② good
③ fantastic
④ sweetly
⑤ delicious

06

A: How did the boy feel yesterday?
B: He felt very _____.

① dizzy
② silly
③ lonely
④ lively
⑤ terribly

07

빈칸에 들어갈 말이 나머지 넷과 <u>다른</u> 것은?

① Grandma told a story _____ us.
② Will you find my bag _____ me?
③ Mom bought a new bike _____ me.
④ Please get some water _____ me.
⑤ Can you make some soup _____ him?

08

빈칸에 들어갈 말이 순서대로 짝지어진 것은?

• He wrote a thank-you letter _____ his teacher.
• I made a paper airplane _____ my little sister.

① to – of
② for – of
③ to – for
④ for – to
⑤ of – for

09

대화의 빈칸에 들어갈 말로 알맞은 것은?

> A: Did you hear the news about them?
>
> B: Yes. It _____.

① sounds like amazing
② sounds like wonderful
③ sounds wonderfully
④ doesn't sound the truth
⑤ doesn't sound like the truth

10

빈칸에 들어갈 말로 알맞은 것을 모두 고르면?

> The girl looks _____.

① sadly   ② lovely   ③ greatly
④ nervous   ⑤ friendly

[11~12] 밑줄 친 동사의 쓰임이 나머지 넷과 다른 것을 고르시오.

11

① I got him a drink.
② She passed me the ball.
③ John told us his life story.
④ They named their son David.
⑤ He cooked his children pasta.

12

① You look tired today.
② Mom's hands feel warm.
③ She became a hair designer.
④ Dad caught a big fish.
⑤ Her face turned red.

13 서술형

두 문장의 의미가 같도록 빈칸에 알맞은 말을 쓰시오.

> My mom bought me a new skateboard.

→ My   mom   bought   a   new   skateboard
   _____.

14

빈칸에 들어갈 수 있는 동사를 두 개 고르면?

> This project _____ difficult.

① sees   ② looks   ③ sounds
④ hears   ⑤ watches

15 서술형

우리말과 일치하도록 괄호 안의 말을 바르게 배열하시오.

> Grace는 주민센터에서 아이들에게 영어를 가르쳤다.
> (English, taught, children, Grace, at the community center)

→ _____

16

다음 중 어법상 틀린 것은? (바르게 고칠 것)

① Kate asked a favor of him.
② Mom made some cookies for us.
③ Dad sent a big present for me.
④ Her boyfriend bought a ring for her.
⑤ He gave a shoulder massage to me.

[17~18] 어법상 틀린 부분을 바르게 고쳐 다시 쓰시오.

17 서술형

> This fish smells badly.

→ _____

18 서술형

> It sounded a beautiful song to my ears.

→ _____

19

우리말을 영어로 바르게 옮긴 것을 모두 고르면?

> 그는 종종 우리에게 어려운 질문들을 했다.

① He often asked us difficult questions.
② He often asked difficult questions of us.
③ He often asked difficult questions for us.
④ He often asked difficult questions us.
⑤ He often asked difficult questions to us.

20 서술형

다음 대화에서 어법상 틀린 부분을 두 군데 찾아 바르게 고치시오.

> A: Fred, you look happy today.
> B: I feel wonderful today. Minho gave two free movie tickets me. Let's go to the movies tonight.
> A: That sounds greatly.

(1) _____ → _____

(2) _____ → _____

21 서술형

대화의 빈칸에 들어갈 말을 괄호 안의 말을 바르게 배열하여 쓰시오.

> A: Does the baby want some milk?
> B: Yes. _____

→ _____

(give, some, him, milk)

22

다음 중 어법상 옳은 것을 모두 고르면? (틀린 것들을 바르게 고칠 것)

① Nancy told to me her story.
② Jake showed her a picture.
③ Could you pass the ketchup to me?
④ They gave some money for him.
⑤ Ms. Lee asked he some questions.

23

(A), (B), (C)의 각 네모 안에서 어법에 맞는 표현으로 순서대로 짝지어진 것은?

> Yesterday was mom's birthday. My sister and I did something special for her. First, I made a birthday cake (A) to / for mom. My sister bought mom a nice present. She also wrote a birthday card (B) to / for mom. Mom looked so (C) happy / happily.

① to - to - happy
② for - to - happy
③ to - for - happy
④ for - for - happily
⑤ to - for - happily

24

다음 중 어법상 옳은 것은 <u>모두</u> 몇 개인가? (<u>틀린</u> 것들을 바르게 고칠 것)

> a. The blanket feels soft.
> b. The trash smells terrible.
> c. His voice sounded sadly.
> d. Jenny looks lovely today.
> e. The boy looks a prince.

① 1개   ② 2개   ③ 3개
④ 4개   ⑤ 5개

25 서술형

다음 글의 밑줄 친 부분 중 어법상 <u>틀린</u> 것을 두 개 골라 바르게 고치시오.

> Jason and his friends ① visit a children's home every Saturday. Jason ② tells funny stories the children. ③ They laugh. Brian and Sally ④ clean the toys. Jane and Bobby ⑤ get some snacks to the children.

_____ → _____

_____ → _____

26 서술형

두 사람이 상대방에게 해 준 일을 조건과 주어진 어구를 이용하여 완성하시오.

> 조건   1. 과거시제로 쓸 것
>   2. 표의 모든 정보를 활용할 것

>   lend her camera
> Lisa ⟺ Tony
>   buy some chocolate

(1) Lisa _____ Tony.

(2) Tony _____ some chocolate.

27 서술형

우리말과 일치하도록 괄호 안의 말을 이용하여 문장을 완성하시오.

> 그 구름은 양처럼 보인다. (a sheep)

→ The cloud _____ _____ _____

_____ .

28 서술형

다음 중 어법상 <u>틀린</u> 것을 <u>모두</u> 골라 바르게 고치시오.

> a. The girl looks friendly.
> b. The man feels powerfully.
> c. This apple tastes very sour.
> d. Bring the magazine to me now.
> e. I gave flowers to my parents.
> f. The soap smells like an orange.
> g. I made a sandwich to my sister.

29 서술형

Paul은 오늘 오후 여동생 Amy를 돌볼 계획이다. 계획표를 보고, 빈칸에 알맞은 말을 쓰시오.

Time	Plan
2:00 p.m.	teach math
3:00 p.m.	read stories
5:00 p.m.	cook pasta

(1) At 2 p.m., Paul will teach _____

_____ .

(2) At 3 p.m., Paul will read _____

_____ Amy.

(3) At 5 p.m., Paul will cook _____

_____ Amy.

Recall My Memory

Answers p.16

다음 문장이 어법상 맞으면 O표, **틀리면** 바르게 고치시오.

01 The man looked a bear. ➲ p. 118

02 Please pass the butter me. ➲ p. 120

03 What tall boy he is! ➲ p. 108

04 Is your brother and sister at home now? ➲ p. 20

05 Where didn't you go camping? – Because I was sick. ➲ p. 104

06 The oven is hot. You don't have to touch it. ➲ p. 92

07 Brian put the soccer ball in the box yesterday. ➲ p. 76

08 These aren't my pens. Are these yours? ➲ p. 58

09 Your son likes tomatoes, does he? ➲ p. 108

10 Two woman are playing badminton. ➲ p. 44

11 The roses in the room smell well. ➲ p. 118

12 He didn't drink milk this morning. ➲ p. 34

13 Do you have some brothers or sisters? ➲ p. 62

14 Was there a pool at the hotel? ➲ p. 106

15 She made a pretty dress to me. ➲ p. 120

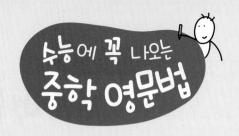

point **1**

🔗 Chapter 5

문맥상 알맞은 시제의 쓰임

The show opens(→ **opened**) in 1996. › 고1 연합
그 공연은 1996년에 시작되었다.

• 시제는 시간이나 빈도를 나타내는 부사(구)와 연관이 있는 경우가 많다.

시제	동사의 형태	쓰임	함께 쓰이는 부사(구)
현재	동사의 현재형	현재의 상태나 성질, 반복되는 일이나 습관, 일반적인 사실이나 변하지 않는 진리	every ~, always, usually, often, sometimes, never 등
과거	동사의 과거형	과거에 일어난 일이나 과거의 상태, 역사적 사실	yesterday, last ~, ~ ago, 「in + 연도」 등
미래	will + 동사원형 be going to + 동사원형	앞으로 일어날 일	tomorrow, tonight, next ~, in the future, soon 등
현재진행	am/are/is + 동사원형-ing	바로 지금 진행되고 있는 일	now, right now, at this time 등
과거진행	was/were + 동사원형-ing	과거의 어떤 순간에 진행되고 있었던 일	then, at that time 등

point **2**

🔗 Chapter 8

목적어가 필요하지 않은 동사 vs. 목적어가 필요한 동사

In America, a host [sits / **seats**] diners. › 고1 연합
미국에서는 호스트가 손님들에게 자리를 안내해 준다.

• 동사 뒤에 목적어가 있는지 없는지에 따라 쓸 수 있는 동사가 다르다.
• 형태나 의미가 비슷한 동사들은 혼동하기 쉬우므로 알아두어야 한다.

목적어가 필요하지 않은 동사		목적어가 필요한 동사	
lie	눕다, 놓여 있다 과거 lay | 과거분사 lain | 현재분사 lying	lay	눕히다, 놓다 과거 laid | 과거분사 laid | 현재분사 laying
rise	오르다, 일어나다 과거 rose | 과거분사 risen | 현재분사 rising	raise	올리다, 일으키다, 키우다 과거 raised | 과거분사 raised | 현재분사 raising
sit	앉다 과거 sat | 과거분사 sat | 현재분사 sitting	seat	앉히다 과거 seated | 과거분사 seated | 현재분사 seating

point **3**

🔗 Chapter 8

주격보어 자리에는 형용사 YES, 부사 NO!

They can feel [**safe** / safely]. › 고1 연합
그들은 안전함을 느낄 수 있다.

• 주격보어 자리에 형용사는 올 수 있지만, 부사는 절대로 올 수 없다.
• 다음 동사들은 주격보어로 형용사를 가진다.
  - 감각동사 look, sound, smell, taste, feel
  - '~이 되다, ~해지다'라는 의미의 become, turn, get 등
  - '~이다'라는 의미의 be동사
  - '~인 채로 있다'라는 의미의 stay 등

---

host ⑲ (식당에서 손님 자리를 배정하는) 호스트, 주인   diner ⑲ 식사하는 사람[손님]

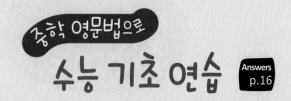

수능 기초 연습 ^{Answers} p.16

A 괄호 안에서 알맞은 말을 고르시오.

1 My uniform looked [perfect / perfectly]. ▸ 고2 학업성취도

2 Last night, a fire [breaks / broke] out in a house. ▸ 고1 연합

3 All the students feel [equal / equally]. ▸ 고1 연합

4 Namibia, Botswana and Zimbabwe [lay / lie] to the north of South Africa. ▸ 고1 연합

5 It was snowing this morning. I [listen / listened] to the radio next to my bed. ▸ 고1 연합

B 밑줄 친 부분이 어법상 맞으면 ○표, 틀리면 바르게 고치시오.

1 Flowers look <u>prettily</u>. ▸ 고1 연합

2 One day I <u>was giving</u> a lecture in New York. ▸ 고1 학업성취도

3 Stores stay <u>open</u> 24 hours a day. ▸ 고1 연합

4 I moved to a new city, and I <u>joined</u> the company baseball team. ▸ 고1 연합

5 Your group and the other group are <u>seating</u> across from each other. ▸ 수능

C 다음 글의 밑줄 친 부분 중, 어법상 <u>틀린</u> 것은? (바르게 고칠 것) ▸ 고1 연합

This picture is twenty years old. I ① <u>am holding</u> a balloon. My father is next to me. He looks ② <u>good</u> in his striped jacket. My mother is next to him. She is wearing hanbok. She ③ <u>is liking</u> to wear it. What a nice family picture!

A perfect ⑱ 완벽한 break out 발생하다 equal ⑱ 동등한, 평등한   B lecture ⑲ 강연, 강의   C striped ⑱ 줄무늬가 있는

수능 독해 적용

Answers p.16

I (A), (B), (C)의 각 네모 안에서 어법에 맞는 표현으로 가장 적절한 것은?

Do you want to (A) rise / raise your English score? Then, write down each new word and look up its meaning in a dictionary. What is its meaning in the story? Sometimes there are many meanings. Study the other meanings. You can also study the other word forms. For example, the word 'pretty' is an adjective. It is also an adverb. As an adverb, it means 'quite' or 'very.' I (B) started / was starting doing this two years ago. It really works. I feel (C) confident / confidently in English now.

	(A)		(B)		(C)
①	rise	⋯⋯	started	⋯⋯	confident
②	rise	⋯⋯	was starting	⋯⋯	confidently
③	raise	⋯⋯	started	⋯⋯	confident
④	raise	⋯⋯	was starting	⋯⋯	confident
⑤	raise	⋯⋯	started	⋯⋯	confidently

2 다음 글의 밑줄 친 부분 중, 어법상 틀린 것은? (바르게 고칠 것) › 고1 연합

On April 6, 1976, I ① was born with no arms and no legs. My father didn't ② show me to my mother right away. After one month, she ③ can see me at last. My father was worried about her. However, she saw me for the first time and said, "④ How cute you are!" She ⑤ looked so happy. My parents were different from other parents. They didn't hide me from people. They took me out with them all the time.

3 (A), (B), (C)의 각 네모 안에서 어법에 맞는 표현으로 가장 적절한 것은? ▸ 고1 연합

Long ago, a great civilization (A) raised / arose in Central America and southern Mexico. This was the Maya civilization. The Maya people had big cities with pyramids. The Maya civilization ended around 1300 AD. The Maya people weren't able (B) rebuild / to rebuild it. Their civilization passed away and left only huge pyramids behind. They tell us, "A great civilization once (C) lives / lived here."

(A)		(B)		(C)
① raised	······	rebuild	······	lives
② raised	······	to rebuild	······	lived
③ raised	······	rebuild	······	lived
④ arose	······	to rebuild	······	lived
⑤ arose	······	rebuild	······	lives

---

1 write down ~을 적다 look up (사전 등에서) ~을 찾다 dictionary 명 사전 form 명 형태 adjective 명 형용사 adverb 명 부사 quite 부 꽤, 상당히 work 동 효과가 있다 confident 형 자신감 있는

2 be born 태어나다 right away 즉시, 곧바로 at last 마침내, 드디어 for the first time 처음으로 be different from ~와 다르다 hide 동 숨기다(-hid-hidden) take ~ out ~를 데리고 나가다 all the time 항상

3 civilization 명 문명 arise 동 생기다, 발생하다(-arose-arisen) around 부 약, ~쯤 rebuild 동 다시 세우다 (-rebuilt-rebuilt) pass away 없어지다, 사라지다 leave ~ behind ~을 남기다 huge 형 거대한

Chapter

동사인 듯 동사 아닌
동사 같은 너,

to부정사와 동명사

Unit
01 명사처럼 쓰이는 to부정사

Unit
02 형용사, 부사처럼 쓰이는 to부정사

Unit
03 명사처럼 쓰이는 동명사

Unit 01 명사처럼 쓰이는 to부정사

부정사는 품사가 정해지지 않았다는 의미로, 동사원형 앞에 to를 붙인 형태를 'to부정사'라고 한다. to부정사는 동사처럼 뒤에 목적어나 보어, 수식어가 이어질 수 있지만, 문장에서 동사가 아닌 명사, 형용사, 부사의 역할을 한다. 그중 명사 역할을 하는 to부정사는 문장에서 주어, 목적어, 보어로 쓰인다.

A 주어 역할

a **To watch** the Olympic Games *is* fun.
  _{주어}

  → **It** is fun **to watch** the Olympic Games.
  _{가짜 주어} _{진짜 주어}

b **To save** energy *is* important.

  → **It** is important **to save** energy.

주어로 쓰여 '~하는 것은'이라는 의미를 나타내며, 3인칭 단수로 취급하여 단수 동사를 쓴다.

☑ to부정사가 주어일 때 주어 자리에 It을 쓰고 to부정사를 문장 뒤로 보내는 것이 자연스럽다. It은 가짜 주어이므로 해석하지 않는다.

B 목적어 역할

a I want **to play** basketball.

b My family is planning **to visit** Busan.

c She decided **not to see** him any more.

동사의 목적어로 쓰여 '~하는 것을'이라는 의미를 나타낸다.

☑ to부정사의 부정형은 to 앞에 not이나 never를 써서 '~하지 않는 것'의 의미를 나타낸다.

to부정사를 목적어로 가지는 동사

동사 want, hope, wish, plan, decide, need, promise, learn, agree 등 뒤에 다른 동사가 목적어로 올 때 to부정사 형태로 쓴다.

I need **to see** a doctor.

She promised **to come** early.

C 보어 역할

a My dream *is* **to become** a soccer player.

b Sam's goal *is* **to be** healthy.

be동사 뒤에 쓰여 '~하는 것(이다)'의 의미를 나타내며, 주어가 무엇인지 설명해 준다.

vocabulary ---------- A save ⑧ 절약하다 B any more 더 이상 agree ⑧ 동의하다 C goal ⑲ 목표 healthy ⑱ 건강한

Answers
p.17

A 밑줄 친 부분이 문장에서 주어, 목적어, 보어 중 어떤 역할을 하는지 쓰시오.

1 She wants <u>to be</u> a scientist.   _____

2 <u>To see</u> is to believe.   _____

3 His dream is <u>to travel</u> to Africa.   _____

4 It is difficult <u>to live</u> without the Internet.   _____

5 I'm planning <u>to go</u> hiking this weekend.   _____

B 어법상 틀린 부분에 밑줄을 긋고 바르게 고치시오.

1 It is wrong tell a lie.   _____

2 They need buying a laptop.   _____

3 My wish is to going to Universal Studios.   _____

4 This is not easy to keep a pet.   _____

5 He decided to not play computer games.   _____

C 우리말과 일치하도록 괄호 안의 말을 이용하여 문장을 완성하시오.

1 우리는 너를 다시 만나기를 바란다. (hope, see)

　　→ We _____ _____ _____ you again.

2 내 계획은 올해 스페인어를 배우는 것이다. (learn)

　　→ My plan _____ _____ _____ Spanish this year.

3 드럼을 연주하는 것은 재미있다. (play)

　　→ _____ is interesting _____ _____ the drums.

4 나는 TV를 보지 않기로 약속했다. (promise, watch)

　　→ I _____ _____ _____ _____ TV.

02 형용사, 부사처럼 쓰이는 to부정사

A 형용사처럼 쓰이는 to부정사

명사나 대명사를 뒤에서 꾸며 주며, '~하는, ~할'이라는 의미를 나타낸다.

a It's time **to go** to school.

b I want something **to drink**.

cf. She needs a chair **to sit on**.

May I have some paper **to write on**?

a 명사 수식

b 대명사 수식

cf. 수식을 받는 (대)명사가 to부정사 뒤에 오는 전치사의 목적어일 때 전치사를 빠뜨리지 않도록 주의한다.

B 부사처럼 쓰이는 to부정사

동사, 형용사 등을 꾸며 주며, 문맥에 따라 목적, 감정의 원인, 결과 등 여러 가지 의미를 나타낸다.

1 목적

a I will go to the store **to buy** milk.

b Ann exercises **to lose** weight.

cf. Ann exercises **in order to lose** weight.

1 '~하기 위해'라는 의미로 동작의 목적을 나타내며, 부사적 의미 중 가장 많이 쓰인다.

cf. 목적의 의미를 더 분명히 나타낼 때는 「in order to + 동사원형」으로 바꿔 쓸 수 있다.

2 감정의 원인

a They were *happy* **to see** me.

b I'm *sorry* **to bother** you.

2 '~해서 (…한)'이라는 의미로, 감정을 나타내는 형용사 뒤에 쓰여 감정을 느끼게 된 원인을 나타낸다.

☑ 감정을 나타내는 형용사: happy, glad, sad, sorry, surprised 등

3 결과

a The boy grew up **to be** a famous actor.

b My grandfather lived **to be** 90 years old.

3 '(그래서, 그 결과) ~하다'라는 의미로, 주로 grow up, live 등의 동사 뒤에 쓰여 결과의 의미를 나타낸다.

vocabulary ⋯⋯⋯⋯ **B** lose weight 체중을 줄이다, 살을 빼다 bother ⑧ 귀찮게 하다 grow up 자라다

Exercise

Answers p.17

A 자연스러운 문장이 되도록 알맞게 연결하시오.

1 I will grow up • • a to drink.

2 We are very sorry • • b to be an artist.

3 She bought a dress • • c to hear the news.

4 They want something • • d to play with his son.

5 He came home early • • e to wear for the party.

B 어법상 틀린 부분에 밑줄을 긋고 바르게 고치시오.

1 I'm happy to being here. _____

2 There is a sofa to sit. _____

3 He went to Italy in order study music. _____

4 I have many friends help me. _____

5 Students study hard for get good grades. _____

C 우리말과 일치하도록 괄호 안의 말을 이용하여 문장을 완성하시오.

1 집에 먹을 것이 있니? (eat, something)

→ Do you have _____ _____ _____ at home?

2 나는 너를 다시 만나서 기쁘다. (glad, see)

→ I'm _____ _____ _____ you again.

3 그들은 배드민턴을 하기 위해 공원에 갔다. (play, badminton)

→ They went to the park _____ _____ _____.

4 나의 삼촌은 살 집을 지었다. (live, a house)

→ My uncle built _____ _____ _____ _____

_____.

Unit 03 명사처럼 쓰이는 동명사

동사원형에 -ing를 붙인 형태를 '동명사'라고 한다. 항상 「동사원형 + -ing」 형태이며, 뒤에 목적어나 보어, 수식어가 이어질 수 있다. 동명사는 명사처럼 쓰여 문장에서 주어, 목적어, 보어 역할을 한다.

A 주어 역할

a **Learning** English *is* fun.

b **Making** sandwiches *is* easy.

주어로 쓰여 '~하는 것은'이라는 의미를 나타내며, 3인칭 단수로 취급하여 단수 동사를 쓴다.

B 목적어 역할

a I finished **painting** a picture.

b He enjoys **not doing** anything on holiday.

c Thank you *for* **inviting** me.

동사나 전치사의 목적어로 쓰여 '~하는 것을'이라는 의미를 나타낸다.

☑ 동명사의 부정형은 동명사 앞에 not이나 never를 써서 '~하지 않는 것'의 의미를 나타낸다.

동명사를 목적어로 가지는 동사

동사 finish, enjoy, stop, keep, practice, mind, quit, avoid, give up 등은 뒤에 다른 동사가 목적어로 올 때 동명사 형태로 쓴다.

Suji stopped **talking** to me.

cf. Suji stopped **to talk** to me. 목적(~하기 위해)을 나타내는 to부정사의 부사적 쓰임

동명사와 to부정사를 모두 목적어로 가지는 동사들도 있는데 like, love, hate, start, begin 등이 대표적이다.

I like **listening** to music. = I like **to listen** to music.

C 보어 역할

a My hobby *is* **making** model airplanes.

b Her job *is* **designing** shoes.

cf. She is designing shoes.

　　　주어　동사(현재진행형)　목적어

be동사 뒤에 쓰여 '~하는 것(이다)'의 의미를 나타내며, 주어가 무엇인지 설명해 준다.

cf. '~하는 것(이다)'로 해석되면 동명사, '~하고 있다, ~하는 중이다'로 해석되면 진행형으로 쓰인 것이다.

D 자주 쓰이는 동명사 표현

a I will **go fishing** with my father.

b **How[What] about going** to the movies?

a go -ing: ~하러 가다

b How[What] about -ing?: ~하는 게 어때?

- be busy -ing: ~하느라 바쁘다
- look forward to -ing: ~하기를 고대하다
- spend + 시간[돈] + -ing: ~하는 데 시간[돈]을 쓰다
- feel like -ing: ~하고 싶다

---

vocabulary ----------

B invite 동 초대하다　mind 동 상관하다, 언짢아하다　quit 동 그만두다(-quit-quit)　avoid 동 피하다

C model airplane 모형 비행기

Exercise

Answers p.17

A 밑줄 친 부분이 문장에서 주어, 목적어, 보어 중 어떤 역할을 하는지 쓰시오.

1 I don't mind <u>waiting</u> for you.

2 <u>Exercising</u> regularly is a good habit.

3 She is good at <u>speaking</u> English.

4 Dad stopped <u>smoking</u> for his health.

5 His hobby is <u>collecting</u> Star Wars toys.

B 밑줄 친 부분이 어법상 맞으면 ○표, 틀리면 바르게 고치시오.

1 It started <u>to rain</u> in the morning.

2 Brushing your teeth <u>are</u> important.

3 Did you finish <u>to wash</u> the dishes?

4 I'm looking forward <u>to see</u> the singer.

5 People enjoy <u>working not</u> on weekends.

C 우리말과 일치하도록 괄호 안의 말을 이용하여 문장을 완성하시오.

1 나는 내일 기타 치는 것을 연습할 것이다. (practice, play)

　　→ I will ＿＿＿＿＿＿＿ ＿＿＿＿＿＿＿ the guitar tomorrow.

2 그녀의 직업은 학생들을 가르치는 것이다. (teach)

　　→ Her job ＿＿＿＿＿＿＿ ＿＿＿＿＿＿＿ students.

3 독서는 모든 사람에게 좋다. (read)

　　→ ＿＿＿＿＿＿＿ ＿＿＿＿＿＿＿ good for everyone.

4 Tyler는 시험공부하느라 바쁘다. (busy, study)

　　→ Tyler ＿＿＿＿＿＿＿ ＿＿＿＿＿＿＿ ＿＿＿＿＿＿＿ for the exam.

Writing Practice

Answers p.17

A 우리말과 일치하도록 괄호 안의 말을 바르게 배열하시오. (필요하면 형태를 바꿀 것)

01 그는 빨래를 끝냈다. (washing, finished, the clothes)

→ He _____ .

02 나는 쓸 종이가 필요하다. (write, need, on, paper, to)

→ I _____ .

03 그들은 뱀을 보고 놀랐다. (see, surprised, were, a snake, to)

→ They _____ .

04 그녀의 계획은 휴가를 토론토에서 보내는 것이다. (spend, is, the holidays, to)

→ Her plan _____ in Toronto.

05 나는 남동생과 싸우지 않기로 결심했다. (fight, to, decided, not)

→ I _____ with my brother.

06 우리는 다음 주말에 캠핑 가기를 고대하고 있다. (go, looking, to, camping, forward)

→ We are _____ next weekend.

07 잠시 기다려 주겠니? (wait, mind, for a minute)

→ Do you _____ ?

08 그는 음악을 듣기 위해 라디오를 켰다. (listen to, music, the radio, turned on)

→ He _____ .

09 너는 마실 물을 좀 원하니? (want, drink, some water)

→ Do you _____ ?

10 규칙적으로 운동하는 것이 중요하다. (important, it, exercise, is)

→ _____ regularly.

B 우리말과 일치하도록 괄호 안의 말을 이용하여 문장을 완성하시오.

01 a 나는 영화 보는 것을 즐긴다. (enjoy, watch)

→ I _____ movies.

b 내 취미는 영화를 보는 것이다.

→ My hobby _____.

02 a 우리는 쉬는 것을 그만두었다. (stop, take)

→ We _____ a break.

b 우리는 쉬기 위해 멈추었다.

→ _____

03 a 나는 일찍 일어나야 한다. (need, get up)

→ I _____ early.

b 나는 계속 일찍 일어난다. (keep)

→ _____

04 a 사야 할 옷들이 있다. (clothes, buy)

→ There are _____.

b 그녀는 옷들을 사서 기분이 좋다. (happy)

→ She is _____.

05 a 그는 우주 비행사가 되고 싶어 한다. (want, become)

→ He _____ an astronaut.

b 그의 꿈은 우주 비행사가 되는 것이다.

→ His dream _____.

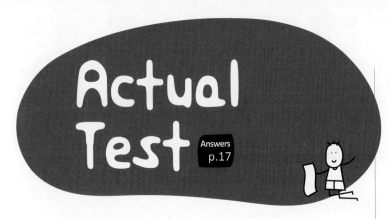

Actual Test

Answers p.17

[01~02] 빈칸에 들어갈 말로 알맞은 것을 고르시오.

01

| What about _____ out for dinner tonight? |

① go　　② went　　③ gone
④ going　　⑤ will go

02

| Mina decided _____ to go to bed late. |

① no　　② none　　③ don't
④ never　　⑤ doesn't

[03~04] 빈칸에 들어갈 말로 알맞지 <u>않은</u> 것을 고르시오.

03

| I _____ to visit my grandmother with my family. |

① want　　② plan　　③ hope
④ avoid　　⑤ like

04

| I _____ doing my homework. |

① like　　② love　　③ wished
④ stopped　　⑤ gave up

05 서술형

두 문장의 의미가 같도록 빈칸에 알맞은 말을 쓰시오.

| To study English is really fun. |

→ _____ is really fun _____ _____ English.

06

밑줄 친 부분이 어법상 틀린 것은? (바르게 고칠 것)

① My job is <u>to teach</u> English.
② Does he need a chair <u>to sit on</u>?
③ I will start <u>jogging</u> from tomorrow.
④ Do you mind <u>opening</u> the door?
⑤ To know you <u>are</u> to love you.

07 서술형

대화의 빈칸에 들어갈 말을 괄호 안의 말을 바르게 배열하여 쓰시오.

| A: Hi, Jisu. What are you going to do this weekend?
B: _____
A: Sounds good. |

→ _____

(am, to, Jeju Island, I, planning, visit)

08

빈칸에 들어갈 말이 순서대로 짝지어진 것은?

| • Thank you for _____ us.
• I am interested in _____. |

① invite – to cook　　② invite – cooking
③ inviting – cook　　④ inviting – to cook
⑤ inviting – cooking

09

대화의 밑줄 친 부분이 어법상 틀린 것은? (바르게 고칠 것)

> A: Charlie, ① wake up! It's time ② to go to school.
> B: Mom, please. Five more ③ minutes.
> A: Sorry ④ for wake you up, but you must not ⑤ be late for school.
> B: Okay, Mom.

[10~11] 우리말과 일치하도록 괄호 안의 말을 이용하여 문장을 완성하시오.

10 서술형

> 나는 건강해지기 위해서 운동을 할 것이다.
> (exercise, be)

→ I will ＿＿＿＿＿ ＿＿＿＿＿ ＿＿＿＿＿ healthy.

11 서술형

> 나는 내 친구들과 함께 수영하러 갈 것이다. (go, swim)

→ I will ＿＿＿＿＿ ＿＿＿＿＿ with my friends.

12

다음 문장에서 not이 들어가기에 알맞은 곳은?

> I (①) decided (②) to (③) leave (④) my (⑤) hometown.

[13~14] 밑줄 친 부분의 쓰임이 보기와 같은 것을 고르시오.

13

| 보기 | Amy needed <u>to get</u> some rest. |

① I promised <u>to do</u> my best.
② His goal is <u>to pass</u> the exam.
③ It is important <u>to use</u> your time wisely.
④ My dream is <u>to become</u> a painter.
⑤ It is exciting <u>to ride</u> a roller coaster.

14

| 보기 | I have lots of work <u>to do</u>. |

① I have no money <u>to spend</u>.
② It is necessary <u>to save</u> water.
③ My hobby is <u>to listen</u> to music.
④ The king lived <u>to be</u> 80 years old.
⑤ She was happy <u>to see</u> her old friends.

15 서술형

그림을 보고, 괄호 안의 말을 이용하여 문장을 완성하시오.

→ The boy wants ＿＿＿＿＿＿＿＿＿ ＿＿＿＿＿＿＿. (something, drink)

16

밑줄 친 부분과 바꿔 쓸 수 있는 것은?

Jinsu went to the bookstore to buy some books.

① in order to buy some books
② in order buying some books
③ on order to buy some books
④ in orders to buy some books
⑤ on order to buying some books

17

빈칸에 전치사를 쓸 필요가 없는 것은?

① She has a house to live _____.
② There is no water to drink _____.
③ Do you have a pen to write _____?
④ We have many things to talk _____.
⑤ Give your puppy a toy to play _____.

18

밑줄 친 부분의 쓰임이 나머지 넷과 다른 것은?

① My job is driving a bus.
② My friend is helping me.
③ My goal is buying a house.
④ My dream is being a musician.
⑤ My hobby is collecting stamps.

19

밑줄 친 부분이 어법상 틀린 것은? (바르게 고칠 것)

①Planting many ②trees ③are good ④for ⑤the environment.

20

다음 문장을 우리말로 바르게 해석한 것은?

The girl grew up to be a scientist.

① 그 소녀는 자라서 과학자가 되었다.
② 그 소녀는 과학자로 자라서 기뻤다.
③ 그 소녀는 과학자로 성장하고 있었다.
④ 그 소녀는 과학자가 되는 것이 꿈이었다.
⑤ 그 소녀는 과학자가 되기 위해 노력했다.

21 서술형

괄호 안의 말을 이용하여 대화의 빈칸에 알맞은 말을 쓰시오.

A: Did you _____ _____ your room? (finish, clean)
B: Of course, Mom.

22

다음 중 어법상 틀린 것은? (바르게 고칠 것)

① Did you practice dancing?
② I really hate to say goodbye.
③ Learning Chinese is interesting.
④ Are you trying to quit to smoke?
⑤ She enjoys not doing anything on Sundays.

23

빈칸에 공통으로 들어갈 수 있는 말로 알맞은 것은?

• Do you _____ to cook?
• I _____ playing the violin.

① like
② keep
③ want
④ enjoy
⑤ finish

24

대화의 밑줄 친 부분과 쓰임이 다른 것은?

> A: Sam, are you glad to see your cousin again?
> B: Yes, Mom. I want to play soccer with him.

① I am sorry to miss the club meeting.
② You will be surprised to see me.
③ He was excited to hear the news.
④ The doctor was sad to lose a patient.
⑤ It was difficult to solve the problem.

25 서술형

다음 대화에서 문맥상 어색한 부분을 찾아 바르게 고치시오.

> A: Please stop to bother me. I'm studying now.
> B: Oh, I'm so sorry.

_____ → _____

26

다음 중 영어 문장을 잘못 해석한 것은?

① I promised to wash my dad's car.
   → 나는 아빠의 차를 세차하기로 약속했다.
② I went to the library to borrow some books.
   → 나는 책을 좀 빌리러 도서관에 갔다.
③ Their job is selling vegetables.
   → 그들의 직업은 채소를 판매하는 것이다.
④ He wishes to send this message.
   → 그는 이 메시지를 보내기를 원한다.
⑤ She has a book to read.
   → 그녀는 독서를 하기 위해서 책을 가지고 있다.

27

다음 중 어법상 옳은 것은? (틀린 것들을 바르게 고칠 것)

① Their children began to walking.
② I hope to learn another language.
③ Drawing pictures are my hobby.
④ Don't worry about make mistakes.
⑤ To know all be to forgive all.

28 서술형

다음 문장을 보기와 같이 바꿔 쓰시오.

> 보기 Mike is good at badminton. (play)
>   → Mike is good at playing badminton.

> You don't have to be afraid of the dog. (play with)

→ _____

_____

29 서술형

다음 글에서 어법상 틀린 부분을 모두 찾아 바르게 고치시오.

> Having good relationships with friends is very important. To getting along well with friends, first we need to start talking to them. Second, listen to your friends carefully. Third, try to be nice to them. Fourth, helping each other is very important, too. Finally, it is necessary to spend time together. Keep to do these and enjoy your school life.

Recall My Memory

Answers p.18

다음 문장이 어법상 맞으면 ○표, <u>틀리면</u> 바르게 고치시오.

01   The actor enjoys to watch musicals.   ⤵ p. 138

02   They have a lot of things to do.   ⤵ p. 136

03   Mr. Kim teaches science for us.   ⤵ p. 120

04   She sends us some potatoes yesterday.   ⤵ p. 76

05   I am happy to hearing from you.   ⤵ p. 136

06   This sweater looks warm and softly.   ⤵ p. 118

07   That is dangerous to play with fire.   ⤵ p. 134

08   I played drums at the school festival.   ⤵ p. 48

09   My father and I am cleaning the living room now.   ⤵ p. 80

10   He is looking forward to meet my sister.   ⤵ p. 138

11   The baby is able to walk well.   ⤵ p. 90

12   Chris were sad to leave his friends.   ⤵ p. 18

13   How early you get up!   ⤵ p. 108

14   My hobby is write poems.   ⤵ p. 134, 138

15   What is your favorite subject, history or social studies?   ⤵ p. 102

말과 글을 살찌우는

형용사와 부사

Unit 01   형용사

Unit 02   부사

Unit 03   원급, 비교급, 최상급

Unit 01 형용사

A 형용사의 쓰임

형용사는 사람이나 사물의 상태, 성질 등을 나타내는 말로, 명사나 대명사를 꾸며 주거나 주어를 자세히 설명해 준다.

1 (대)명사를 꾸며 주는 역할

a BTS is a **famous** boy band.

b Let's do something **special** for her.

2 주어를 설명해 주는 역할

a The game was **exciting**.

b My socks smelled **terrible**.

c The light turned **green**.

1 형용사는 보통 명사를 앞에서 꾸며 주지만, -thing, -body, -one으로 끝나는 대명사는 뒤에서 꾸며 준다.

2 be동사, 감각동사(look, smell, sound, taste, feel), '~이 되다, ~해지다라는 의미의 become, turn, get 등의 동사 뒤에 쓰여 주어의 상태나 성질을 설명해 준다.

B 수와 양을 나타내는 형용사

명사 앞에서 명사의 수나 양을 나타내며, 뒤에 오는 명사의 종류에 따라 쓰이는 형용사가 다르다.

1 수를 나타내는 형용사

a He doesn't have **many** friends.

b I have **a few** friends.

c She has **few** friends.

2 양을 나타내는 형용사

a He doesn't need **much** money.

b I need **a little** money.

c She needs **little** money.

3 수와 양을 모두 나타내는 형용사

a We ate **a lot of**[**lots of**] cookies.

b They ate **a lot of**[**lots of**] bread.

1 셀 수 있는 명사의 복수형 앞에 쓴다.

a many: 많은, 다수의

b a few: 조금 있는, 약간의

c few: 거의 없는

2 셀 수 없는 명사 앞에 쓴다.

a much: 많은, 다량의

b a little: 조금 있는, 약간의

c little: 거의 없는

3 a lot of와 lots of는 '많은'이라는 의미로, 셀 수 있는 명사와 셀 수 없는 명사 앞에 모두 쓸 수 있다.

많은	many	+ 셀 수 있는 명사의 복수형	much	+ 셀 수 없는 명사
	a lot of[lots of]		a lot of[lots of]	
조금 있는, 약간의	a few		a little	
거의 없는	few		little	

vocabulary .... A special 휑 특별한   exciting 휑 신나는, 흥미진진한   terrible 휑 지독한   light 몡 신호등

A 괄호 안에서 알맞은 말을 고르시오.

1 I bought [a few / a little] color pencils.

2 His idea is [interest / interesting].

3 I want to drink [something cold / cold something].

4 There aren't [many / much] people in the street.

B 그림을 보고, 빈칸에 알맞은 형용사를 보기에서 골라 쓴 후, 그 형용사가 (대)명사를 꾸며 주는지, 주어를 설명해 주는지를 쓰시오.

| 보기 | slow | fun | popular | lovely |

1 Mary is a _____ girl. _____

2 The turtle is very _____. _____

3 The singer became _____. _____

4 There isn't anything _____ on TV. _____

C 빈칸에 알맞은 말을 보기에서 골라 쓰시오. (한 번씩만 쓸 것)

| 보기 | few | a few | little | a little | a lot of |

1 I will go out for a walk. I need _____ fresh air.

2 Kate is always happy. She has _____ problems.

3 This cupcake is very sweet. It has _____ sugar in it.

4 Mark has _____ free time. He can't even watch a movie.

5 They want a small wedding. They will invite just _____ friends.

Unit 02 부사

A 부사의 쓰임

부사는 동사, 형용사, 다른 부사, 또는 문장 전체를 꾸며 주어 내용을 풍부하게 해 주는 말이다.

a My teacher smiled **happily**.

b Park Gyeong is **very** smart.

c The news spread **so** quickly.

d **Suddenly**, someone knocked on the door.

a 동사 수식

b 형용사 수식

c 다른 부사 수식

d 문장 전체 수식

B 부사의 형태

a Could you speak **slowly**?

b He found the answer **easily**.

c Bolt can run **fast**. *cf.* Bolt is a **fast** man.

d I **hardly** know him. *cf.* She studies **hard**.

대부분의 부사는 형용사에 -ly를 붙여 만든다.

c 어떤 부사들은 형용사와 형태가 같다.

d 부사에 -ly가 붙어 다른 뜻을 갖는 부사들이 있다.

형용사를 부사로 만드는 법

대부분 형용사의 부사	형용사 + -ly	real → really	slow → slowly	sudden → suddenly
-y로 끝나는 형용사의 부사	y를 i로 바꾸고 + -ly	easy → easily	happy → happily	lucky → luckily
형용사와 형태가 같은 부사	fast(형 빠른) → **fast**(부 빨리)　early(형 이른) → **early**(부 일찍)　late(형 늦은) → **late**(부 늦게) high(형 높은) → **high**(부 높이)　hard(형 어려운, 열심인, 딱딱한) → **hard**(부 열심히)			
「부사 + -ly」가 다른 뜻을 갖는 부사	**hard**(부 열심히) – **hardly**(부 거의 ~ 않다)　　**high**(부 높이) – **highly**(부 매우) **late**(부 늦게) – **lately**(부 최근에)　　**near**(부 가까이) – **nearly**(부 거의)			
예외	good(형 좋은, 잘 된, 괜찮은) → **well**(부 잘) *cf.* well 형 건강한			

cf. -ly로 끝나는 형용사: lovely(사랑스러운), friendly(친절한), lonely(외로운), costly(많은 돈이 드는)

C 빈도를 나타내는 부사

1 빈도부사의 종류

0% ──→ 50% ──→ 70% ──→ 90% ──→ 100%
never　　sometimes　　often　　usually　　always
(결코 ~ 않다)　(가끔)　(자주, 종종)　(보통, 대개)　(항상)

2 빈도부사의 자리

a He **always** wakes up early.

b She is **often** late for school.

c We will **never** eat fast food again.

1 어떤 일이 얼마나 자주 일어나는지를 나타내는 부사를 '빈도부사'라고 한다.

2 빈도부사는 일반동사 앞, be동사나 조동사 뒤에 쓴다.

Exercise

Answers
p.18

A 괄호 안에서 알맞은 말을 고르시오.

1 I stayed up [late / lately] last night.

2 My father can speak Chinese [good / well].

3 That horse runs very [fast / fastly].

4 Mike [sometimes listens / listens sometimes] to classical music.

5 She [is usually / usually is] quiet in school.

B 빈칸에 들어갈 말을 보기에서 골라 알맞은 부사형으로 쓴 후, 그 부사가 꾸며 주는 말에 밑줄을 그으시오. (한 번씩만 쓸 것)

보기	lucky	hard	real	heavy	near

1 I will study _____ for the exam.

2 The food smells _____ good.

3 _____, the firefighters put out the fire quickly.

4 It rained _____ yesterday.

5 The desert is _____ always hot and dry.

C 괄호 안의 말을 알맞은 곳에 넣어 문장을 다시 쓰시오.

1 I help my father in the kitchen. (often)

→ _____

2 Daniel is very friendly. (usually)

→ _____

3 Cindy tells a lie. (never)

→ _____

4 You should wear a helmet. (always)

→ _____

 **원급, 비교급, 최상급**

형용사나 부사의 형태를 원급, 비교급, 최상급으로 바꾸어 둘 이상의 사람이나 사물의 상태, 성질 등의 정도를 비교할 수 있다.

A 원급

원급은 둘을 비교하여 정도가 같음을 나타낼 때 쓰는 형용사나 부사의 원래 형태이다.

a My little brother is **as tall as** me.

b Jimin dances **as well as** Daniel.

「as + 원급 + as」로 '~만큼 …한/하게'의 의미를 나타낸다.

B 비교급

비교급은 둘을 비교하여 정도의 차이를 나타낼 때 쓰는 형용사나 부사의 형태이다.

a Sam's dog is **bigger than** yours.

b Math is **more difficult than** science for me.

c Hot water freezes **faster than** cold water.

cf. Fried chicken is **much[very] tastier than** pizza.

「비교급 + than」으로 '~보다 더 …한/하게'의 의미를 나타낸다.

cf. 비교급 앞에 much, even, still, far, a lot 등을 쓰면 '~보다 훨씬 더 …한/하게'의 의미가 된다. very는 쓸 수 없음에 주의한다.

C 최상급

최상급은 셋 이상을 비교하여 정도가 가장 최고임을 나타낼 때 쓰는 형용사나 부사의 형태이다.

a Seoul is **the largest** city in Korea.

b Spring is **the most beautiful** season of all.

c The blue whale is **the heaviest** animal on Earth.

「the + 최상급」으로 '가장 ~한/하게'의 의미를 나타낸다.

비교급과 최상급 만드는 법

대부분의 형용사/부사	원급 + -er/-est	fast – fast**er** – fast**est**	tall – tall**er** – tall**est**
-e로 끝나는 형용사/부사	원급 + -r/-st	large – larger – largest	nice – nicer – nicest
「단모음 + 단자음」으로 끝나는 형용사/부사	마지막 자음을 한 번 더 쓰고 + -er/-est	big – big**ger** – big**gest** sad – sad**der** – sad**dest**	hot – hot**ter** – hot**test** thin – thin**ner** – thin**nest**
「자음 + y」로 끝나는 형용사/부사	y를 i로 바꾸고 + -er/-est	easy – eas**ier** – eas**iest** pretty – prett**ier** – prett**iest**	heavy – heav**ier** – heav**iest** tasty – tast**ier** – tast**iest**
일부 2음절 및 3음절 이상의 형용사/부사	more/most + 원급	famous(2음절: fa/mous) – **more** famous – **most** famous beautiful(3음절: beau/ti/ful) – **more** beautiful – **most** beautiful	
불규칙하게 변하는 형용사/부사	good/well – **better** – **best** many/much – **more** – **most**	bad – **worse** – **worst** little – **less** – **least**	

vocabulary ---------- **B** freeze 동 얼다(-froze-frozen) tasty 형 맛있는 **C** blue whale 흰긴수염고래

A

괄호 안에서 알맞은 말을 고르시오.

1 Janghun is as [strong / stronger] as Hodong.

2 Yura draws pictures [well / better] than me.

3 Turtles live [very / much] longer than rabbits.

4 John is the [taller / tallest] boy in his class.

5 This is the [popularest / most popular] song these days.

B

그림을 보고, 빈칸에 들어갈 말을 보기에서 골라 알맞은 형태로 쓰시오.

보기	thin	good	heavy	expensive

1 Elephants are _____ than pigs.

2 The pink bag is the _____ bag in this shop.

3 The storybook is _____ than the dictionary.

4 My car is as _____ as yours.

C

우리말과 일치하도록 괄호 안의 말을 이용하여 문장을 완성하시오.

1 내 컴퓨터는 Henry의 것만큼 좋다. (nice)

→ My computer is _____ _____ _____ Henry's.

2 이 침대가 저 침대보다 더 편안하다. (comfortable)

→ This bed is _____ _____ _____ that one.

3 오늘이 어제보다 훨씬 더 덥다. (much, hot)

→ Today is _____ _____ _____ yesterday.

4 Ellsa는 우리 학교에서 가장 예쁜 소녀이다. (pretty)

→ Ellsa is _____ _____ girl in our school.

Writing Practice

Answers p.19

A 우리말과 일치하도록 괄호 안의 말을 바르게 배열하시오. (필요하면 형태를 바꿀 것)

01 새 스웨터는 따뜻하다. (new, the, sweater, warm, is)

→ _____

02 그녀는 겨울에 자주 아프다. (often, she, sick, is)

→ _____ in winter.

03 우리는 새로운 무언가를 만들어내야 한다. (something, make, new)

→ We have to _____.

04 나는 내 숙제에 약간의 도움이 필요하다. (little, need, I, a, help)

→ _____ with my homework.

05 호랑이는 사자만큼 빨리 달린다. (a lion, as, runs, a tiger, as, fast)

→ _____

06 스쿨버스는 항상 8시에 도착한다. (arrive, the school bus, always)

→ _____ at eight.

07 나래는 그녀의 학교에서 가장 재미있는 소녀이다. (funny, the, in her school, girl)

→ Narae is _____.

08 상어는 바다에서 매우 위험한 동물이다. (are, sharks, high, animals, dangerous)

→ _____ in the sea.

09 나는 어제 몇 가지 컴퓨터 게임을 했다. (played, I, a, computer game, few)

→ _____ yesterday.

10 건강이 돈보다 훨씬 더 중요하다. (money, is, health, much, than, important)

→ _____

B 우리말과 일치하도록 괄호 안의 말을 이용하여 문장을 완성하시오.

01 a Clara는 훌륭한 바이올린 연주자이다. (wonderful)

→ Clara is a _____ violin player.

b Clara는 바이올린을 훌륭하게 연주한다.

→ Clara plays _____.

02 a 그는 돈이 많지 않다. (money)

→ He doesn't have _____.

b 그는 친구가 많지 않다. (friend)

→ _____

03 a 수박은 사과보다 더 크다. (big)

→ Watermelons are _____ than apples.

b 수박은 농구공만큼 크다. (basketballs)

→ _____

04 a 금요일이 일주일 중 최고의 요일이다. (good)

→ Friday is the _____ day of the week.

b 금요일이 월요일보다 더 좋다. (Monday)

→ _____

05 a 냉장고에 달걀이 거의 없다. (egg)

→ There are _____ in the fridge.

b 냉장고에 우유가 거의 없다. (milk)

→ _____

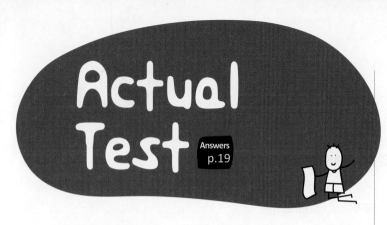

[01~02] 짝지어진 두 단어의 의미 관계가 나머지 넷과 <u>다른</u> 것을 고르시오.

01

① sad – sadly　　② quick – quickly
③ final – finally　　④ friend – friendly
⑤ real – really

02

① wise – wisely　　② slow – slowly
③ high – highly　　④ nice – nicely
⑤ sweet – sweetly

03

빈칸에 들어갈 말로 알맞은 것을 <u>모두</u> 고르면?

| Joe is as _____ as Henry. |

① rich　　　　　② heavier
③ smart　　　　④ more handsome
⑤ most popular

04

빈칸에 들어갈 말로 알맞은 것은?

| Hulk is _____ of all the superheroes. |

① stronger　　　② more strong
③ strongest　　④ the strongest
⑤ the most strong

05

다음 문장에서 nice가 들어가기에 알맞은 곳은?

| She (①) wanted (②) to buy (③) something (④) for her boyfriend (⑤). |

[06~07] 빈칸에 들어갈 말로 알맞지 <u>않은</u> 것을 고르시오.

06

| Amy looks _____. |

① angry　　② kindly　　③ lovely
④ smart　　⑤ lonely

07

| Eric came home _____ earlier than usual. |

① far　　② very　　③ even
④ much　　⑤ a lot

08

밑줄 친 부분이 어법상 <u>틀린</u> 것은? (바르게 고칠 것)
① <u>Luckily</u>, I got a free ticket.
② I made a <u>really</u> big mistake.
③ The girl smiled at me <u>brightly</u>.
④ We can <u>easily</u> win the game.
⑤ My uncle's socks smelled <u>terribly</u>.

09

(A), (B), (C)의 각 네모 안에서 어법에 맞는 표현으로 순서대로 짝지어진 것은?

> Jason went to bed (A)| late / lately | last night. And, he didn't sleep (B)| good / well |. So, he feels (C)| tired / tiredly | now.

① late – good – tired
② lately – good – tiredly
③ late – well – tired
④ lately – well – tired
⑤ late – well – tiredly

[10~11] 두 문장의 의미가 같도록 빈칸에 알맞은 말을 쓰시오.

10 서술형

> My father is a hard worker.

→ My father works _____.

11 서술형

> Lisa is a quick learner.

→ Lisa learns _____.

12

밑줄 친 부분의 쓰임이 나머지 넷과 <u>다른</u> 것은?

① Her face turned <u>red</u>.
② This lemon tastes <u>sour</u>.
③ You look <u>different</u> today.
④ It is a very <u>delicious</u> pie.
⑤ The movie was so <u>exciting</u>.

13

다음 문장에서 sometimes가 들어가기에 알맞은 곳은?

> We (①) can (②) see (③) each other (④) after (⑤) school.

[14~15] 괄호 안의 말을 알맞은 곳에 넣어 문장을 다시 쓰시오.

14 서술형

> Dad is late for work. (never)

→ _____

15 서술형

> Tom comes right home after school. (usually)

→ _____

16 서술형

다음은 민수의 여가활동과 그 빈도를 나타낸 표이다. 표를 보고, 보기와 같이 괄호 안의 말을 이용하여 문장을 완성하시오.

listen to music		100%
play soccer		90%
read books		50%
play the piano		0%

| 보기 | Minsu always listens to music. (always) |

(1) Minsu _____. (sometimes)

(2) Minsu _____. (never)

(3) Minsu _____. (usually)

17

빈칸에 공통으로 들어갈 말로 알맞은 것은?

• There are _____ books in my bag.
• I have _____ work to do.

① many ② much ③ a little
④ a few ⑤ a lot of

18

우리말을 영어로 옮길 때 빈칸에 들어갈 말로 알맞은 것은?

그는 이제 기운이 거의 없다.
→ He has _____ energy now.

① few ② a few ③ little
④ a little ⑤ some

[19~20] 다음 중 어법상 틀린 것을 고르시오. (바르게 고칠 것)

19

① I bought a few apples.
② There are few toys in the box.
③ She put a little sugar in the coffee.
④ He saw a little movies on the weekend.
⑤ There were many children at the park.

20

① I never will forget this day.
② They often go to the park.
③ She is always kind to her students.
④ He sometimes reads comic books.
⑤ I usually go shopping on weekends.

21

대화의 빈칸에 들어갈 말로 알맞은 것은?

A: When did Jane go out?
B: _____ minutes ago.

① Few ② Little ③ Much
④ A few ⑤ A little

22

비교급과 최상급이 잘못 연결된 것은? (바르게 고칠 것)

① little – less – least
② cold – coldder – colddest
③ sad – sadder – saddest
④ tasty – tastier – tastiest
⑤ famous – more famous – most famous

23 서술형

빈칸에 들어갈 말을 괄호 안에서 골라 알맞은 형태로 쓰시오.

Julie is taller than me. I am taller than Lucy.
So, Lucy is _____ than Julie.
(tall / short)

24 서술형

다음 글의 내용과 일치하도록 괄호 안의 말과 최상급을 이용하여 문장을 완성하시오.

There are three kinds of fruits in the store.
Each peach is 2 dollars. Each pear is 3
dollars. Each watermelon is 10 dollars.

→ _____ is _____
fruit in the store. (expensive)

25 서술형

그림을 보고, 괄호 안에서 알맞은 말을 골라 두 과일의 무게를 비교하는 문장을 완성하시오.

→ The orange is _____ the apple.
  (light / heavy)

26

다음 글에서 밑줄 친 부분이 어법상 틀린 것은? (바르게 고칠 것)

My sister, Mina, is ① older than me. She is taller and ② thinner than me. And she is ③ more beautiful than me. But I'm ④ too smarter than she is. And I am ⑤ better at sports than my sister.

27 서술형

다음 중 어법상 틀린 것을 모두 골라 바르게 고치시오.

a. She is as tall as her brother.
b. Brian is the most smart boy in my class.
c. The sun is bigger than the moon.
d. Love is most important thing in life.
e. I feel more healthy than before.
f. My room is cleaner than my brother's.
g. She is even more intelligent than her sister.

[28~29] 우리말과 일치하도록 괄호 안의 말을 이용하여 문장을 완성하시오.

28 서술형

나의 언니는 나보다 책을 더 많이 읽는다.

→ My sister reads _____ books than I do. (many)

29 서술형

농구는 가장 흥미진진한 운동이다.

→ Basketball is _____ sport.
  (exciting)

30 서술형

다음은 Tony와 그 형제들을 비교하는 표이다. 표를 보고, 보기의 말을 이용하여 형제들을 비교하는 글을 완성하시오. (중복 가능)

	Tony	Jake	Peter
age	15	16	18
height	168 cm	175 cm	173 cm
weight	60 kg	60 kg	62 kg

보기	old	tall	heavy

Tony has two brothers, Jake and Peter. As for age, Peter is (1)_____ _____ of the three. As for height, Jake is (2) _____ _____ of the three. As for weight, Tony is (3)_____ _____ _____ Jake. And Peter is (4)_____ _____ of the three.

Recall My Memory

Answers p.20

다음 문장이 어법상 맞으면 ○표, **틀리면** 바르게 고치시오.

01 She gave some food for poor children. → p. 120

02 I can run as fastly as Kevin. → p. 152

03 Drawing cartoons are very interesting to me. → p. 138

04 We were going to travel to Croatia next month. → p. 78

05 He drinks three cups of coffee a day. → p. 46

06 I have a little friends to play with. → p. 148

07 Is there some flowers in the garden? → p. 106

08 A basketball is much bigger than a baseball. → p. 152

09 She must go to the hospital last week. → p. 92

10 He sleeps often in the living room. → p. 150

11 My sisters doesn't want to go to the party. → p. 34

12 Yesterday was coldest day this winter. → p. 152

13 He'll go to the movies tonight, doesn't he? → p. 108

14 I don't have some money in my pocket. → p. 62

15 Can you get me something to drink? → p. 136

나를 이끌어 줘,
명사의 가이드

전치사

Unit 01 **시간을 나타내는 전치사**

Unit 02 **장소를 나타내는 전치사**

Unit 03 **그 밖의 전치사**

Unit 01 시간을 나타내는 전치사

전치사는 '앞에 놓이는 말'이라는 뜻으로, 명사나 대명사, 동명사 앞에 쓰여 시간, 장소, 방법 등을 나타낸다.

A at, on, in

1 at

a I get up **at** 7 o'clock.

b I was having dinner **at** that time.

2 on

a The summer vacation begins **on** July 30th.

b I will go to the amusement park **on** Saturday.

c She sent me a card **on** my birthday.

3 in

a It usually snows a lot **in** January.

b Korea hosted the Winter Olympics **in** 2018.

c We have Chuseok **in** fall.

d What do you usually do **in** the evening?

1 at은 '~에'의 의미로, 구체적인 시각이나 특정한 시점을 나타낼 때 쓴다.

2 on은 '~에'의 의미로, 날짜, 요일, 특정한 날을 나타낼 때 쓴다.

3 in은 '~에'의 의미로, 월, 연도, 계절, 오전, 오후, 저녁 등을 나타낼 때 쓴다.

B before, after

a I must finish the work **before** tonight.

b He always drinks coffee **after** breakfast.

cf. The train will leave **in** 5 minutes.

before는 '~ 전에', after는 '~ 후에'라는 의미이다.

cf. 이때의 in은 '(지금부터) ~ 후에'의 의미이다.

C for, during

a I exercise **for** an hour every day.

b Don't use your phone **during** class.

둘 다 '~ 동안'의 의미이지만, for는 계속된 시간을 나타내는 숫자의 기간 앞에, during은 특정한 기간을 나타내는 명사 앞에 쓴다.

D by, until

a They have to arrive at the airport **by** 6 p.m.

b I studied **until** 11 o'clock yesterday.

둘 다 '~까지'의 의미이지만, by는 어떤 일이 특정 기한까지 끝나는 것을 나타내고, until은 특정 기한까지 계속되는 것을 나타낸다.

vocabulary ----- **A** amusement park 놀이공원 a lot 많이 host ⑧ 주최하다 **B** leave ⑧ 떠나다(-left-left)

A 괄호 안에서 알맞은 말을 고르시오.

1 I was born [on / in] 2005.

2 Americans eat turkey [at / on] Thanksgiving Day.

3 Don't stay up late [at / in] night.

4 We have good weather [on / in] fall.

5 My family will go on a picnic [at / on] Sunday.

6 I will call you back [at / in] ten minutes.

B 빈칸에 알맞은 말을 보기에서 골라 쓰시오. (한 번씩만 쓸 것)

보기	before	after	for	during	by	until

1 I waited for a bus _____ thirty minutes.

2 Bats sleep _____ the day.

3 The concert went on _____ eleven o'clock.

4 You should wash your hands _____ meals.

5 Suho and I will ride our bikes _____ school.

6 You must hand in your homework _____ Monday.

C 빈칸에 알맞은 전치사를 써서 대화를 완성하시오.

1 A: When is your birthday?　　　　　　　B: _____ August eighth.

2 A: How long will you stay there?　　　　B: _____ five days.

3 A: What time do you have breakfast?　　B: _____ seven o'clock.

4 A: When does the rainy season start?　　B: _____ June.

5 A: How long did the party last?　　　　　B: _____ midnight.

Unit 02 장소를 나타내는 전치사

A at, in, on

1 at

a I left my phone **at** home.

b Let's meet **at** the bus stop.

2 in

a The actor lives **in** Los Angeles.

b She put her letters **in** the box.

3 on

a He hung a picture **on** the wall.

b A lamp is **on** the table.

1 at은 '~에'의 의미로, 비교적 좁은 장소나 한 지점을 나타낼 때 쓴다.

2 in은 '~에, ~ 안에'의 의미로, 비교적 넓은 장소나 장소 안에 있음을 나타낼 때 쓴다.

3 on은 '~에, ~ 위에'의 의미로, 표면에 붙어 있는 상태를 나타낼 때 쓴다.

B under, over

a A horse is standing **under** the tree.

b Some birds are flying **over** the tree.

under는 '~ 아래에', over는 '~ 위에'라는 의미로, 둘 다 표면에 붙어 있지 않은 상태를 나타낸다.

C in front of, behind, next to, across from

a There was a bike **in front of** the house.

b You can park **behind** the building.

c May I sit **next to** the window?

d The hotel is **across from** the park.

a in front of: ~ 앞에

b behind: ~ 뒤에

c next to: ~ 옆에(= beside, by)

d across from: ~의 맞은편에[건너편에]

D between A and B, from A to B

a I sat **between** Mina **and** Suho.

b How long does it take **from** Seoul **to** Daegu?

cf. The post office is open **from** 9 a.m. **to** 6 p.m.

a between A and B: A와 B 사이에

b from A to B: A부터 B까지

cf. from A to B는 시간에도 쓸 수 있다.

at

in   on

over
under

in front of   behind
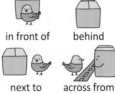
next to   across from

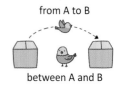
from A to B
between A and B

A 괄호 안에서 알맞은 말을 고르시오.

1 They are lying [in / on] the beach.

2 He first met his wife [at / on] university.

3 We can see wild animals [at / in] Africa.

4 There are a lot of people [at / on] the bus.

5 Students are sitting [in / on] the classroom.

B 그림을 보고, 빈칸에 알맞은 말을 보기에서 골라 쓰시오.

보기	under	over	in front of	next to

1 The plants are _____ the window.

2 The cat is _____ the table.

3 The lamp is _____ the sofa.

4 The clock is _____ the TV.

C 우리말과 일치하도록 괄호 안의 말을 이용하여 문장을 완성하시오.

1 어린 소녀가 문 뒤에 숨었다. (the door)

→ The little girl hid _____ _____ _____.

2 독일은 폴란드와 프랑스 사이에 있다. (Poland, France)

→ Germany is _____ _____ _____ _____.

3 극장은 서점 건너편에 있다. (the bookstore)

→ The theater is _____ _____ _____ _____.

4 그는 공항에서 호텔까지 버스를 탔다. (the airport, the hotel)

→ He took a bus _____ _____ _____

_____ _____.

03 그 밖의 전치사

A with

a Yerim went fishing **with** her father.

b Japanese eat their soup **with** chopsticks.

a (사람과 함께 쓰여) ~와 함께

b (도구와 함께 쓰여) ~을 가지고, ~으로

B by

a Bill goes to school **by** bus.

cf. I go to school **on** foot.

b Please send your homework **by** email.

a (교통수단과 함께 쓰여) ~으로

cf. on foot: 걸어서

b (통신수단과 함께 쓰여) ~으로

C for

a You have to work hard **for** your dream.

b France is famous **for** wine.

c They will leave **for** Canada on Friday.

a ~을 위해[위한]

b (이유·원인을 나타내어) ~ 때문에

c ~을 향해

D about

a Don't worry **about** the test.

b What do you think **about** the movie?

~에 대해

E of

a She is a member **of** a girl group.

b James climbed to the top **of** the mountain.

~의

vocabulary ············ A go fishing 낚시하러 가다   chopsticks ⑲ 젓가락 (한 쌍)   C be famous for ~로[때문에] 유명하다   wine ⑲ 와인, 포도주   E member ⑲ 구성원, 일원   climb ⑧ 오르다   top ⑲ 꼭대기, 정상

Exercise

Answers p.20

A 괄호 안에서 알맞은 말을 고르시오.

1 I ordered pizza [by / with] phone.

2 Can you tell me [for / about] the festival?

3 Sarah played tennis [with / by] her brother.

4 Bach is a master [of / about] classical music.

5 You should exercise [about / for] good health.

B 빈칸에 알맞은 말을 보기에서 골라 쓰시오. (한 번씩만 쓸 것)

보기	of	by	about	for	with

1 My father goes to work _____ subway.

2 Children cut paper _____ scissors.

3 Mark read a book _____ Korean culture.

4 The plane left LA _____ Seattle at 10 a.m.

5 Lincoln was the 16th president _____ the United States.

C 우리말과 일치하도록 괄호 안의 말을 이용하여 문장을 완성하시오.

1 그는 이메일로 내게 더 많은 정보를 보내 주었다. (email)

　→ He sent me more information _____ _____.

2 벨기에는 초콜릿으로 유명하다. (chocolate)

　→ Belgium is famous _____ _____.

3 우리는 좋아하는 책에 관해 이야기했다. (our favorite books)

　→ We talked _____ _____ _____ _____.

4 나는 친구와 함께 영화를 보러 갔다. (my friend)

　→ I went to the movies _____ _____ _____.

Writing Practice

Answers p.20

A 우리말과 일치하도록 괄호 안의 말을 바르게 배열하시오. (필요하면 단어를 추가할 것)

01 그녀는 작년에 시드니에서 살았다. (Sydney, she, in, lived)

→ _____ last year.

02 너는 7월에 수영을 배울 거니? (swim, in, learn, July, to)

→ Will you _____ ?

03 우리 집 옆에 도서관이 있다. (my house, is, next, there, a library, to)

→ _____

04 버스 정류장은 경찰서 건너편에 있다. (across, is, from, the police station)

→ The bus stop _____ .

05 우체국은 소방서와 병원 사이에 있다. (between, the hospital, is, the fire station, and)

→ The post office _____ .

06 여기서부터 너의 학교까지 얼마나 머니? (here, your school, to)

→ How far is it _____ ?

07 그는 보통 아침 식사 전에 조깅을 한다. (usually, jogging, goes, breakfast, he)

→ _____

08 몇몇 나라에서는 사람들이 손으로 먹는다. (eat, people, their hands)

→ In some countries, _____ .

09 어머니는 자전거를 타고 시장에 가신다. (goes, bike, the market, to)

→ My mother _____ .

10 크리스마스이브에 파티를 하자. (a party, have, Christmas Eve)

→ Let's _____ .

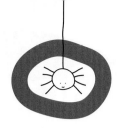

B   우리말과 일치하도록 괄호 안의 말을 이용하여 문장을 완성하시오.

01 a 그녀는 1시간 동안 영어 문법 공부를 했다. (an hour)

→ She studied English grammar _____ .

b 그는 방학 동안 영어 문법 공부를 했다. (the vacation)

→ _____

02 a 나는 9월 15일에 태어났다. (September 15th)

→ I was born _____ .

b 그는 봄에 태어났다. (spring)

→ _____

03 a 그녀는 정오까지 집에 올 것이다. (noon)

→ She will come home _____ .

b 나는 정오까지 그녀를 기다릴 것이다. (wait for)

→ _____

04 a 은행은 서점 앞에 있다. (the bookstore)

→ The bank is _____ .

b 빵집은 서점 뒤에 있다. (the bakery)

→ _____

05 a 책상 위에 책 두 권이 있다. (the desk)

→ There are two books _____ .

b 책상 아래에 책가방이 있다. (a school bag)

→ _____

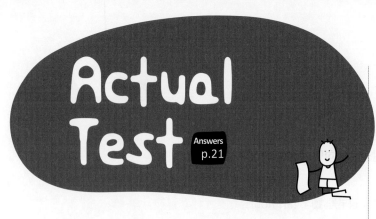

Actual Test

Answers p.21

[01~03] 빈칸에 공통으로 들어갈 말로 알맞은 것을 고르시오.

01

- I ate dinner _____ 8 o'clock.
- He was so happy _____ that time.
---

① over　　　② for　　　③ on
④ at　　　⑤ in

02

- You should work hard _____ your future.
- She studies English _____ three hours every day.
---

① by　　　② on　　　③ for
④ after　　　⑤ about

03

- We will go skiing _____ Sunday.
- He will visit Seoul _____ July 2nd.
---

① at　　　② on　　　③ in
④ for　　　⑤ about

04　서술형

우리말과 일치하도록 빈칸에 알맞은 말을 쓰시오.

Peter는 수업 시간 동안 선생님의 말씀을 귀담아들었다.

→ Peter listened to the teacher carefully _____ the class.

05

밑줄 친 부분이 어법상 틀린 것은? (바르게 고칠 것)

① What do you do in your birthday?
② He gave me a present on Christmas Day.
③ The spring sale will go on for a week.
④ I watched TV until 10 o'clock yesterday.
⑤ She wants to finish her homework before dinner.

06

밑줄 친 부분의 쓰임이 나머지 넷과 다른 것은?

① I often catch a cold in winter.
② I wake up early in the morning.
③ She met Chris in June this year.
④ We began our new project in 2017.
⑤ The taxi will arrive here in ten minutes.

07　서술형

우리말과 일치하도록 괄호 안의 말을 바르게 배열하시오.

우리는 점심 식사 후에 자주 공원을 산책한다.
(often, in, walk, after, the park, we, lunch)

→ _____

08

밑줄 친 부분이 어법상 옳은 것은? (틀린 것들을 바르게 고칠 것)

① She slept during seven hours.
② He was playing basketball on noon.
③ We can finish the work by 2 o'clock.
④ They had a lot of fun for this festival.
⑤ I have to hand in my report until tomorrow.

09 서술형

대화의 빈칸에 들어갈 말을 보기에서 골라 쓰시오.

보기	on	in	for	during

A: What are you going to do (1)_____ lunchtime?

B: I am going to read some books (2)_____ the school library.

10

밑줄 친 부분의 쓰임이 문맥상 알맞지 <u>않은</u> 것은? (바르게 고칠 것)

① We don't want to hear <u>about</u> it.

② The place is famous <u>for</u> its beauty.

③ You have to do your best <u>in</u> your dream.

④ He played computer games <u>with</u> his brother.

⑤ We can do many things <u>with</u> our cell phones.

11

다음 중 영어 문장을 바르게 해석한 것은?

① The table is behind the sofa.

→ 탁자는 소파 앞에 있다.

② A car is in front of the truck.

→ 자동차 한 대가 트럭 뒤에 있다.

③ Who is the man next to Jenny?

→ Jenny 앞에 있는 남자는 누구니?

④ She sat down across from him.

→ 그녀는 그의 바로 옆에 앉았다.

⑤ Is the police station between the school and the park?

→ 경찰서는 학교와 공원 사이에 있나요?

[12~13] 빈칸에 들어갈 말이 순서대로 짝지어진 것을 고르시오.

12

How long does it take _____ here _____ the airport?

① by – at
② by – to
③ from – at
④ from – to
⑤ from – in

13

• I will wait _____ the bus stop.

• My cousin lives _____ Australia.

• A boy is sitting _____ the bench.

① at – in – in
② at – in – on
③ at – at – on
④ in – at – in
⑤ in – in – on

14 서술형

그림을 보고, 빈칸에 알맞은 말을 쓰시오.

→ There is a pen _____ the desk.

15

밑줄 친 부분의 쓰임이 문맥상 알맞지 <u>않은</u> 것은? (바르게 고칠 것)

We ① should brush our ② teeth ③ for meals ④ to have ⑤ healthy teeth.

16

빈칸에 들어갈 말이 나머지 넷과 <u>다른</u> 것은?

① I love to travel _____ train.

② She cut the bread _____ a knife.

③ He went to Jeju Island _____ ship.

④ Please send it to me _____ email.

⑤ We have to make a decision _____ tomorrow.

17 서술형

우리말과 일치하도록 괄호 안의 단어 중 필요한 단어만을 바르게 배열하여 문장을 완성하시오.

> 나는 내 우산을 집에 두고 왔다.
> (left, leave, my, I, umbrella, in, at, home)

→ _____

18

다음 중 빈칸에 on이 들어갈 수 <u>없는</u> 것은?

① There is nothing _____ the shelf.

② People are walking _____ the street.

③ The painting _____ the wall is beautiful.

④ You were happy _____ your wedding day.

⑤ I visited my grandmother _____ the end of the week.

19

밑줄 친 부분이 어법상 <u>틀린</u> 것은? (바르게 고칠 것)

> ①The theater ②is ③right across ④between the gas ⑤station.

20

다음 중 어법상 옳은 것은? (틀린 것들을 바르게 고칠 것)

① Let's go for a walk.

② What can I do of you?

③ Is this a book by flowers?

④ She is a member at our team.

⑤ He doesn't like traveling from plane.

21

대화의 빈칸에 들어갈 말이 순서대로 짝지어진 것은?

> A: What do you think _____ his new book?
> B: It was so interesting. I finished it _____ a day.
> A: Yeah, me too.

① for – in   ② for – on

③ about – at   ④ about – in

⑤ about – on

22 서술형

그림을 보고, 괄호 안의 말을 이용하여 문장을 완성하시오.

→ A kite is _____ _____ _____. (fly, the trees)

23

밑줄 친 부분의 쓰임이 보기와 <u>다른</u> 것은?

> 보기　　I brought a gift <u>for</u> you.

① He bought a ticket <u>for</u> Paris.
② I am doing this <u>for</u> my country.
③ She did many things <u>for</u> America.
④ We planned a birthday party <u>for</u> him.
⑤ They will open a school <u>for</u> young children.

24

다음 중 어법상 <u>틀린</u> 것은? (바르게 고칠 것)

① The cat is under the bed.
② Matthew came here at night.
③ Korea held the World Cup in 2002.
④ I read the newspaper before breakfast.
⑤ She gave a flower to her mom in Mother's Day.

25

다음 그림을 영어로 바르게 설명한 것은?

① A dog is sleeping under the table.
② A dog is sleeping on the table.
③ A dog is sleeping next to the table.
④ A dog is sleeping in front of the table.
⑤ A dog is sleeping behind the table.

26 서술형

대화의 밑줄 친 우리말을 영어로 쓰시오.

> A: What are the opening hours of the bank?
> B: <u>그것은 오전 9시부터 오후 4시까지 열어요.</u>
> A: Okay, thanks.

→ _____

27 서술형

빈칸에 공통으로 들어갈 말을 쓰시오.

> • I am worried _____ the math test.
> • What was the phone call _____?

→ _____

28 서술형

다음 글에서 어법상 틀린 부분을 <u>모두</u> 찾아 바르게 고치시오.

> I went hiking of my father in the morning. The weather was great for hiking, but it was hard to climb the mountain. However, with my father's help, I finally climbed to the top by the mountain after two hours of climbing. From the top, the view was beautiful. And I could see a beautiful rainbow. We stayed there during an hour and went down the mountain. It was a great experience.

Recall My Memory

Answers
p.22

다음 문장이 어법상 맞으면 O표, 틀리면 바르게 고치시오.

01 These pink sneakers aren't her.   ➔ p. 58

02 Will you meet me in the airport at seven?   ➔ p. 164

03 He studied hardly to pass the exam.   ➔ p. 150

04 This ice cream tastes strawberries.   ➔ p. 118

05 May I use a computer during lunchtime?   ➔ p. 162

06 Lisa can't speak any Korean three years ago.   ➔ p. 90

07 Is there anything wrong with my cell phone?   ➔ p. 148

08 Many children go to school on foot.   ➔ p. 166

09 A mother kangaroo has a pouch over her stomach.   ➔ p. 164

10 A triangle had three corners.   ➔ p. 76

11 We were happy to winning the game.   ➔ p. 136

12 What smart that dog is!   ➔ p. 108

13 The school festival will start in October 2nd.   ➔ p. 162

14 Sally is good at playing the table tennis.   ➔ p. 48

15 The main character of this animation is a little penguin.   ➔ p. 166

너와 나를 이어 주는 오작교,

접속사

Unit 01	and, but, or, so
Unit 02	when, while, before, after
Unit 03	because, if, that

Unit 01 and, but, or, so

접속사는 단어와 단어, 구와 구, 절과 절을 연결해 주는 말이다. 그중 접속사 and, but, or, so는 문장에서의 역할이나 형태가 같은 단어, 구, 절을 서로 연결한다.

A and

a I bought a skirt **and** a jacket.
　　　　 단어(명사)　　　　 단어(명사)

b He played the piano, **and** she sang.
　　　 절　　　　　　　　　　 절

c I studied math, science, **and** English.
　　　 단어(명사)　 단어(명사)　　　 단어(명사)

'그리고, ~와/과'라는 의미로, 서로 비슷한 내용을 연결한다.

c 셋 이상의 말을 연결할 때는 「A, B, and C」와 같은 형태로 쓴다.

B but

a My little sister is young **but** smart.
　　　　　　　　　　 단어(형용사)　　　 단어(형용사)

b I eat fish, **but** I don't eat meat.
　　　 절　　　　　　　 절

'그러나, ~지만'이라는 의미로, 서로 반대되는 내용을 연결한다.

C or

a You can have tea **or** coffee.
　　　　　　　　 단어(명사)　　 단어(명사)

b Will you stay in **or** go out?
　　　　　　 구　　　 구

'또는, ~이나'라는 의미로, 둘 이상의 선택 사항을 연결한다.

연결할 때 주의할 점

and, but, or는 형용사와 형용사, 동사와 동사, 동명사와 동명사처럼 문법적으로 형태나 역할이 같은 말을 연결해야 한다. 특히, 동사와 동사를 연결할 때는 동사의 수와 시제를 같게 해야 한다.

I love reading **and** writing[to write].
　　　　 동명사　　　 동명사

He plays tennis **or** swims[swim] every day.
　　 3인칭 단수 현재형　　 3인칭 단수 현재형

D so

a It was raining, **so** I took my umbrella.
　　　 절(원인)　　　　 절(결과)

b He was tired, **so** he went to bed early.

'그래서'라는 의미로, 절과 절을 연결한다. so 앞은 원인, 뒤는 결과를 나타낸다.

---

vocabulary ·········· **C** stay in (밖으로) 나가지 않다, 집에 있다　**D** tired ⑱ 피곤한

Exercise

Answers p.22

A 괄호 안에서 알맞은 말을 고르시오.

1 I can't snowboard, [so / but] I can ski.

2 He is cute [and / or] funny.

3 Do you want milk [or / but] juice?

4 She was cold, [but / so] she turned on the heater.

5 I stayed at home and [help / helped] my mother.

B 빈칸에 알맞은 말을 보기에서 골라 쓰시오. (한 번씩만 쓸 것)

보기	and	but	or	so

1 I called, _____ he didn't answer.

2 He bought some fruits _____ vegetables.

3 We can go there by bus _____ by train.

4 She is my best friend, _____ I tell her my problems.

C 우리말과 일치하도록 괄호 안의 말을 이용하여 문장을 완성하시오.

1 Tommy는 축구와 야구를 좋아한다. (football, baseball)

→ Tommy likes _____ _____ _____.

2 TV가 켜져 있지만, 그들은 그것을 보고 있지 않다. (watch)

→ The TV is on, _____ _____ _____ _____ _____ it.

3 나는 우산이 없어서 비에 젖었다. (get wet)

→ I didn't have an umbrella, _____ _____ _____ _____.

4 너는 재킷을 입을 거니, 점퍼를 입을 거니? (a jacket, a jumper)

→ Will you wear _____ _____ _____ _____ _____?

02 when, while, before, after

when, while, before, after, because, if는 절과 절을 연결한다. 접속사가 이끄는 절은 문장에서 부사 같은 역할을 하여 부사절이라고 하며, 부사절이 앞에 올 때는 부사절 끝에 콤마(,)를 붙인다. when, while, before, after는 시간을 나타내는 대표적인 접속사이다.

A when

a **When** I have time, I take pictures.

　　└─────절─────┘　　　절
　　　　부사절

b Mom was beautiful **when** she was young.

cf. **When** do you go to school?

'~할 때'라는 의미이다.

cf. 접속사 when은 뒤에 「주어+동사」가 오지만, 의문문의 when은 '언제'라는 의미로, 뒤에 「(조)동사+주어」가 온다.

B while

a **While** I was running to school, I fell down.

　　　　　　　진행형

b Dad listens to music **while** he is driving.

'~하는 동안'이라는 의미로, 두 가지 일이 동시에 일어남을 나타낸다. 진행형과 함께 잘 쓰인다.

C before

a **Before** I go to bed, I brush my teeth.

b I wash my hands **before** I eat.

'~하기 전에'라는 의미이다.

D after

a **After** she took the medicine, she felt better.

b He drinks water **after** he wakes up.

'~한 후에'라는 의미이다.

시간의 부사절에서
미래를 표현하는 방법

시간을 나타내는 부사절에서는 미래의 일을 현재시제로 나타낸다.

I will start **when** I am[~~will be~~] ready.

She will call you **after** she arrives[~~will arrive~~].

 vocabulary ──────── **B** fall ⑤ 넘어지다; 떨어지다(-fell-fallen)　**D** medicine ⑲ 약

Exercise

Answers
p.22

A 괄호 안에서 알맞은 말을 고르시오.

1 We rested [before / after] we rode our bikes.

2 [After / While] she was reading the book, she felt sad.

3 When he [goes / will go] to London, he will visit Windsor Castle.

4 [When / While] I get up, I check the weather.

5 She washes her hair [before / after] she goes out.

B 빈칸에 알맞은 말을 보기에서 골라 쓰시오. (한 번씩만 쓸 것)

보기	when	while	before	after

1 We didn't speak _____ we were eating.

2 She makes a shopping list _____ she goes shopping.

3 _____ you need my help, I will give it.

4 They drink coffee _____ they finish their housework.

C 우리말과 일치하도록 괄호 안의 말을 이용하여 문장을 완성하시오.

1 내가 그곳에 도착했을 때 거의 9시가 되었다. (arrive, there)

→ It was almost nine _____ _____ _____ _____ .

2 그녀는 열심히 일한 후에 몹시 피곤했다. (work, hard)

→ She was very tired _____ _____ _____ _____ .

3 그는 요리하는 동안 데었다. (cook)

→ He burned himself _____ _____ _____ _____ .

4 나는 결정하기 전에 신중하게 생각할 것이다. (make a decision)

→ I will think carefully _____ _____ _____ _____

_____ .

because와 if는 각각 이유와 조건을 나타내는 부사절 접속사이다. 반면, that은 절을 이끌어 문장에서 명사 같은 역할을 하여 명사절 접속사라고 한다.

A because

a He is in the hospital **because** he is sick.

b The train was late **because** it snowed heavily.

cf. The train was late **because of** heavy snow.
　　　　　　　　　　　　　　　　　명사구

'~하기 때문에'라는 의미로, 이유나 원인을 나타낸다.

cf. because 뒤에는 절이 오지만, because of 뒤에는 명사(구)가 온다.

B if

a **If** you freeze water, it becomes ice.

b You can get a discount **if** you bring your own cup.

cf. **If** it **is**[will be] sunny tomorrow, we will go to the park.

'만약 ~하다면'의 의미로, 조건을 나타낸다.

cf. 조건을 나타내는 부사절에서도 미래의 일을 현재시제로 나타낸다.

C that

that이 이끄는 절은 문장에서 명사처럼 쓰여 주어, 목적어, 보어 역할을 한다.

a **That** he likes her is true.
　　　└───┬───┘
　　　　절
　　　명사절(주어)

→ **It** is true **that** he likes her.
　가짜 주어　　　　진짜 주어

b I know **(that)** he likes her.
　　　　　명사절(목적어)

c The fact *is* **that** he likes her.
　　　　　　　명사절(보어)

a 주어로 쓰여 '~하는 것은'의 의미를 나타낸다. that절이 주어일 때는 주어 자리에 It을 쓰고 that절을 문장 뒤로 보내는 것이 자연스럽다. It은 가짜 주어이므로 해석하지 않는다.

b 동사 know, think, believe, hope, tell, say 등의 목적어로 쓰여 '~하는 것을'의 의미를 나타낸다. 이때의 that은 생략할 수 있다.

c be동사의 보어로 쓰여 '~하는 것(이다)'의 의미를 나타내며, 주어가 무엇인지 설명해 준다.

 vocabulary -------- **B** freeze ⑧ 얼다[얼리다](-froze-frozen)　discount ⑱ 할인　own ⑲ 자기 자신의　**C** fact ⑲ 사실

Exercise

Answers p.22

A 괄호 안에서 알맞은 말을 고르시오.

1 [If / That] I finish early, I will watch a movie.

2 It is surprising [that / if] his grades went up a lot.

3 I didn't buy the watch [if / because] it was expensive.

4 We believe [because / that] she will do a great job.

5 If you [won't hurry / don't hurry], you will miss the plane.

B 빈칸에 알맞은 말을 보기에서 골라 쓰시오. (중복 가능)

보기	because	because of	if	that

1 Everyone likes Yunji _____ she dances well.

2 The fact is _____ he is a honest man.

3 _____ you study hard, you will pass the exam.

4 I hope _____ you will enjoy your holiday.

5 Many students were absent from school _____ the flu.

C 우리말과 일치하도록 괄호 안의 말을 이용하여 문장을 완성하시오.

1 비가 오고 있었기 때문에 우리는 해변에 가지 않았다. (rain)

→ We didn't go to the beach _____ _____ _____

_____ .

2 나는 그녀가 대회에서 우승할 것으로 생각한다. (will, win, the contest)

→ I think _____ _____ _____ _____ _____

_____ .

3 네가 지금 이 편지를 보내면 그가 내일 그것을 받을 것이다. (send, this letter)

→ _____ _____ _____ _____ _____ now,

he will receive it tomorrow.

Writing Practice

Answers p.22

A 우리말과 일치하도록 괄호 안의 말을 바르게 배열하시오.

01 우리는 꽃들을 심은 후에 물을 주었다. (we, after, planted, them)

→ We watered the flowers _____.

02 그는 요리하기를 좋아하기 때문에 요리사가 되고 싶어 한다. (because, likes, he, cooking)

→ He wants to be a cook _____.

03 나는 내 책을 도서관에 두고 온 것 같다. (I, my book, that, left)

→ I think _____ in the library.

04 엘리베이터가 작동하지 않아서 나는 계단을 이용해야 했다. (I, take, so, had to, the stairs)

→ The elevator didn't work, _____.

05 그녀는 시장에 갈 때 장바구니를 가져간다. (goes, when, she, the market, to)

→ _____, she takes a shopping bag.

06 그 남자는 차가 있지만, 자전거를 타고 다닌다. (he, but, rides, his bike)

→ The man has a car, _____.

07 그들은 낚시하는 것과 테니스 하는 것을 좋아한다. (play, and, like, tennis, to, fish)

→ They _____.

08 그녀는 집안일을 하는 동안 라디오를 듣는다. (doing, is, while, she, the housework)

→ She listens to the radio _____.

09 내가 네 휴대 전화를 발견하면 네게 말해 줄게. (find, if, I, your cell phone)

→ _____, I'll tell you.

10 그는 오늘 호텔 방과 비행기 표를 예약했다. (a flight, booked, and, he, a hotel room)

→ _____ today.

B 우리말과 일치하도록 괄호 안의 말을 이용하여 문장을 완성하시오.

01 a 그녀는 책을 샀고, 그것을 읽었다. (read)

→ She bought a book, _____.

b 그는 책을 샀지만, 그것을 읽지 않았다.

→ _____

02 a 너는 먹기 전에 손을 씻어야 한다. (eat)

→ You should wash your hands _____.

b 너는 먹은 후에 이를 닦아야 한다. (brush, teeth)

→ _____

03 a 내가 자고 있는 동안에 아빠가 집에 오셨다. (sleep)

→ My dad came home _____.

b 아빠가 집에 오셨을 때 나는 자고 있었다.

→ _____

04 a 그는 아파서 병원에 갔다. (go to the hospital)

→ He was sick, _____.

b 그는 아팠기 때문에 병원에 갔다.

→ _____

05 a 나는 그녀를 만날 때 그녀에게 이 편지를 줄 것이다. (meet)

→ _____, I will give her this letter.

b 만약 내가 그녀를 만나면 그녀에게 이 편지를 줄 것이다.

→ _____

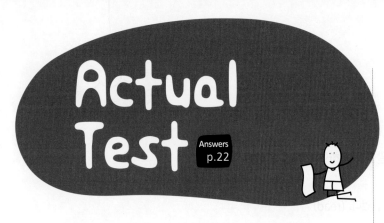

Actual Test

Answers p.22

[01~02] 빈칸에 들어갈 말로 알맞은 것을 고르시오.

01

There are some apples, oranges, _____ bananas on the table.

① so   ② or   ③ if
④ and   ⑤ but

02

If it _____ tomorrow, I will make a snowman.

① snow   ② snows   ③ snowed
④ will snow   ⑤ will be snowing

[03~04] 밑줄 친 부분이 어법상 **틀린** 것을 고르시오. (바르게 고칠 것)

03

① She felt hungry <u>but</u> tired.
② You can stay here <u>or</u> leave now.
③ Peter <u>and</u> Alex are my friends.
④ He tried again <u>but</u> he failed.
⑤ Which would you like, tea <u>or</u> coffee?

04

① I'm sorry, <u>but</u> I can't help you.
② Call 119 <u>if</u> you are in danger.
③ We can go by bus <u>or</u> we can walk.
④ He didn't know <u>so</u> there was a big fire.
⑤ I went to bed <u>after</u> I changed into my pajamas.

[05~07] 대화의 빈칸에 들어갈 말로 알맞은 것을 고르시오.

05

A: Why does he look so worried?
B: I heard _____ his mom is very sick.

① if   ② when   ③ that
④ after   ⑤ before

06

A: Oh, no! We're late.
B: Don't worry. We will get there in time _____ we leave now.

① or   ② if   ③ and
④ while   ⑤ that

07

A: Could you turn off the TV _____ turn down the volume? I can't focus on my work.
B: I'm sorry. I'll just turn it off.

① or   ② if   ③ but
④ when   ⑤ that

08

빈칸에 공통으로 들어갈 말로 알맞은 것은?

• Thanks for inviting me, _____ I have to go now.
• I wasn't tired, _____ I went to bed early.

① if   ② or   ③ so
④ but   ⑤ and

[09-10] 밑줄 친 부분의 쓰임이 나머지 넷과 <u>다른</u> 것을 고르시오.

09

① <u>When</u> I get there, I will call you.
② <u>When</u> I feel lonely, I listen to music.
③ <u>When</u> are you going to do the dishes?
④ <u>When</u> I was young, I wanted to be a pilot.
⑤ <u>When</u> you finish your work, what do you like to do?

10

① I think <u>that</u> she likes you.
② The fact is <u>that</u> he said no.
③ Look at <u>that</u> bird in the tree.
④ It is true <u>that</u> he is a good man.
⑤ I don't believe <u>that</u> he is lying.

[11-12] 두 문장의 의미가 같도록 주어진 말로 시작하여 다시 쓰시오.

11 서술형

He did warm-up exercises, then he went into the water.

→ Before _____
_____.

12 서술형

Everyone arrived, then they started the meeting.

→ After _____
_____.

13 서술형

우리말과 일치하도록 괄호 안의 말을 바르게 배열하시오.

엄마가 요리하는 동안 나는 상을 놓았다.
(cooking, mom, was, while)

→ _____,

I set the table.

14 서술형

밑줄 친 부분이 어법상 틀린 것을 골라 바르게 고치시오.

Jane ①and I ②went out ③and ④see ⑤a movie last night.

_____ → _____

[15~16] 빈칸에 들어갈 말이 순서대로 짝지어진 것을 고르시오.

15

• The chair is cheap, _____ the table is expensive.
• Sam can speak _____ write Chinese.

① or – but   ② so – or
③ but – so   ④ and – but
⑤ but – and

16

• _____ she came home, her brother was eating a snack.
• I couldn't call him _____ my phone battery died.

① If – that   ② If – because
③ When – that   ④ When – because
⑤ Because – that

17

대화의 밑줄 친 부분이 어법상 <u>틀린</u> 것은? (바르게 고칠 것)

A: Mom, can I have more ice cream?

B: No, ①you can't. You ②will get a stomachache if you ③will eat too much ice cream.

A: ④But I want to have more. It tastes really good.

B: Okay, ⑤but just one more scoop of ice cream.

18 서술형

어법상 틀린 곳을 바르게 고쳐 다시 쓰시오.

We were late because the heavy traffic.

→ _____

19

다음은 Tim의 어제 일정표이다. 빈칸에 들어갈 말이 나머지 넷과 <u>다른</u> 것은?

4 p.m.	play soccer
5 p.m.	take a shower
6 p.m.	have dinner
7 p.m.	do his homework
8 p.m.	watch TV
10 p.m.	go to bed

① Tim played soccer _____ he took a shower.

② _____ Tim had dinner, he took a shower.

③ Tim had dinner _____ he did his homework.

④ Tim watched TV _____ he did his homework.

⑤ _____ Tim went to bed, he watched TV.

20 서술형

우리말과 일치하도록 괄호 안의 말을 이용하여 영어로 쓰시오.

그가 돌아올 때 그는 너에게 전화할 것이다.
(call, come back)

→ _____

[21~22] 괄호 안의 말을 이용하여 두 문장을 한 문장으로 쓰시오.

21 서술형

I was so hungry. So, I ate a lot. (because)

→ _____

22 서술형

She will get well soon. I believe it. (that)

→ _____

23

다음 중 어법상 옳은 것으로 바르게 짝지어진 것은? (<u>틀린</u> 것들을 바르게 고칠 것)

a. Because the noise, I couldn't hear the bell.

b. Call me if you need my help.

c. Please take care of my dog while I'm away.

d. I will welcome you when you will arrive.

① a, b   ② a, d   ③ b, c

④ c, d   ⑤ b, c, d

24

다음 중 어법상 <u>틀린</u> 것은? (바르게 고칠 것)

① You can call her now or later.
② He is honest, so I trust him.
③ She likes singing and to dance.
④ I lifted and carried the box.
⑤ The exam was difficult, but I passed it.

25 서술형

두 문장을 한 문장으로 만들 때 빈칸에 알맞은 말을 쓰시오.

> He can speak five languages. It is amazing.

→ _____ is amazing _____ he can speak five languages.

26 서술형

다음은 날씨에 따른 Kate의 이번 주말 계획이다. 주어진 말을 이용하여 글을 완성하시오.

| | sunny, ride her bike in the park |
| | rain, watch a movie at home |

Kate made some plans for this weekend. If
(1) _____ ,
_____ .
If (2) _____ ,
_____ .
She thinks that she will have a wonderful weekend.

[27~28] 그림을 보고, after 또는 before를 이용하여 문장을 완성하시오.

27 서술형

(wash your hands)   (make sandwiches)

→ Wash your hands _____
_____ .

28 서술형

(take a long walk)   (feel very tired)

→ He felt very tired _____
_____ .

29 서술형

다음 중 어법상 <u>틀린</u> 것을 <u>모두</u> 골라 바르게 고치시오.

a. Lily is good at math and science.
b. Now I know that I'm not alone.
c. It was cold but windy outside.
d. It was expensive, so I didn't buy it.
e. It is strange that nobody knows the news.
f. Would you like beef or chicken?
g. Grandma will be sad if you won't come.

Recall My Memory

다음 문장이 어법상 맞으면 O표, **틀리면** 바르게 고치시오.

01 There is a lot of geese on the farm. ➲ p. 106

02 If I will have to work tomorrow, I won't go on a picnic. ➲ p. 180

03 Does Thomas Edison invent the light bulb? ➲ p. 34

04 My dog is more heavy than your dog. ➲ p. 152

05 I like watching movies and play soccer. ➲ p. 176

06 When are you going to clean your room? ➲ p. 104

07 I will arrive at the airport by three o'clock. ➲ p. 162

08 While he was a child, he lived in the city. ➲ p. 178

09 The teacher needs a pen to write. ➲ p. 136

10 I think that you should do some volunteer work. ➲ p. 180

11 Did your dad finish to clean his car? ➲ p. 138

12 The music was loud, because I couldn't sleep. ➲ p. 176

13 We have to take care of us. ➲ p. 58

14 You must take a shower after you go into the pool. ➲ p. 178

15 Angela can't be at home. The lights are on in her house. ➲ p. 92

point 1

🔗 Chapter 9

동사의 목적어: to부정사 vs. 동명사

He decided working(→ **to work**) on stress management. › 고1 연합
그는 스트레스 관리를 시작하기로 마음먹었다.

- to부정사를 목적어로 가지는 동사와 동명사를 목적어로 가지는 동사를 구분해서 알아둔다.

to부정사를 목적어로 가지는 동사	want, hope, wish, plan, decide, need, promise, learn, agree 등
동명사를 목적어로 가지는 동사	finish, enjoy, stop, keep, practice, mind, quit, avoid, give up 등
to부정사, 동명사 둘 다 목적어로 가지는 동사	like, love, hate, start, begin 등

- stop은 뒤에 동명사와 to부정사 둘 다 올 수 있는데, 둘의 쓰임과 의미가 다름에 주의해야 한다.
  - stop + 동명사: '~하는 것을 멈추다'라는 의미로, 동명사는 stop의 목적어이다.
  - stop + to부정사: '~하기 위해 멈추다'라는 의미로, to부정사는 stop의 목적어가 아니라 부사처럼 쓰여 '목적(~하기 위해)'을 나타낸다.

point 2

🔗 Chapter 10

원급 vs. 비교급 vs. 최상급

After half time, England played [**better** / best] than Holland. › 고1 연합
하프 타임 이후에는 영국이 네덜란드보다 더 잘했다.

- 원급, 비교급, 최상급을 이용한 비교 표현의 형태를 알아둔다.

원급 비교	비교급 비교	최상급 비교
as + 원급 + as (~만큼 …한/하게)	비교급 + than (~보다 더 …한/하게)	the + 최상급 (가장 ~한/하게)

- 원급 비교에서 as와 as 사이에 형용사가 들어가는지 부사가 들어가는지는 as를 가리고 생각해 본다.
  - be동사, become 등의 보어 자리 / 명사를 꾸며 주는 자리 → 형용사
  - 동사를 꾸며 주는 자리 → 부사
- 비교되는 두 대상은 문법적으로 형태나 성격이 서로 같아야 한다.
- 비교급을 강조하여 '훨씬'이라는 의미를 나타낼 때는 much, even, still, far, a lot 등을 쓴다. very, so, too, more 등은 비교급을 강조할 수 없다.

point 3

🔗 Chapter 12

문법적으로 비슷한 것들을 연결하는 and, but, or

He says, "How's it going, George?" and [keep / **keeps**] on walking. › 고1 연합
그는 "요즘 어떻게 지내, George?"라고 말하고는 계속해서 걸어간다.

- and, but, or는 단어와 단어, 구와 구, 절과 절을 연결한다.
- 연결되는 대상들은 문법적으로 형태나 성격이 서로 같아야 한다. 특히, 동사와 동사를 연결할 때는 동사의 수와 시제를 일치시키는 데 주의한다.

---

work on ~을 시작하다   stress management 스트레스 관리   keep (on) -ing ~을 계속하다

A 괄호 안에서 알맞은 말을 고르시오.

1 Many families enjoy [to travel / traveling] on holidays. › 고1 연합

2 Few plants are as [useful / usefully] as the yucca plant. › 고1 연합

3 Martin thought life would be [much / more] better. › 고1 연합

4 Avoid [touching / to touch] a wild animal. › 고1 연합

5 People work longer, go to meetings at night, eat dinner late, or [go / going] out until late. › 고1 연합

B 밑줄 친 부분이 어법상 맞으면 ○표, 틀리면 바르게 고치시오.

1 The dog was as <u>bigger</u> as a lion. › 고1 연합

2 At what age should a child learn <u>to use</u> a computer? › 고1 연합

3 After finishing his program and <u>received</u> his degree, Martin moved to Boulder. › 고1 연합

4 At first, the machine made a lot of noise, and later, it stopped <u>to work</u>. › 수능

5 He went to New York City to find a job, and never <u>returned</u> to the South. › 고1 연합

C 다음 글의 밑줄 친 부분 중, 어법상 틀린 것은? (바르게 고칠 것) › 고1 연합

Three important inventions came out of Mesopotamia: the wheel, the plow, and the sailboat. Carts with wheels carried more goods to market ① <u>more quickly</u>. Animals pulled plows and turned over the soil. They were ② <u>far</u> more efficient than humans. By sailboat, people went to other countries across the sea and ③ <u>trade</u> with them. *plow: 쟁기

A wild 형 야생의　**B** program 명 (학업) 과정　degree 명 학위　machine 명 기계　**C** invention 명 발명품　come out of ~에서 나오다　wheel 명 바퀴　sailboat 명 범선　goods 명 상품　pull 동 끌다　turn over ~을 뒤집다　soil 명 흙　efficient 형 효율적인　trade 동 거래[무역]하다

1 (A), (B), (C)의 각 네모 안에서 어법에 맞는 표현으로 가장 적절한 것은?

Eating too little or not (A) to eat / eating at all is not a good way of dieting. Diet doesn't mean 'not eating.' It means 'eating right.' If you diet too much, you may lose your health, not your weight. Young people need good nutrition (B) to grow / growing. If you really want to keep your body in good shape, you need to eat well and (C) exercise / exercising well. That is the best way to stay healthy.

(A)		(B)		(C)
① to eat	......	to grow	......	exercise
② eating	......	to grow	......	exercise
③ to eat	......	growing	......	exercise
④ eating	......	to grow	......	exercising
⑤ to eat	......	growing	......	exercising

2 다음 글의 밑줄 친 부분 중, 어법상 틀린 것은? (바르게 고칠 것) ▸ 고1 연합

What makes a great vacation? People have ① many different ideas about it. Some people like to go for long walks in the forest. They ② won't see anyone for days there. Others like to spend their holiday in an exciting city. There they can visit museums, theaters, and good restaurants. Still others enjoy the fresh air at the seashore. They can spend their days at the beach and ③ listen to the ocean waves at night. ④ A few people decide to stay at home and do some major housework. They may spend their vacation painting a front door or ⑤ to wash all the windows in their apartment.

3 (A), (B), (C)의 각 네모 안에서 어법에 맞는 표현으로 가장 적절한 것은? › 고1 연합

Australia is home to the most dangerous animals on the earth. For example, the Australian taipan is a snake. Its poison can kill 199 people with just one bite. Great white sharks with about 300 teeth are as deadly (A) than / as taipans, too. But Australian wild dogs kill (B) very / much more people than great white sharks. Also, the box jellyfish has strong poison. If its poison gets into your body, your heart will stop (C) to beat / beating after only three minutes.

	(A)		(B)		(C)
①	as	......	very	......	beating
②	than	......	very	......	to beat
③	as	......	much	......	to beat
④	than	......	much	......	beating
⑤	as	......	much	......	beating

---

1 diet ⑧ 식이 요법을 하다 ⑲ 식이 요법 lose ⑧ 잃다(-lost-lost) nutrition ⑲ 영양 in good shape (몸의) 상태가 좋은

2 some ~, others …, still others – 어떤 사람들은 ~, 다른 사람들은 …, 또 다른 사람들은 – seashore ⑲ 해변 wave ⑲ 파도 major ⑲ 중요한 front door 현관

3 poison ⑲ 독 deadly ⑲ 치명적인 get into ~에 들어가다 beat ⑧ (심장이) 뛰다(-beat-beaten)

수학 개념을 쉽게 이해하는 방법?
개념수다로 시작하자!

수학의 진짜 실력자가 되는 비결 -
나에게 딱 맞는 개념서를 술술 읽으며 시작하자!

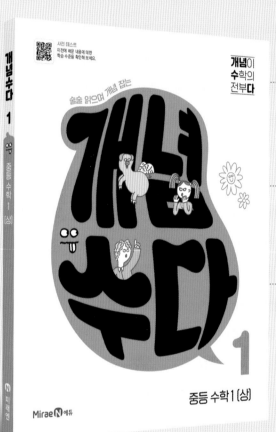

개념 이해
친구와 수다 떨듯 쉽고 재미있게,
베테랑 선생님의 동영상 강의로 완벽하게

개념 확인·정리
깔끔하게 구조화된 문제로 개념을 확인하고,
개념 전체의 흐름을 한 번에 정리

개념 끝장
온라인을 통해 개개인별 성취도 분석과
틀린 문항에 대한 맞춤 클리닉 제공

| 추천 대상 |
• 중등 수학 과정을 예습하고 싶은 초등 5~6학년
• 중등 수학을 어려워하는 중학생

수학은 순서를 따라 학습해야 효과적이므로,
초등 수학부터 꼼꼼하게 공부해 보자.

개념이 수학의 전부다
수학 개념을 제대로 공부하는 EASY 개념서

개념수다 시리즈 (전7책)

0_초등 핵심 개념
1_중등 수학 1(상), 2_중등 수학 1(하)
3_중등 수학 2(상), 4_중등 수학 2(하)
5_중등 수학 3(상), 6_중등 수학 3(하)

초등 핵심 개념
한 권으로 빠르게 정리!

중등 도서안내

비주얼 개념서 ─────────────

룩 LOOK

이미지 연상으로 필수 개념을 쉽게 익히는
비주얼 개념서

국어   문학, 문법
역사   ①, ②

필수 개념서 ─────────────

올리드

자세하고 쉬운 개념,
시험을 대비하는 특별한 비법이 한가득!

국어   1-1, 1-2, 2-1, 2-2, 3-1, 3-2
영어   1-1, 1-2, 2-1, 2-2, 3-1, 3-2
수학   1(상), 1(하), 2(상), 2(하), 3(상), 3(하)
사회   ①-1, ①-2, ②-1, ②-2
역사   ①-1, ①-2, ②-1, ②-2
과학   1-1, 1-2, 2-1, 2-2, 3-1, 3-2

* 국어, 영어는 미래엔 교과서 관련 도서입니다.

국어 독해·어휘 훈련서 ─────────────

깨독

수능 국어 독해의 자신감을 깨우는
단계별 훈련서

독해   0_준비편, 1_기본편, 2_실력편, 3_수능편
어휘   1_종합편, 2_수능편

영문법 기본서 ─────────────

GRAMMAR
BITE

중학교 핵심 필수 문법 공략,
내신·서술형·수능까지 한 번에!

문법   PREP
        Grade 1, Grade 2, Grade 3
        SUM

영어 독해 기본서 ─────────────

READING
BITE

끊어 읽으며 직독직해하는
중학 독해의 자신감!

독해   PREP
        Grade 1, Grade 2, Grade 3
        PLUS 수능

GRAMMAR BITE

핵심 문법만 콕! 쉽게 이해하는
중등 영문법

Workbook

Grade
1

GRAMMAR
BITE

Grade 1

Workbook

Unit 01 be동사의 현재형과 과거형

Answers p.26

A 빈칸에 알맞은 be동사를 각각 쓰시오.

1 This book _____ very interesting.

These books _____ very boring.

2 My brother _____ 10 years old last year.

He _____ 11 years old now.

3 Cindy and Amy _____ fans of the boy band.

They _____ at their concert yesterday.

B 밑줄 친 부분이 어법상 맞으면 ○표, **틀리면** 바르게 고치시오.

1 She <u>are</u> very diligent.

_____

2 I <u>was</u> from Sweden.

_____

3 Coffee and tea <u>is</u> on the table.

_____

4 They <u>were</u> in the room a minute ago.

_____

5 The bread <u>was</u> delicious.

_____

C 우리말과 일치하도록 괄호 안의 말을 이용하여 문장을 완성하시오.

1 그는 어제 학교에 늦었다. (late)

→ _____ _____ _____ for school yesterday.

2 그들은 친절하고 잘생겼다. (kind)

→ _____ _____ _____ and handsome.

3 그녀는 그 책의 작가이다. (the writer)

→ _____ _____ _____ _____ of the book.

4 그 편지들은 책상 위에 있었다. (the letters)

→ _____ _____ _____ on the desk.

be동사의 부정문과 의문문

Answers
p.26

A 괄호 안에서 알맞은 말을 고르시오.

1 She [is not / not is] a nurse.

2 [Is / Are] your father at home?

3 [I amn't / I'm not] a good singer.

4 [Are / Were] they tired yesterday?

5 The children [wasn't / weren't] careful.

B 대화의 빈칸에 알맞은 말을 쓰시오.

1 A: Are you from Mexico?

 B: _____, _____ _____. I'm from Canada.

2 A: _____ _____ a cook?

 B: Yes, he was.

3 A: Is your grandmother sick?

 B: _____, _____ _____. She is in the hospital.

4 A: _____ _____ tall then?

 B: No, they weren't. _____ _____ short then.

C 다음 문장을 괄호 안의 지시대로 바꿔 쓰시오.

1 The food is delicious.

 (1) _____ (부정문으로)

 (2) _____ (의문문으로)

2 Nick was at the party last night.

 (1) _____ (부정문으로)

 (2) _____ (의문문으로)

Unit 01 일반동사의 현재형

A 괄호 안에서 알맞은 말을 고르시오.

1 Kate [play / plays] the piano every day.

2 We [brush / brushes] our teeth after meals.

3 My aunts [live / lives] in Sydney.

4 The baby [crys / cries] all the time.

5 They [work / works] at the department store.

B 주어진 동사를 현재형으로 써서 문장을 완성하시오.

1 love   **a** Brian _____ rock music.

 b We _____ dance music.

2 read   **a** Dad _____ newspapers in the evening.

 b I _____ books in the evening.

3 study   **a** Kate's friends _____ French.

 b Kate _____ German.

4 go   **a** He _____ to school by bike.

 b They _____ to school by bus.

C 밑줄 친 부분에 유의하여 어법상 틀린 부분을 바르게 고쳐 문장을 다시 쓰시오.

1 <u>Jenny</u> do her homework after dinner.

 → _____

2 <u>A bird</u> flys in the sky.

 → _____

3 <u>My parents</u> has bread and coffee for breakfast.

 → _____

Unit 02 일반동사의 과거형

Answers p.26

A 괄호 안의 동사를 과거형으로 써서 문장을 완성하시오.

1 Julia _____ a cup. (break)

2 My grandfather _____ at the post office. (work)

3 Ben and Jack _____ in the pool. (swim)

4 I _____ my bag on the table. (put)

5 They _____ a strange sound last night. (hear)

B 밑줄 친 부분이 어법상 맞으면 ○표, 틀리면 바르게 고치시오.

1 I <u>ate</u> lunch an hour ago. _____

2 They <u>buy</u> a small house in 2015. _____

3 Lucy and Cindy <u>study</u> English last night. _____

4 He <u>read</u> the storybook this morning. _____

5 John <u>plays</u> tennis yesterday. _____

C 다음 문장을 주어진 내용에 맞게 바꿔 쓰시오.

1 She dances at the party.

→ _____ last night.

2 We plan a trip to Hawaii.

→ _____ yesterday.

3 Dad and I go fishing.

→ _____ last weekend.

4 He writes a letter to his family.

→ _____ two weeks ago.

Unit 03 일반동사의 부정문과 의문문

Answers
p.26

A 괄호 안에서 알맞은 말을 고르시오.

1 My dad [don't / doesn't] have breakfast.

2 I didn't [ride / rode] my bike yesterday.

3 Does Bomi [have / has] long hair?

4 They [don't / doesn't] speak English well.

5 [Does / Did] he wash his car last week?

B 대화의 빈칸에 알맞은 말을 쓰시오.

1 A: Does Minho study Chinese?

　 B: Yes, _____ _____ .

2 A: Do they play baseball after school?

　 B: No, _____ _____ . They play basketball.

3 A: _____ _____ watch TV in the evening?

　 B: No, she didn't. She wrote a science report.

C 우리말과 일치하도록 괄호 안의 말을 이용하여 문장을 완성하시오.

1 그들은 일주일 전에 이곳을 떠났니? (leave)

　 → _____ _____ _____ here a week ago?

2 나는 햄버거를 좋아하지 않는다. (like)

　 → I _____ _____ hamburgers.

3 그녀는 어젯밤에 그에게 전화하지 않았다. (call)

　 → She _____ _____ him last night.

4 너는 매일 아침에 요가를 하니? (do yoga)

　 → _____ _____ _____ _____ every morning?

Unit 01 셀 수 있는 명사

A 주어진 명사의 복수형을 쓰시오.

1 leaf _____   6 flower _____

2 baby _____   7 piano _____

3 man _____   8 foot _____

4 class _____   9 sheep _____

5 tomato _____   10 child _____

B 밑줄 친 부분이 어법상 맞으면 ○표, 틀리면 바르게 고치시오.

1 Two house are on the street.   _____

2 The cook has many knifes.   _____

3 Sam and Tony are my friend.   _____

4 I have three puppy.   _____

5 Many sheep eat the grass on the field.   _____

C 우리말과 일치하도록 괄호 안의 말을 이용하여 문장을 완성하시오.

1 나는 아침으로 사과 한 개를 먹는다. (apple)

→ I eat _____ _____ for breakfast.

2 물고기 다섯 마리가 어항에서 헤엄친다. (fish)

→ _____ _____ swim in the fishbowl.

3 그들은 시장에서 감자를 판다. (potato)

→ They sell _____ in the market.

4 그는 한 번에 두 상자를 옮긴다. (box)

→ He carries _____ _____ at a time.

Unit 02 셀 수 없는 명사

Answers p.26

A 다음을 셀 수 있는 명사와 셀 수 없는 명사로 구분하여 쓰시오.

milk	child	egg	cheese	potato
love	computer	paper	animal	sugar
health	bread	friend	money	water

1 셀 수 있는 명사: _____

2 셀 수 없는 명사: _____

B 밑줄 친 부분이 어법상 맞으면 ○표, 틀리면 바르게 고치시오.

1 He studied in <u>a France</u>. _____

2 We didn't buy <u>salts</u>. _____

3 <u>The meats</u> aren't fresh today. _____

4 I don't have any <u>money</u> in my wallet. _____

5 John ate <u>three piece of cakes</u>. _____

C 우리말과 일치하도록 괄호 안의 말을 이용하여 문장을 완성하시오.

1 나는 물 한 잔을 마셨다. (water)

→ I drank _____ _____ _____ _____.

2 행복은 우리에게 있어서 중요하다. (happiness, be)

→ _____ _____ important to us.

3 그녀는 청바지가 다섯 벌 있다. (jean)

→ She has _____ _____ _____ _____.

4 그는 어제 올리브 오일 세 병을 샀다. (olive oil)

→ He bought _____ _____ _____ _____ _____

yesterday.

Unit 03 관사

Answers p.26

A 빈칸에 a, an, the 중 알맞은 말을 쓰시오. (필요 없으면 ×로 표시할 것)

1 Her brother is _____ university student.

2 My family has _____ dinner at 7 p.m.

3 I want _____ egg sandwich and a coke.

4 She goes to _____ church on Sundays.

5 Did you lock _____ door?

B 밑줄 친 부분이 어법상 맞으면 ○표, 틀리면 바르게 고치시오.

1 He bought a umbrella. _____

2 She wore an yellow dress yesterday. _____

3 I take a bath once a week. _____

4 A hour has sixty minutes. _____

5 A sun sets in the west. _____

C 괄호 안의 말 앞에 알맞은 관사를 쓰거나 생략하여 문장을 완성하시오.

1 a He has _____. (car)

  b She goes to work by _____. (bike)

2 a I play _____ every Saturday. (basketball)

  b My sister plays _____ every day. (violin)

3 a _____ shone in the sky. (moon)

  b _____ shines brightly in the sky. (star)

4 a The man is _____. (animal doctor)

  b Do you know _____ in the picture? (animal)

Answers
p.27

Unit 01 인칭대명사, 재귀대명사

A 괄호 안에서 알맞은 말을 고르시오.

1 The doctor helps [his / him].

2 Kate and I studied hard. [We / They] are tired now.

3 Do you know [their / theirs] names?

4 He bought a ring for [hers / her].

5 I don't wash my cat. Cats clean [them / themselves].

B 빈칸에 밑줄 친 부분을 대신하는 알맞은 대명사를 쓰시오.

1 This is not our car. _____ is red.

2 Lisa cut _____ on a knife.

3 Daniel and Mark are my friends. _____ are active.

4 This is Mike's report. He wrote it _____.

5 I saw a giraffe at the zoo. _____ neck is so long.

C 대화의 빈칸에 알맞은 대명사를 쓰시오.

1 A: Is this your room?

   B: Yes, it's _____.

2 A: Does Tom like baseball?

   B: Yes, it's _____ favorite sport.

3 A: Do you listen to K-pop music?

   B: Of course. I love _____.

4 A: Did you enjoy _____ at the party?

   B: Yes, I had a lot of fun.

Unit 02 this, that, it

Answers p.27

A

괄호 안에서 알맞은 말을 고르시오.

1 [This / These] are nice watches.

2 [That / Those] resort has a big garden.

3 [This / It] is rainy today.

4 Is [this / that] your notebook here?

5 I know [these / those] men over there.

B

그림을 보고 this, that, it을 이용하여 문장을 완성하시오. (필요하면 형태를 바꿀 것)

1 **2** **3** **4** **5**

1 _____ is the Eiffel Tower.

2 Are _____ your keys?

3 _____ flowers are beautiful.

4 I like _____ hat.

5 _____ is December 25th.

C

우리말과 일치하도록 괄호 안의 말을 바르게 배열하시오.

1 5시 정각이다. (five, it, o'clock, is)

→ _____

2 이 사람은 내 여자 형제이다. (sister, this, my, is)

→ _____

3 저것들이 네 양말이니? (those, socks, your, are)

→ _____

4 이 개들은 그녀의 것이다. (hers, these, are, dogs)

→ _____

Unit 03 one, some, any

Answers p.27

A 괄호 안에서 알맞은 말을 골라 대화를 완성하시오.

1 A: Do you like that jumper?

B: No, I like this [one / ones].

2 A: Does Mary have a bike?

B: Yes, but she doesn't ride [one / it].

3 A: I need new white shorts.

B: Sorry, we have only blue [one / ones].

B 빈칸에 some 또는 any를 넣어 문장을 완성하시오.

1 She bought _____ bread.

2 Our teacher didn't give _____ homework to us.

3 We met _____ friends after school yesterday.

4 Do you have _____ brothers or sisters?

5 I didn't eat _____ salad, but Suho ate _____.

C 우리말과 일치하도록 괄호 안의 말을 이용하여 문장을 완성하시오.

1 몇몇 사람들이 그 록 밴드를 좋아한다. (people)

→ _____ _____ like the rock band.

2 나는 우산이 필요해. 네게 하나 있니? (have)

→ I need an umbrella. Do you _____ _____ ?

3 그녀는 TV를 조금도 보지 않는다. (TV)

→ She doesn't watch _____ _____ .

4 그는 이어폰을 잃어버려서 새것을 샀다. (new)

→ He lost his earphones, so he bought _____ _____ .

현재시제, 과거시제

Answers p.27

A 괄호 안에서 알맞은 말을 고르시오.

1 I [take / took] a yoga class twice a week.

2 Daniel [buys / bought] a new car last month.

3 Mr. Kim [teaches / taught] at a middle school.

4 [Does / Did] Edison invent the light bulb?

5 Mom [drinks / drank] a cup of coffee every morning.

B 괄호 안의 말을 빈칸에 알맞은 형태로 각각 쓰시오.

1 It _____ rainy last night. It _____ sunny now. (be)

2 I _____ sweet food before. Now I _____ spicy food. (like)

3 She always _____ a sandwich for breakfast. She _____ an egg sandwich yesterday. (eat)

4 My uncle _____ at a hotel now. He _____ at a restaurant before. (work)

C 밑줄 친 부분을 알맞은 형태로 바꿔 문장을 다시 쓰시오.

1 They <u>be</u> not busy yesterday.

→ _____

2 The store <u>open</u> at 8 every morning.

→ _____

3 Water <u>freeze</u> at 0℃.

→ _____

4 My brother <u>study</u> hard last night.

→ _____

Unit 02 미래시제

Answers p.27

A 두 문장의 의미가 같도록 빈칸에 알맞은 말을 쓰시오.

1 We will travel to Mexico.

→ We _____ _____ _____ to Mexico.

2 He won't eat fast food.

→ He _____ _____ _____ _____ fast food.

3 Will you watch the soccer game tonight?

→ _____ _____ _____ _____ the soccer game tonight?

B 밑줄 친 부분이 어법상 맞으면 ○표, 틀리면 바르게 고치시오.

1 A new teacher will <u>comes</u> to our school soon. _____

2 We're going to <u>selling</u> our clothes at the school event. _____

3 Tom <u>will not do</u> his homework before dinner. _____

4 Are you going to <u>listen</u> to the radio? _____

5 My cousin <u>is going not to</u> leave tonight. _____

C 괄호 안의 말을 이용하여 미래시제 문장으로 바꿔 쓰시오.

1 I go shopping. (be going to)

→ _____ tomorrow.

2 Does she see a doctor? (will)

→ _____ this afternoon?

3 They don't buy a new computer. (be going to)

→ _____ next week.

4 He is a firefighter. (will)

→ _____ in the future.

Unit 03 진행시제

Answers p.27

A 괄호 안에서 알맞은 말을 고르시오.

1 Is it [rain / raining] hard now?

2 She's [wears / wearing] a pretty jacket.

3 I [know / am knowing] the answer.

4 Billy is [singing not / not singing] a song.

5 Minji [is writing / was writing] her blog last night.

B 현재시제 문장은 현재진행시제로, 과거시제 문장은 과거진행시제로 바꿔 쓰시오.

1 My brother draws a picture.

→ _____

2 Did you practice the piano?

→ _____

3 I didn't call my friend.

→ _____

4 The man doesn't cut the grass.

→ _____

C 준호의 오늘 일과표를 보고, 빈칸에 알맞은 말을 쓰시오. (진행시제를 사용할 것)

07:00~07:40	have breakfast	14:00~17:00	play basketball
09:00~11:00	study math	19:00~19:30	have dinner
11:50~12:30	have lunch	20:00~22:00	watch TV

1 Junho _____ _____ _____ at 10 a.m.

2 He _____ _____ _____ at noon.

3 He _____ _____ at 4 p.m.

4 It's 9 in the evening. He _____ _____ _____ now.

can, may

Answers p.27

A 그림을 보고, 보기에서 알맞은 말을 골라 문장을 완성하시오. (한 번씩만 쓸 것)

1   2   3   4

1   Chickens _____ fly high.

2   You _____ eat here.

3   Rabbits _____ run fast.

4   It's very cloudy. It _____ rain soon.

보기	can
	can't
	may
	may not

B 밑줄 친 부분이 어법상 맞으면 ○표, 틀리면 바르게 고치시오.

1   They <u>can</u> go camping that weekend.   _____

2   <u>May</u> I read the comic book?   _____

3   Bora <u>is able not to</u> play the cello.   _____

4   He has a nice car. He <u>is able to</u> be rich.   _____

5   <u>May</u> you carry this bag?   _____

C 우리말과 일치하도록 괄호 안의 말을 이용하여 문장을 완성하시오.

1   나는 스키를 잘 못 탄다. (ski)

   → I _____ _____ well.

2   Daniel은 지금 집에 있을지도 모른다. (be)

   → Daniel _____ _____ at home now.

3   그녀는 제시간에 이곳에 도착할 수 있니? (arrive)

   → _____ _____ _____ here on time?

4   그들은 파티에 올 수 없다. (come)

   → They _____ _____ _____ _____ to the party.

Unit 02 must, have to, should

Answers p.27

A 괄호 안에서 알맞은 말을 고르시오.

1 You [must / must not] chew gum during class.

2 [Must / Does] Alex have to clean his room?

3 The light is off in his room. He [must / should] be sleeping now.

4 It's a free gift. You [must not / don't have to] pay for it.

5 Turn off the air conditioner. We [should / can't] save energy.

B 밑줄 친 조동사에 유의하여 해석하시오.

1 a Tom didn't answer his phone. He <u>must</u> be busy.

→ _____

  b Cathy is an honest girl. She <u>can't</u> be a liar.

→ _____

2 a You <u>must not</u> fight with your friends.

→ _____

  b You <u>don't have to</u> take off your shoes.

→ _____

C 빈칸에 알맞은 말을 보기에서 골라 쓰시오. (필요하면 형태를 바꿀 것)

보기	• should not go outside	• should exercise every day
	• don't have to buy it	• have to get some sleep

1 Mike is getting fat. He _____ .

2 I'm very tired. I _____ .

3 It's raining hard. We _____ .

4 Lisa has the book. She _____ .

who, what, which 의문문

Answers p.28

Unit 01

A 대화의 빈칸에 알맞은 말을 보기에서 골라 쓰시오.

| 보기 | who | whose | what | which |

1 A: _____ is this backpack?　　　　B: It's Minho's.

2 A: _____ are you reading now?　　　B: I'm reading a novel.

3 A: _____ is that man in the picture?　B: It's my father.

4 A: _____ is my pen, this one or that one?　B: That one is yours.

B 우리말과 일치하도록 괄호 안의 말을 바르게 배열하시오.

1 너는 지난 주말에 뭐 했니? (you, what, do, did)

→ _____ last weekend?

2 너는 사과와 배 중 어느 과일을 원하니? (you, do, which, fruit, want)

→ _____, apples or pears?

3 누가 이 질문에 답할 수 있니? (answer, can, who)

→ _____ this question?

4 지금 누구의 전화기가 울리고 있는 거니? (phone, ringing, whose, is)

→ _____ now?

C 의문사를 이용하여 대답에 알맞은 질문을 완성하시오.

1 A: _____ _____ that woman?　　B: She's my math teacher.

2 A: _____ _____ is on the table?　B: It's my wallet.

3 A: _____ _____ can you play, soccer or basketball?

　B: I can play basketball.

4 A: _____ _____ does the train arrive?

　B: It arrives at eight thirty.

Unit 02 when, where, why, how 의문문

Answers p.28

A 대화의 빈칸에 알맞은 말을 보기에서 골라 쓰시오.

보기	when	where	why	how

1 A: _____ are you going to pay?   B: I'll pay with cash.

2 A: _____ is Logan's birthday?   B: It's December 10th.

3 A: _____ did you go in Busan?   B: We went to Haeundae Beach.

4 A: _____ is she late for school?   B: Because she missed the bus.

B 질문에 알맞은 응답을 바르게 연결하시오.

1 Where is your sister? •   • a At nine.

2 Why are they at home today? •   • b In the kitchen.

3 When does the store close? •   • c Fifteen dollars.

4 How much does it cost? •   • d Because it's snowing hard.

C 우리말과 일치하도록 괄호 안의 말을 이용하여 문장을 완성하시오.

1 너는 왜 나에게 화가 났니? (angry)

→ _____ _____ _____ _____ with me?

2 그는 페이스북 친구들이 몇 명이니? (Facebook friend)

→ _____ _____ _____ _____ _____ he have?

3 그들은 다음 주말에 어디에 갈 거니? (will, go)

→ _____ _____ _____ next weekend?

4 그녀는 언제 그 일을 끝냈니? (finish)

→ _____ _____ _____ the work?

03 명령문, Let's ~, There is/are ~

Answers p.28

A 괄호 안에서 알맞은 말을 고르시오.

1 [Have / Has] a cup of tea.

2 Let's [play / playing] badminton after school.

3 There [is / are] some salt on the table.

4 [Don't / Doesn't] smoke inside the building.

5 [Is / Are] there many animals in the zoo?

B 어법상 틀린 부분에 밑줄을 긋고 바르게 고치시오.

1 Please makes your bed.　　　　　　　　　　_____

2 Not let's waste time.　　　　　　　　　　_____

3 There aren't any paper in the printer.　　　_____

4 Don't afraid of the dog.　　　　　　　　　_____

5 Was there lots of people at the festival?　　_____

C 우리말과 일치하도록 괄호 안의 말을 이용하여 문장을 완성하시오.

1 뜨거운 난로를 만지지 마시오. (touch)

　→ _____ _____ the hot stove.

2 이번 토요일에 스키 타러 가자. (go)

　→ _____ _____ skiing this Saturday.

3 들판에 소들이 있니? (cow)

　→ _____ _____ _____ in the field?

4 냉장고에 치즈가 조금도 없다. (any cheese)

　→ _____ _____ _____ _____ in the fridge.

04 감탄문, 부가의문문

Answers p.28

A 괄호 안에서 알맞은 말을 고르시오.

1 [What / How] a rude man he is!

2 [What / How] beautifully she sings!

3 He's a cook, [is he / isn't he]?

4 [What / What a] nice presents these are!

5 She did not come to the party, [did she / didn't she]?

B 밑줄 친 부분이 어법상 맞으면 ○표, **틀리면** 바르게 고치시오.

1 <u>How interesting</u> stories they are! _____

2 You cannot ride a bike, <u>do you</u>? _____

3 <u>What nice</u> smile he has! _____

4 You and Emily are very close, <u>aren't they</u>? _____

5 <u>How cute</u> your puppy is! _____

C 우리말과 일치하도록 괄호 안의 말을 이용하여 문장을 완성하시오.

1 오늘 정말 바람이 많이 부는구나! (windy)

→ _____ _____ it is today!

2 미나는 영어를 좋아하지, 그렇지 않니? (like)

→ Mina _____ English, _____ _____ ?

3 그는 정말 용감한 소년이구나! (brave, boy)

→ _____ _____ _____ _____ he is!

4 아이들은 TV를 보는 중이 아니었어, 그렇지? (watch)

→ The kids _____ _____ TV, _____ _____ ?

Chapter 8

Unit 01 감각동사

Answers
p.28

A 밑줄 친 부분이 어법상 맞으면 ○표, **틀리면** 바르게 고치시오.

1 I feel <u>thirst</u>. I want some water. _____

2 His ring tone <u>sounds</u> a bird. _____

3 You look so <u>lovely</u> in the picture. _____

4 Lemons taste very <u>sour</u>. _____

5 Fresh bread smells <u>wonderfully</u>. _____

B 빈칸에 알맞은 말을 보기에서 골라 현재형으로 쓰시오. (한 번씩만 쓸 것)

보기	feel	smell	taste	sound

1 Your idea _____ great.

2 These grapes _____ very sweet.

3 The shampoo _____ like roses.

4 This silk scarf _____ very soft.

C 우리말과 일치하도록 괄호 안의 말을 이용하여 문장을 완성하시오.

1 이 꽃들에서 좋은 향기가 난다. (nice)

→ These flowers _____ _____.

2 그녀의 목소리가 전화로 이상하게 들린다. (strange)

→ Her voice _____ _____ on the phone.

3 칠면조고기에서 닭고기 같은 맛이 난다. (chicken)

→ Turkey _____ _____ _____.

4 그 축구 선수들은 지쳐 보였다. (tired)

→ The soccer players _____ _____.

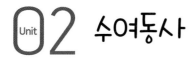

A 두 문장의 의미가 같도록 빈칸에 알맞은 말을 쓰시오.

1 I gave my aunt a cup of coffee.

→ I gave a cup of coffee _____ _____ _____.

2 Can I ask you some questions?

→ Can I ask _____ _____ _____ _____?

3 He bought her a new computer.

→ He bought _____ _____ _____ _____ _____.

B 빈칸에 들어갈 말을 보기에서 골라 알맞은 형태로 쓰시오.

보기	tell	teach	lend	cook

1 I can't find my textbook. Can you _____ me yours?

2 He _____ Chinese to us. He is very kind.

3 Did you solve the question? Please _____ me the answer.

4 Daniel visited his grandmother. She _____ dinner for him.

C 우리말과 일치하도록 괄호 안의 말을 이용하여 문장을 완성하시오.

1 나는 그에게 사진들을 보내 주었다. (send, the pictures)

→ I _____ _____ _____ _____.

2 저에게 운동화 좀 보여 주시겠어요? (show, some sneakers)

→ Could you _____ _____ _____ _____?

3 아빠는 아침에 우리에게 샌드위치를 만들어 주신다. (make, sandwiches)

→ Dad _____ _____ _____ _____ in the morning.

4 그녀는 부모님께 편지를 쓸 것이다. (write, a letter, her parents)

→ She will _____ _____ _____ _____ _____ _____.

Unit 01 명사처럼 쓰이는 to부정사

Answers p.28

A 밑줄 친 부분이 문장에서 주어, 목적어, 보어 중 어떤 역할을 하는지 쓰고 해석하시오.

1 She wants <u>to live</u> in the country.

→ _____ / _____

2 <u>To worry</u> is to waste time.

→ _____ / _____

3 His plan is <u>to start</u> a business.

→ _____ / _____

4 It is exciting <u>to watch</u> baseball games.

→ _____ / _____

B 어법상 틀린 부분에 밑줄을 긋고 바르게 고치시오.

1 He hopes meets you soon.   _____

2 My dream is travel around the world.   _____

3 She promised keeping the secret.   _____

4 That is not easy to be honest.   _____

5 I decided to not buy a car.   _____

C 서로 같은 뜻이 되도록 빈칸에 알맞은 말을 쓰시오.

1 My brother wants to become a pilot. He wishes for it.

→ My brother wishes _____ _____ a pilot.

2 Don't drive fast in the rain. It is dangerous.

→ _____ is dangerous _____ _____ fast in the rain.

3 I have to read an English newspaper. It's my homework.

→ My homework _____ _____ _____ an English newspaper.

02 형용사, 부사처럼 쓰이는 to부정사

Answers
p.28

A 밑줄 친 부분이 문장에서 형용사, 부사 중 어떤 역할을 하는지 쓰고 해석하시오.

1 There are many places to visit in Korea.

→ ＿＿＿＿＿＿＿＿＿ / ＿＿＿＿＿＿＿＿＿＿＿＿＿

2 The boy was very happy to win first prize.

→ ＿＿＿＿＿＿＿＿＿ / ＿＿＿＿＿＿＿＿＿＿＿＿＿

3 Many people went to the park to see the band's concert.

→ ＿＿＿＿＿＿＿＿＿ / ＿＿＿＿＿＿＿＿＿＿＿＿＿

B 자연스러운 문장이 되도록 알맞게 연결하시오.

1 I grew up · · **a** to wash.

2 I'm calling · · **b** to play in.

3 He was surprised · · **c** to see me.

4 She has some jeans · · **d** to be a writer.

5 The children need a garden · · **e** to ask you about our homework.

C 우리말과 일치하도록 괄호 안의 말을 바르게 배열하시오.

1 그녀는 100세까지 살았다. (a hundred, to, be)

→ She lived ＿＿＿＿＿＿＿＿＿＿＿＿＿＿＿＿＿＿ .

2 그는 말할 누군가가 필요하다. (to, talk, someone, to)

→ He needs ＿＿＿＿＿＿＿＿＿＿＿＿＿＿＿＿＿＿ .

3 나는 엄마에게 드릴 선물을 사기 위해 쇼핑을 갔다. (buy, to, a gift)

→ I went shopping ＿＿＿＿＿＿＿＿＿＿＿＿＿＿＿＿ for my mom.

4 나는 너의 안 좋은 소식을 듣게 되어 유감이다. (hear, sorry, to, your bad news)

→ I'm ＿＿＿＿＿＿＿＿＿＿＿＿＿＿＿＿＿＿ .

Unit 03 명사처럼 쓰이는 동명사

Answers p.29

A 밑줄 친 부분이 문장에서 주어, 목적어, 보어 중 어떤 역할을 하는지 쓰고 해석하시오.

1 His hobby is <u>taking</u> pictures.

→ _____ / _____

2 My parents started <u>helping</u> children in Africa.

→ _____ / _____

3 <u>Walking</u> fast is good for your health.

→ _____ / _____

B 괄호 안에서 알맞은 말을 고르시오.

1 Her job is [selling / to selling] fruits.

2 I enjoy [to watch / watching] horror movies.

3 Having close friends [are / is] wonderful.

4 They finished [to clean / cleaning] the kitchen.

5 He spent time [writing / to writing] a report.

C 우리말과 일치하도록 괄호 안의 말을 이용하여 문장을 완성하시오.

1 회의에 늦어서 죄송합니다. (be, late)

→ I'm sorry for _____ _____ for the meeting.

2 창문을 좀 열어 주겠니? (mind, open)

→ Do you _____ _____ the window?

3 너는 밤에 먹는 것을 그만두어야 한다. (stop, eat)

→ You should _____ _____ at night.

4 나는 바닷가에 가고 싶다. (feel like, go)

→ I _____ _____ _____ to the beach.

Unit 01 형용사

Answers p.29

A 빈칸에 알맞은 형용사를 보기에서 골라 쓴 후, 그 형용사가 (대)명사를 꾸며 주는지, 주어를 설명해 주는지를 쓰시오. (한 번씩만 쓸 것)

보기	different	smart	friendly	wrong

1 The teacher is kind and _____. Students like him. _____

2 Suho is a _____ student. He learns very fast. _____

3 You look _____. What happened to your hair? _____

4 You're in perfect health. We couldn't find anything _____.

_____

B 괄호 안에서 알맞은 말을 고르시오.

1 I have [a few / a little] good friends. I'm not lonely.

2 We must be quick. We have [few / little] time.

3 Listen carefully. I'm going to give you [little / a little] advice.

4 The movie isn't very good. There are [few / a few] people at the cinema.

5 I don't have [many / much] water. I'll buy some at the shop.

C 우리말과 일치하도록 괄호 안의 말을 바르게 배열하시오.

1 래프팅은 매우 흥미진진한 스포츠이다. (sport, is, rafting, a, exciting, very)

→ _____

2 그녀는 매일 많은 영어 단어를 외운다. (a, she, English, lot, memorizes, of, words)

→ _____ every day.

3 나는 네게 중요한 것을 말해 줄 것이다. (you, will, important, tell, I, something)

→ _____

4 너는 여행에 필요한 모든 것을 샀니? (you, did, everything, buy, necessary)

→ _____ for your trip?

Answers
p.29

Unit 02 부사

A 두 문장의 의미가 같도록 밑줄 친 단어를 부사형으로 바꿔 문장을 완성하시오.

1 Jennifer is a <u>good</u> singer. → Jennifer sings _____.

2 Cheetahs are <u>fast</u> animals. → Cheetahs run _____.

3 The couple had a <u>happy</u> life. → The couple lived _____.

4 My father is a <u>careful</u> driver. → My father drives _____.

B 괄호 안의 말을 알맞은 곳에 넣어 문장을 다시 쓰시오.

1 Tom makes his bed. (always)

→ _____

2 I can hear my neighbor's TV. (never)

→ _____

3 Mina is late for class. (often)

→ _____

C 우리말과 일치하도록 주어진 말을 이용하여 문장을 완성하시오.

1 그는 방 청소를 빠르게 끝냈다. (finish, quick)

→ He _____ cleaning his room _____.

2 우리의 드론이 높이 날고 있다. (fly, high)

→ Our drone is _____ _____.

3 그녀는 대개 토요일에 늦게 일어난다. (usual, get up)

→ She _____ _____ _____ late on Saturdays.

4 나는 그것이 좀처럼 믿어지지가 않는다. (can, hard, believe)

→ I _____ _____ _____ it.

03 원급, 비교급, 최상급

Answers p.29

A 괄호 안의 말을 빈칸에 알맞은 형태로 쓰시오.

1 Ronaldo is the _____ player on the team. (good)

2 Tomorrow will be the _____ day this summer. (hot)

3 My sister gets up as _____ as me. (early)

4 The English test was _____ than the math test. (difficult)

5 Cities are _____ than villages. (busy)

B 서로 의미가 같도록 비교 표현을 이용하여 문장을 완성하시오.

1 Jack is 14 years old. Brian is 14 years old.

→ Jack is _____ _____ _____ Brian.

2 This tower looks smaller than that building.

→ That building looks _____ _____ this tower.

3 Sophie can't swim as fast as Maria.

→ Maria swims _____ _____ Sophie.

C 표를 보고, 괄호 안의 말을 이용하여 비교하는 문장을 완성하시오.

	age	height	weight
Alex	15	177 cm	70 kg
Chris	15	164 cm	62 kg
Sam	14	170 cm	58 kg

1 Alex is _____ _____ Chris. (tall)

2 Sam is _____ _____ Chris. (young)

3 Chris is _____ _____ of the three. (short)

4 Alex is _____ _____ Sam. (heavy)

Unit 01 시간을 나타내는 전치사

Answers
p.29

A 빈칸에 알맞은 전치사를 쓰시오.

1 It is very hot _____ summer.

2 The movie will start _____ 7:30.

3 I do yoga every day _____ the morning.

4 Would you wait for me _____ ten minutes?

5 Our school picnic will be _____ May 2nd.

B 밑줄 친 부분을 어법상 바르게 고치시오.

1 I will play computer games <u>by</u> 3 o'clock.   _____

2 John came back to Korea <u>on</u> 2018.   _____

3 It rained a lot <u>during</u> three days.   _____

4 We went shopping <u>in</u> Saturday afternoon.   _____

5 Does the restaurant open <u>on</u> five?   _____

C 우리말과 일치하도록 괄호 안의 말을 이용하여 문장을 완성하시오.

1 그녀는 밤에 커피를 마시지 않는다. (night)

→ She doesn't drink coffee _____ _____.

2 너는 다음 주 월요일까지 그 책을 돌려줘야 한다. (next Monday)

→ You have to return the book _____ _____ _____.

3 나는 저녁 식사 후에 숙제를 할 것이다. (dinner)

→ I will do my homework _____ _____.

4 주말 동안에 많은 사람들이 놀이공원을 방문했다. (the weekend)

→ A lot of people visited the amusement park _____ _____

_____.

_{Unit}02 장소를 나타내는 전치사

Answers
p.29

A 빈칸에 알맞은 전치사를 쓰시오.

1 Can I watch TV _____ the room?

2 A man is standing _____ the bus stop.

3 They hung their socks _____ the Christmas tree.

4 I bought the wine _____ France.

5 There is a bridge _____ the river.

B 그림을 보고, 빈칸에 알맞은 전치사를 쓰시오.

1 The bookstore is _____ _____ the restaurant.

2 The bank is _____ _____ the bookstore.

3 The restaurant is _____ _____ _____ the park.

4 The police station is _____ the bank _____ the hospital.

C 우리말과 일치하도록 괄호 안의 말을 이용하여 문장을 완성하시오.

1 Tom은 집 뒤에 있는 언덕에 올랐다. (his house)

→ Tom climbed the hill _____ _____ _____.

2 벽에 세계지도가 있다. (the wall)

→ There is a world map _____ _____ _____.

3 나는 나무 아래에 내 자전거를 놓았다. (the tree)

→ I put my bike _____ _____ _____.

그 밖의 전치사

Answers
p.29

A 괄호 안에서 알맞은 말을 고르시오.

1 I learned [about / for] Chinese history.

2 Gandhi was a great leader [of / with] India.

3 He received the package [by / for] mail.

4 Grandma made a lot of food [for / of] my birthday.

5 We enjoyed playing soccer [with / of] a new ball.

B 밑줄 친 부분을 어법상 바르게 고치시오.

1 May I play <u>by</u> your dog?   _____

2 The color <u>in</u> the table is white.   _____

3 He knows much <u>for</u> cars.   _____

4 Let's go to Busan <u>with</u> KTX.   _____

5 Andersen wrote many fairy tales <u>of</u> children.   _____

C 우리말과 일치하도록 괄호 안의 말을 이용하여 문장을 완성하시오.

1 나는 한국전쟁에 관한 영화를 보았다. (the Korean War)

→ I saw a movie _____ _____ _____ _____.

2 그는 지하철을 타고 박물관에 갔다. (subway)

→ He went to the museum _____ _____.

3 그녀는 칼로 수박을 잘랐다. (a knife)

→ She cut the watermelon _____ _____ _____.

4 너는 다음 달에 토론토로 떠날 거니? (Toronto)

→ Will you leave _____ _____ next month?

Unit 01 and, but, or, so

Answers p.29

A 괄호 안에서 알맞은 말을 고르시오.

1 Science is interesting, [and / but] it isn't easy.

2 He plays golf [but / or] swims on Sundays.

3 My cousin can speak English [but / and] German.

4 The roller coaster is scary [but / so] exciting.

5 The museum was closed, [or / so] I couldn't see the painting.

B 자연스러운 문장이 되도록 알맞게 연결하시오.

1 My name is Mark, •   • a or I will go rafting.

2 I like playing basketball, •   • b so I can't play with you.

3 I will ride a zip-line, •   • c but I'm not very good at it.

4 I have a lot of homework, •   • d and I'm a new student.

C 우리말과 일치하도록 괄호 안의 말을 바르게 배열하시오.

1 디즈니랜드는 런던에 있니, 파리에 있니?

(a Disneyland, London, is, or, in, Paris, there)

→ _____

2 칼은 날카로워서 위험하다. (sharp, the knife, is, it, dangerous, so, is)

→ _____

3 그는 열심히 일해서 돈을 많이 벌었다. (hard, worked, he, money, and, made, a lot of)

→ _____

4 그녀는 그 비밀을 알지만, 그것을 말하지 않고 있다.

(the secret, she, but, knows, not, it, she, telling, is)

→ _____

Unit 02 when, while, before, after

Answers
p.30

A 빈칸에 알맞은 말을 보기에서 골라 쓰시오. (한 번씩만 쓸 것)

보기	when	while	before	after

1 _____ he got off the train, he took a taxi.

2 Would you like to sit down _____ you are waiting?

3 She always warms up _____ she exercises.

4 _____ you ride a bike, you should wear a helmet.

B 자연스러운 문장이 되도록 알맞게 연결하시오.

1 He packs his school bag •　　•**a** when he heard it.

2 He washes his hands •　　•**b** before he goes to bed.

3 He cleaned the table •　　•**c** after he gets home.

4 He couldn't believe the news •　　•**d** while she was doing the dishes.

C 두 문장을 주어진 말로 시작하는 한 문장으로 쓰시오.

1 I always listen to music. I am studying.

→ While _____.

2 You use the computer. You should turn it off.

→ After _____.

3 Cindy came home. She talked to me.

→ When _____.

4 Lock all doors and windows. You leave.

→ Before _____.

Unit 03 because, if, that

Answers p.30

A 괄호 안에서 알맞은 말을 고르시오.

1 We will catch the train [if / that] we hurry.

2 They canceled their trip [because / if] the weather was bad.

3 My thought is [that / because] happiness is within us.

4 If he [wakes / will wake] up early, he will go jogging.

5 Some sailors believed [because / that] cats brought good luck.

B 두 문장을 괄호 안의 말을 이용하여 한 문장으로 쓰시오.

1 It may rain tomorrow. He won't wash his car today. (because)

→ _____

2 Sally is studying at the library. I know it. (that)

→ _____

3 He isn't hungry. He doesn't have breakfast. (if)

→ _____

C 우리말과 일치하도록 괄호 안의 말을 이용하여 문장을 완성하시오.

1 버스가 고장 났기 때문에 나는 학교에 늦었다. (the bus, break down)

→ I was late for school _____ _____ _____ _____ _____.

2 그가 시험에 떨어졌다는 것은 사실이 아니다. (true)

→ _____ _____ _____ _____ _____ he failed the test.

3 나는 이 무서운 영화를 보면 잠을 잘 수 없을 것이다. (watch, this scary movie)

→ I won't be able to sleep _____ _____ _____ _____

_____ _____.

4 의사들은 웃는 것이 우리의 건강에 좋다고 말한다. (laughing, good, for, our health)

→ Doctors say _____ _____ _____ _____ _____ _____

_____.

Overall Test

Answers p.30

이름: 맞은 개수:

01

다음 중 어법상 옳은 것을 <u>모두</u> 고르면? (틀린 것들을 바르게 고칠 것)

① The boxes is very heavy.
② Are you sick yesterday?
③ Are Jason and you friends?
④ Math is not my favorite subject.
⑤ Were the boy hungry and tired?

02 서술형

다음 문장을 괄호 안의 지시대로 바꿔 쓰시오.

(1) The students studied hard for the exam.

(부정문으로)

→ _____

(2) Lily has big eyes. (의문문으로)

→ _____

03

명사의 복수형이 <u>잘못</u> 연결된 것은? (바르게 고칠 것)

① sheep – sheeps   ② goose – geese
③ photo – photos   ④ potato – potatoes
⑤ country – countries

04

빈칸에 공통으로 들어갈 말로 알맞은 것은?

• This is _____ car.
• The keys on the table are _____.

① my   ② her   ③ his
④ your   ⑤ their

05

빈칸에 정관사 the가 들어가는 것을 <u>모두</u> 고르면?

① Look at the stars in _____ sky.
② Did you have _____ breakfast?
③ Let's play _____ soccer together.
④ I went to _____ bed late last night.
⑤ Who can play _____ piano?

06 서술형

그림을 보고, 괄호 안의 말을 이용하여 대화를 완성하시오.

A: What is the queen doing?
B: She is _____ _____ _____
   in the mirror. (look at)

07 서술형

빈칸에 알맞은 be동사를 넣어 글을 완성하시오.

Hi, my name (1)_____ Julie Anderson.
I (2)_____ 14 years old. I (3)_____
a little short. My hair (4)_____ long,
and my eyes (5)_____ big. I have a
dog. My dog Max (6)_____ brown. Its
legs (7)_____ short. We (8)_____
good friends.

08

빈칸에 들어갈 말이 순서대로 짝지어진 것은?

> • I _____ have time to play now.
> • _____ he call you last night?

① don't – Do
② didn't – Did
③ don't – Did
④ didn't – Does
⑤ don't – Does

09

빈칸에 들어갈 말로 알맞은 것을 <u>모두</u> 고르면?

> Henry is doing his homework now. After doing his homework, he _____.

① played soccer
② will ride his bike
③ read comic books
④ watches a baseball game
⑤ is going to eat dinner

10

밑줄 친 부분의 쓰임이 나머지 넷과 <u>다른</u> 것은?

① She <u>may</u> be right.
② He <u>may</u> catch a cold.
③ You <u>may</u> like Italian food.
④ They <u>may</u> need a bigger house.
⑤ You <u>may</u> leave now if you wish.

11 서술형

대화의 빈칸에 들어갈 말을 보기에서 골라 쓰시오.

> 보기   it   one   some   any

> A: This towel is dirty. Do you have a clean (1) _____?
> B: Yes. There are (2) _____ on the shelf over there.

12

다음 중 어법상 옳은 것으로 바르게 짝지어진 것은? (틀린 것들을 바르게 고칠 것)

> **a.** It is snowing heavily now.
> **b.** Peter is sleeping at that time.
> **c.** Mike is having lunch with Tom.
> **d.** The Korean War ended in 1953.
> **e.** One day was 24 hours.
> **f.** She is knowing your secret.

① a, b, e
② a, c, d
③ a, c, f
④ b, d, e, f
⑤ c, d, e, f

13 서술형

표지판의 의미를 must와 괄호 안의 말을 이용하여 완성하시오.

(1)   (2)

(1) You _____ your cell phone. (turn off)

(2) You _____ food in here. (bring)

14

다음 중 어법상 옳은 것은 <u>모두</u> 몇 개인가? (틀린 것들을 바르게 고칠 것)

> **a.** The girl looks lovely.
> **b.** She told her story them.
> **c.** Your plan sounds greatly.
> **d.** I asked a favor of him.
> **e.** She looks like a model.

① 1개
② 2개
③ 3개
④ 4개
⑤ 5개

15 서술형

(A)~(E)의 각 네모 안에서 알맞은 것을 골라 쓰시오.

My family went on a picnic yesterday. Mom brought a big basket. There was (A)many / much food in the basket. There (B)was / were some cookies. There were (C)many / much apples. And there (D)was / were some bread. But there weren't (E)some / any drinks in the basket.

(A) _____ (B) _____ (C) _____

(D) _____ (E) _____

16 서술형

두 문장의 의미가 같도록 빈칸에 알맞은 말을 쓰시오.

I couldn't help her.

→ I was _____ _____ _____ help her.

17

우리말을 영어로 바르게 옮긴 것은?

너는 뛸 필요가 없다.

① You cannot run.
② You may not run.
③ You must not run.
④ You should not run.
⑤ You don't have to run.

18

밑줄 친 부분이 어법상 틀린 것은? (바르게 고칠 것)

I ①thanked ②him ③for ④tell ⑤me the truth.

19 서술형

다음 문장을 감탄문으로 바꿔 쓰시오.

(1) It is a very beautiful dress.

→ What _____!

(2) The tower is very tall.

→ How _____!

20 서술형

우리말과 일치하도록 괄호 안의 말을 이용하여 문장을 완성하시오.

그는 커피 한 잔을 마시고, 빵 두 덩어리를 먹었다.
(cup, loaf, coffee, bread)

→ He drank _____ _____ _____

_____ and ate _____ _____

_____ _____.

21 서술형

두 사람이 어제 상대방에게 해 준 일을 주어진 어구를 이용하여 완성하시오.

Jane ⇄ make some cookies / give some books ⇄ Fred

(1) Jane _____ Fred.

(2) Fred _____ Jane.

22

다음 중 어법상 틀린 것은? (바르게 고칠 것)

① His job is to fix bikes.
② Did you practice singing?
③ Reading books are important.
④ I decided not to invite him.
⑤ The boy has many toys to play with.

23

밑줄 친 부분이 어법상 옳은 것은? (틀린 것들을 바르게 고칠 것)

① I was having dinner on noon.
② Dad cleans the bathroom in Sundays.
③ I worked by 12 o'clock yesterday.
④ The man slept during the movie.
⑤ We will travel to New Zealand at January.

24

밑줄 친 부분이 어법상 틀린 것은? (바르게 고칠 것)

① She felt happy and excited.
② Will you stay but leave now?
③ Do you have a dog or a cat?
④ He was tired, so he went to bed early.
⑤ Those shoes look nice, but I won't buy them.

25 서술형

다음 지호와 미나의 어제 방과 후 일정표를 보고, 대화를 완성하시오.

	Jiho	Mina
at 4	play soccer	do my homework
at 5	study math	take a walk

Mina: Jiho, what did you do after school yesterday?
Jiho: I (1)_____. Then I (2)_____. What about you, Mina?
Mina: I (3)_____. Then I (4)_____.

26

빈칸에 들어갈 말로 알맞은 것은?

If she _____ the train, she will be on time.

① catch
② catches
③ caught
④ will catch
⑤ was catching

27 서술형

그림을 보고, 괄호 안의 말을 이용하여 문장을 완성하시오.

→ The red cap is _____ of the three. (expensive)

28 서술형

다음 중 어법상 틀린 것을 모두 골라 바르게 고치시오.

a. Her dress is prettier than mine.
b. My bag is as heavier as yours.
c. She feels a lot better than yesterday.
d. It was the saddest moment of my life.
e. Jason is the most popular boy in my school.
f. He came very earlier than usual.
g. She often is late for school.

GRAMMAR BITE Grade 1

Workbook

Contact Mirae-N

www.mirae-n.com

(우)06532 서울시 서초구 신반포로 321

1800-8890

모바일
홈페이지
바로가기

수학 EASY 개념서

개념이 수학의 전부다! 술술 읽으며 개념 잡는 EASY 개념서

수학 0_초등 핵심 개념,
      1_1(상), 2_1(하),
      3_2(상), 4_2(하),
      5_3(상), 6_3(하)

수학 필수 유형서

 유형완성

체계적인 유형별 학습으로 실전에서 더욱 강력하게!

수학 1(상), 1(하), 2(상), 2(하), 3(상), 3(하)

미래엔 교과서 연계 도서

자습서

 자습서

핵심 정리와 적중 문제로 완벽한 자율학습!

국어	1-1, 1-2, 2-1, 2-2, 3-1, 3-2	역사	①, ②
영어	1, 2, 3	도덕	①, ②
수학	1, 2, 3	과학	1, 2, 3
사회	①, ②	기술·가정	①, ②
		생활 일본어, 생활 중국어, 한문	

평가 문제집

 평가 문제집

정확한 학습 포인트와 족집게 예상 문제로 완벽한 시험 대비!

국어 1-1, 1-2, 2-1, 2-2, 3-1, 3-2
영어 1-1, 1-2, 2-1, 2-2, 3-1, 3-2
사회 ①, ②
역사 ①, ②
도덕 ①, ②
과학 1, 2, 3

내신 대비 문제집

 시험직보 문제집

내신 만점을 위한 시험 직전에 보는 문제집

국어 1-1, 1-2, 2-1, 2-2, 3-1, 3-2

예비 고1을 위한 고등 도서

룩 LOOK

이미지 연상으로 필수 개념을 쉽게 익히는
비주얼 개념서

국어 문법
영어 분석독해

손쉬운

작품 이해에서 문제 해결까지
손쉬운 비법을 담은 문학 입문서

현대 문학, 고전 문학

수학중심

개념과 유형을 한 번에 잡는
개념 기본서

고등 수학(상), 고등 수학(하),
수학Ⅰ, 수학Ⅱ, 확률과 통계, 미적분, 기하

유형중심

체계적인 유형별 학습으로
실전에서 더욱 강력한 문제 기본서

고등 수학(상), 고등 수학(하),
수학Ⅰ, 수학Ⅱ, 확률과 통계, 미적분

올리드

탄탄한 개념 설명, 자신있는 실전 문제

사회 통합사회, 한국사
과학 통합과학

수능 국어에서 자신감을 갖는 방법?
깨독으로 시작하자!

고등 내신과 수능 국어에서 1등급이 되는 비결 -
중등에서 미리 깨운 독해력, 어휘력으로 승부하자!

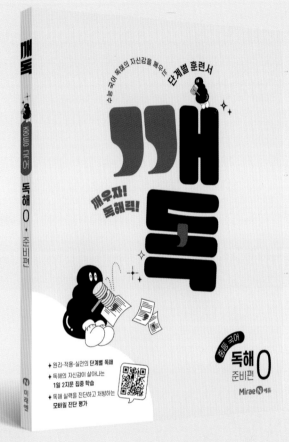

단계별 훈련 — 독해 원리 → 적용 문제 → 실전 문제로 단계별 독해 훈련

교과·수능 연계 — 중학교 교과서와 수능 연계 지문으로 수준별 독해 훈련

독해력 진단 — 모바일 진단 평가를 통한 개인별 독해 전략 처방

| 추천 대상 |

· 중등 학습의 기본이 되는 문해력을 기르고 싶은 초등 5~6학년
· 중등 전 교과 연계 지문을 바탕으로 독해의 기본기를 습득하고 싶은 중학생
· 고등 국어의 내신과 수능에서 1등급을 목표로 훈련하고 싶은 중학생

중등 국어 교과 필수 개념 및 어휘를 '종합편'으로,
수능 국어 기초 어휘를 '수능편'으로 대비하자.

수능 국어 독해의 자신감을 깨우는
단계별 독해 훈련서

깨독 시리즈 (전6책)

[독해] 0_준비편, 1_기본편, 2_실력편, 3_수능편
[어휘] 1_종합편, 2_수능편

독해의 시작은 어휘력에서!